# Designing the Landscape

## An Introductory Guide for the Landscape Designer

Tony Bertauski

*Trident Technical College*

PEARSON

Prentice Hall

Upper Saddle River, New Jersey 07458

**Library of Congress Cataloging-in-Publication Data**

Bertauski, Tony.
  Designing the landscape : an introductory guide for the
landscape designer / Tony Bertauski.
     p.  cm.
  ISBN 0-13-033041-8
1.  Landscape design.  I. Title.

SB472.45.B47  2005
712—dc22                                    2003025241

**Publisher:** Stephen Helba
**Executive Editor:** Debbie Yarnell
**Associate Editor:** Kimberly Yehle
**Production Editor:** Pat Anglin, Carlisle Publishers Services
**Production Liaison:** Janice Stangel
**Director of Manufacturing and Production:** Bruce Johnson
**Managing Editor:** Mary Carnis
**Manufacturing Buyer:** Cathleen Petersen
**Creative Director:** Cheryl Asherman
**Cover Design Coordinator:** Christopher Weigand
**Cover Design:** Kevin Kall
**Cover Illustrations:** Top left: Water feature in the backyard, courtesy of Big Sky Landscaping. Middle: Broad, sweeping
driveway constructed with pavers, courtesy of Blue Ribbon Design/Build. Bottom left: Wide, flowing flagstone entry walk,
courtesy of Tony Bertauski.
**Marketing Manager:** Jimmy Stephens
**Formatting:** Carlisle Communications, Ltd.
**Printing and Binding:** Banta Harrisonburg

**Pearson Prentice Hall**™ is a trademark of Pearson Education, Inc.
**Pearson**® is a registered trademark of Pearson plc
**Prentice Hall**® is a registered trademark of Pearson Education, Inc.

Pearson Education Ltd.
Pearson Education Singapore Pte. Ltd.
Pearson Education Canada, Ltd.
Pearson Education—Japan
Pearson Education Australia Pty. Limited
Pearson Education North Asia Ltd.
Pearson Educación de Mexico, S. A. de C.V.
Pearson Education Malaysia Pte. Ltd.

PEARSON
Prentice
Hall

10 9 8 7 6 5 4
ISBN: 0-13-033041-8

To an original design, unduplicated and immeasurable: *my family*

# Contents

# Preface

Why another landscape design book? There are numerous books on designing the landscape, many of which are very good at presenting the design process and design principles. Among all of these books, there is a great deal of variety regarding illustrations, depth of coverage, and cost. Although I have great admiration for some of these publications, they were not the most suitable books for our horticulture program.

Like many horticulture programs, especially at two-year colleges, students take one class in landscape design with the hope that they will gain an understanding and appreciation of the functionality and aesthetics of design, and to be able to read and understand plan drawings as well as to draw their own. Since students are limited to one semester to study landscape design, the typical textbook, although very informative and thorough, is difficult for students to digest because of the arrangement and/or overwhelming amount of information. As a result, the majority of students end up spending a lot of money on a text they hardly use except for looking through illustrations. Although many texts make great references for advanced learning, they may not be the most useful in an introductory landscape design class.

The intention of this text is to present an approach to landscape design starting with interviewing a client and ending with presenting the design in a format that is concise, readily illustrated to facilitate learning, and, most importantly, can be easily applied in the landscape design industry. This book focuses on residential design, although many of the concepts and steps can be applied to commercial projects as well. In early chapters it covers the roles of a designer and how to find work. Then begins a successive approach to the design process beginning with interviewing the client: how to present yourself, what to bring to the interview, and what questions should be answered. The chapters following Chapter 1, "The Interview," discuss how to take and record measurements (Chapter 2, "The Base Map") and what observations should be made to formulate a design plan (Chapter 3, "Inventory and Analysis") while on site. The book then proceeds with chapters that investigate the function, or usefulness, of the design (Chapter 4, "Functional Principles") and how to draw a concept plan (Chapter 5, "The Concept Plan"); a chapter on design principles (Chapter 6, "Design Principles") looks at creating a visually appealing plan and how to use design principles to draw a preliminary design (Chapter 7, "The Preliminary Design"); a chapter on plant selection and hardscape (Chapter 8) discusses the materials that will be used to formulate the master plan, the final design (Chapter 9, "The Master Plan"). The final chapter addresses how to present a design (Chapter 10, "The Presentation") to clients or in the classroom, which most design books do not cover. Presentation skills cover how to make an effective presentation, making the point that presentation is not reading the plant list but rather how the needs of the site analysis are addressed functionally and aesthetically, as well as why plants and hardscape material are selected and their role in the design. The appendices cover topics such as estimating materials, computer design, attracting and repelling wildlife, and research resources.

My hope is that students will be able to use this text cover to cover over the course of a semester, making it easier to understand and effectively supplement their learning in class and provide them with the skills to be effective landscape designers.

# Acknowledgments

There were many contributions made to this book—photos, interviews, support, and otherwise—that without such it would not have been possible. The people and companies below supplied photos (many from Web sites) or consultation that proved invaluable:

Anne Muecke and Horticopia (www.horticopia.com)

Bill Hoch at the University of Wisconsin (www.midwestlandscapeplants.org)

Chris Briand at Salisbury University (www.salisbury.edu/arboretum/)

Robert Kleinberg Landscaping in East Lansdowne, PA (www.kleinberg.com)

Big Sky Landscaping in Clackamas, OR (www.bigskylandscaping.com)

Thomas Riccardi and Visual Impact Software (www.visualimpactimaging.com)

Craig Smith and Blue Ribbon, LLC in Maryland (www.blueribbonllc.com)

Mary Ann Patterson at American Horticultural Society (www.ahs.org)

Thom Hood at Good Earth Landscaping in Charleston, SC (www.thegoodearthinc.com)

Gary Pribyl and King's Materials, Inc. in Cedar Rapids, IA (www.kingsmaterials.com)

Ron Spiller and JRW Decks in Seattle, WA (www.jrwdecks.com)

Jim Watson and Decks by JRW in Portland, OR (www.decksbyjrw.com)

Doug Hihn and Monet's Gardens in Mt. Pleasant, SC

Trish Emery at Confederate Rose Designs in Goose Creek, SC

Those who provided moral support, professional guidance, or just sound advice and friendship also made this book possible:

Ann Lovering for her home

Sandy Plance for her expertise with CAD

The Horticulture program at Trident Technical College, including Mack Fleming, Sharon Coke, Gray Spencer, and many others

Prentice Hall for answering all my silly questions

The reviewers of this book:

John Kahre—Tulsa Community College
Lin Frye—Johnston Community College
Kathryn Johnson—Gateway Technical College
Gregory Davis—Kansas State University

And all those who have had a creative impact on my life, the list would be too long for this page.

# Introduction

To many people, the landscape design industry is a very satisfying endeavor. It offers the opportunity to be creative, starting on paper with a concept and seeing it come to completion, watching it grow and change over the years, and also having the chance to help clients beautify their property and satisfy their expectations. Students in a horticulture program should be aware of what the job of landscape designer entails. It is not always sitting at a table in an air-conditioned office drawing plans for a contractor to install. Quite often, the landscape designer is part of a design/install company that offers design as a part of their services. Oftentimes, these large companies employ only one or two designers. With small landscape companies, the designer may be the installation contractor as well. Many of the freelance designers who avoid the dirty end of the job still find themselves involved in the installation part, even if only in a supervisory capacity.

Even though the number of job opportunities for the landscape designer is small in comparison to the rest of the horticulture industry, there are encouraging trends. The American Nursery and Landscape Association (www.anla.org) notes that the amount of money spent on landscape designs doubled from 1994 to 1999, although the design spending in 1999 has still only 2 percent of the total landscape service expenditures.

The design job that works exclusively at the table is less often a landscape designer than it is the landscape architect. What's the difference between these positions?

Landscape architects are registered professionals, often referred to as an "L.A." They are required to complete 5 years of study at an accredited institution. They often work on larger, more complex projects that may be commercial or residential. It requires skill in layout and planning, in addition to a good understanding of construction as well as plants. This position often requires in-depth site analysis, plan drawing (drafting and computer), and installation supervision. Drawing skills may include everything from planting plans to full-colored perspective drawings for presentation.

Landscape designers, on the other hand, may be certified through a program of study. The length of study varies greatly between programs, from as little as a few classes in related subjects to a 4-year degree from an accredited institution. Designers are often considered more of a "plant person," working with landscape and nursery businesses and on residential and commercial projects. Depending on the position, the landscape designer is often responsible for the plan drawing, selling the design, and installation supervision. In many cases, the landscape designer serves more as a salesperson than he or she does as a designer.

There are many landscape designers who do freelance design. They often focus on designing for residents or homebuilders. In some cases, when the design is complete and accepted, depending on the designer and agreement, their obligations to the project are over. The client takes the design and finds someone to install it, or the client does the installation. In many cases, it behooves the client as well as the designer for the designer to be involved in the installation in a supervisory capacity. This bodes well for the client and designer to ensure that the design is installed according to their plans. Small changes to the layout and placement can have a large impact on the design. In this case, the landscape designer prepares a materials list and installation specifications that are passed on to a landscape contractor, or placed out for bids among several companies. Many freelance designers quickly establish relationships with companies they can trust.

# People and Business Management

This book is not intended to address business management, however, it is a good idea to briefly mention a few important details pertaining to business. It is advisable to do more research and education in this area from other sources.

As with many facets of horticulture, it is often said that plant knowledge has only been part of the success of designing and managing plants. Just as important is dealing with people and managing the business. As much as the general public dislikes public speaking, it is one of the most important skills to learn. Designers will need to be able to clearly discuss and present ideas to clients. Oftentimes this means working interpersonally with a few people but also may expand to presenting work to a group of people, such as a board of directors. Taking a class in public speaking will help develop invaluable skills of communication.

Often, regardless of design talent, poor business management can eventually cause the company to fail. At the very least, take a small business management class to learn how to write a business plan, know what the liability issues are if the company is a sole proprietor business, and other legal issues. What should the designer consider before launching a landscape design company?

## Business License

Check with the county, or counties, in which your company will be doing business. Each county will require a business license. The cost will vary with the county and the amount of business the company does.

## Business Plan

Write a business plan that will identify the company's niche in the industry and determine if the company will be financially viable. Who are the clients? What are the company's services? What are the costs? What is the profit? If the company cannot make money it will eventually fail. Writing a business plan will set the company in a successful direction.

## Financing

Once a business plan determines overhead, the company will need to invest in supplies and space. Designing may require a minimum investment of drafting supplies that can be used at home, or as much as computer hardware and software and surveying and installation equipment that will require storage. Once the investment amount is determined, a loan will need to be secured to finance the company. Besides discussing options with a banker, look into government programs that can provide funding and consultation at low interest rates or for free.

## Accounting

Become familiar with accounting principles. Keeping receipts, automobile mileage, and home office hours are important components of tax deductions. Consider hiring a certified public accountant (CPA) to handle the company's finances. A CPA will help you balance books and prepare taxes.

# Finding Work

There are many ways to work as a landscape designer. One is with a landscape contractor company or nursery. These positions often vary on the number of designers kept on staff and the role of the designer. Some companies utilize designers as salespeople to find prospective clients, other companies use designers only part-time in the office and the rest of the time in the field for installation.

These positions can sometimes be found in the classified ads of the newspaper. College students should continuously watch the classified ads for design work to get experience and build a portfolio. Also let the professor know you are interested in part-time design work since many people will call a local college to hire students. There are also job bulletins specifically for the horticulture industry that list landscape design openings. A couple of very good Internet job bulletins for job searching are:

http://www.landscapejobs.com/

http://www.hortjobs.com/

Graduating students would benefit from sending out resumes to landscape companies. Call the company as a follow-up to see if they received the resume and schedule a time to come by and present your portfolio.

Some designers prefer to start with a design company to "learn the ropes" before starting their own business as a freelance designer. Freelance designers work for themselves. As a result, they will find design work on their own. To start the business, the word has to get out. Advertising in the Yellow Pages can be effective as well as expensive. The local daily newspaper is another source of advertising. Do not forget small community newspapers that publish once or twice a week. These can be very inexpensive to advertise in and very effective.

Spread the word of the business to all acquaintances. Discuss and give business cards/brochures to your doctor, dentist, real estate agents, lawyer, friends, and family. Often they will talk to someone on this topic with your business in mind.

Once the business becomes more established, word of mouth often becomes the primary method of getting the next project. In a survey done by the Gallup poll (www.anla.org/industry/facts/consumerswant.html), the number one value people looked for in landscape services was *good references and reputation.* This is the driving force of referrals; somebody in the neighborhood or a friend of the client sees the work and contacts your business. If the design is being installed, placing a sign to identify your company will help.

A business card can also be posted at plant nurseries where people often request help for their landscape needs. Other options can also include contacting *construction companies* to inquire if they need designs for new subdivisions. Contact the *county municipality* to get the names of companies that are building in the area.

Starting out in landscape design can be challenging and very time consuming until your design and drawing skills develop and become more time-efficient. Be patient. Take whatever work you can get in the beginning for experience and to build your portfolio. Be sure you charge a fair fee for your work. Do not do too many free designs. Sell your expertise and plan for word of mouth to spread for more work.

# 1 The Interview

## Objectives

- Learn how to conduct an interview
- Learn how to appear professional
- Know what to bring to an interview
- Know what information to get from the client
- Understand about contract and design fees

The **interview** is the initial meeting with the prospective client for whom design services will be provided. This is a meeting not only for the client to interview the designer, but for the designer to interview the client as well. The designer may choose not to work with a client who can be difficult to work with or unreasonable in what they want for what they are willing to pay.

The interview takes place whether the designer is working for a landscape company or as a freelance designer. In some cases there is no interview, such as working for a building contractor before a home is occupied.

The interview may have been the result of a **referral** from a previous client or answering an advertisement. There are a few general guidelines for setting up and proceeding with the interview.

# Setting Up the Interview

## Screen the Client

Before agreeing to meet every person who inquires about design services, **screen** the client by asking a few questions to ensure they understand the scope of services and fees. This could save a lot of time with a person who only wants a few recommendations on plants along the foundation. Usually referrals are good clients because they are familiar with work done for previous clients.

If the prospective client wants to schedule an interview, ask them to do a little homework before the appointment. First, have them consider landscapes they like whether they come up with locations or pictures from magazines. The client should also understand what a site survey is and how they can locate it. Next, have them think about how much money they want to spend on the installation.

## Meet at the Residence

Plan for the interview to take place at the residence. This way observations can be made while on site. It also helps the clients show and explain the areas of concern.

## Meet All the Clients

If working for a couple, it is preferable to schedule the interview while both people are present, whenever possible. In many cases this will be difficult because one of them is working. Meeting in the evening or weekends can make this more possible. Not having one of them there can create communication problems. The designer can avoid call-backs that change design requests, or worse, cancellation of the entire project because the spouse doesn't agree with the fee.

## The One-Hour Interview

One hour is often sufficient to meet the clients, gather site information, and come to an agreement on services. Depending on the project and scope of services, as much as a couple of hours may be required. Much of the time will be spent gathering information about the clients. What services do they want? What are their personalities? What plants do they like? Do they have kids or a dog?

### Free Interview or Consultation Fee?

Many designers do not charge for the initial meeting because screening the calls determines how serious the client is about contracting the company's services. Some designers charge a consultation fee, such as $100, in lieu of a free interview. This would include a little more than just an interview, such as helping the client with design ideas around the yard in a very general sense. The consultation fee is often rolled into the design fee if the client chooses to contract the company for a design. If the client decides not to hire the designer then the time is not wasted.

# Appear Professional

Be presentable at your initial meeting to convey a sense of confidence and quality (Fig. 1–1). Some people place a great deal of importance on appearance and how it relates to work. Make a good first impression.

## Neatly Dressed

Most clients will feel confident in a designer who is clean and tidy instead of one who comes out of the field sloppy and unkempt. Although you are competent, don't let an untucked shirt change the client's perception.

## Clean Hands, Hair, and Clothes

Although this may seem silly, this is an industry that moves soil. It is easy to forget dirt under fingernails and grass stains on the knees because the designer was helping with an installation before the interview. Carry hand soap and towels in the car so that you can clean up before any meeting and smell fresh. As the designer, your professional appearance should be clean.

# What to Bring

There are several items to include on every site visit to get necessary information and be efficient with time. Find a way to bundle these items into an easy to carry package (Fig. 1–2).

(a)

(b)

***Figure 1–1*  Meeting the Client**
(a) Dress professionally. (b) The initial meeting should take place at the residence with both husband and wife. The designer spends about an hour in the interview presenting the portfolio and assessing the clients' needs and wants.

(a)                                                                                                  (b)

***Figure 1–2*  Interview Tools**
Several items that should come along on the interview: business card (a) brochure (b), portfolio (c), compass (d), measuring wheel (e), clipboard (f), contract (g), tape measure (h), and camera (i).

# Clipboard or Notebook

Take notes during the first visit. A clipboard will allow you to walk around the property while securely carrying several documents and scratch paper.

## Measuring Wheel or 200′ Tape Measure

Even with a site survey provided by the client, several measurements may be necessary. A measuring wheel is easier to handle for one person than a measuring tape. However, a tape measure will be required to make some measurements on rough terrain or around objects in the way.

## Compass

Use the **compass** to find magnetic north (Fig. 1–3). This is especially helpful when a site survey is not readily available.

## Camera (Digital or Film)

Photos, taken by either a film or digital **camera,** are helpful to refer back to when at the design table, as well as to store in a portfolio as before and after photos.

## Contract

Some designers like to have a simple contract to be signed by the end of the first meeting. Others prefer to send a proposal and contract after the initial interview.

## Portfolio

Present clients with previous design projects via a **portfolio** (Fig. 1–4). Also have a couple of addresses of previous projects that have been installed that clients can drive by to see. This can also be a time to discuss the cost of various projects to gauge how their budget compares.

*Figure 1–3* **Compass**
A compass is necessary to verify magnetic north.

# Laptop Computer

A **laptop computer** can be used to present a digital portfolio (Fig. 1–5). Software can be used to demonstrate various effects, such as lighting (See Chapter 10).

# Business Card and Brochure

Make sure clients get a **business card** (Fig. 1–6). A good idea is to give the client three business cards: one for each spouse and another to give to a friend. This is an excellent opportunity to have referrals passed along to other people by word of mouth. **Brochures** are even better. They can provide several photos of work and present design philosophy and achievements. Business cards and brochures can be easily designed and printed on a home computer.

*Figure 1–4* **Portfolio**
This is a concise portfolio assembled in a three-ring binder that contains pictures, sketches, and reduced plan drawings. It is helpful to show clients past design work. *(Photo courtesy of Big Sky Landscaping, Inc., Clackamas, OR.)*

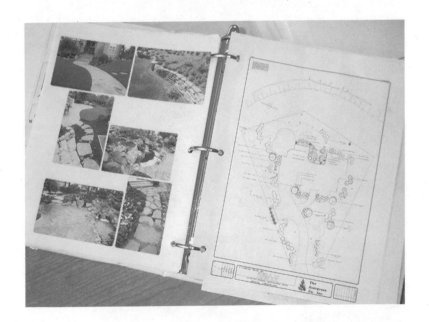

*Figure 1–5* **Laptop Computer**
For those designers who will utilize design software or present a portfolio digitally, the laptop computer can easily show the client ideas and past projects.

# green jeans
creative landscape design and installation

**marge puckhaber.owner**
phone.843.559.1710
greenjns2@aol.com

PHONE 884-6114
FAX 884-6178

## The Good Earth, Inc.
CREATIVE LANDSCAPING

THOM HOOD
VICE PRESIDENT

1495 HARBORGATE BLVD.
MT. PLEASANT, SC 29464

# Monet's Gardens
In Charleston

The Good Earth, Inc.
1495 Harborgate Blvd.
Mt. Pleasant, South Carolina 29464

## Figure 1–6 Business Cards and Brochures

There are several ways to leave company information. A business card is the easiest, although tri-fold brochures are good to include photos of projects and description of services and accomplishments.

## Other Good Ideas

*Door hanger.* Develop a small sign to hang on the client's front door in case they have not arrived for the appointment. It tells the client that you were there.

*Compact disc.* With CD burners being affordable, create a CD of business goals and services along with a digital portfolio containing before and after designs. This will provide clients with a database of plant and landscape images that they can get ideas. This may be the Web site burned on CD (Fig. 1–7).

**Figure 1–7  Compact Disc**
Burning a CD of your company's services along with a digital portfolio can be an inexpensive way to advertise.

*Web site.* Have a Web site created that has similar information as the CD. The Web address can appear on your business card, brochure, and other items. It is easy to pass around and allows prospective clients to look at design work on their own time (Fig. 1–8). Good examples of portfolio Web sites are the following

*http://www.blueribbonllc.com*

*http://www.bigskylandscaping.com*

*http://www.jrwdecks.com*

**Figure 1–8  Web Site**
With most people connected to the Internet, having an inexpensive Web site that displays a portfolio and services is a convenient way to advertise. Having the Web site address on the business card can draw easy traffic. *(Photo courtesy of Courtney Smith.)*

*Catalogs.* Some larger firms keep in touch with clients by publishing a catalog with news and tips about the clients' landscapes (Fig. 1–9).

# THE GOOD EARTH LANDSCAPE COMPANY
# The Good News

QUARTERLY NEWSLETTER                                              SUMMER 2001

## SUMMER CALENDAR

### June

*Plant Iris* – Bearded types can be transplanted while in bloom. Actually, that is the best time to buy because you can see the color. You can also divide and replant existing clumps after they bloom.

*Seeds* – It's not too late to plant annuals. And if your needs are large or your budget small, consider sowing seeds directly into prepared garden beds. Zinnias and Sunflowers respond well.

*Flowers* – Annual and perennial beds, as well as roses, can use a boost, especially where the soil is sandy or the season has been rainy. Apply slow-release fertilizer for maximum benefit with minimum effort.

*Vines* – Train the new growth of clematis, yellow jessamine, and other twining vines to guide them onto the trellis. The new canes of climbing roses usually need some help too. Use loose, dark green twist ties to hold the new growth in place.

### July

*Pumpkins* – If you're going to grow your own jack-o'-lantern, it's time to plant. Choose a sunny spot with plenty of room for the vine. Plant three seeds on a small mound of enriched soil.

*Photographs* – Take pictures of your garden several times during the growing season. This will help you remember what plants to consider when it comes time to start your garden for next year.

*Annuals* – Deadhead your annuals to promote continued blooming.

### August

*Collecting* – It's time to gather grasses, pods and flowers for dried wreaths and arrangements. Wreaths are easier to make while the plant material is fresh; let it dry after it is attached.

*Compost* – This is a good time to begin a compost pile. Although you can get very scientific about it, all you really need is an inconspicuous corner where you can take spent plants, fallen leaves, and vegetable trimmings from the kitchen. Turn the pile occasionally, and you have good soil amendments by spring.

*Pecans* – During drought, water your pecan tree to prevent the nuts from dropping prematurely. Place a soaker hose beneath the outer edge of the canopy and allow it to run until the soil is thoroughly soaked.

**ATTA BOY AWARDS**

**JANUARY:**
Shane Johnson,
Bobby Potter
**FEBRUARY:**
Don Beck,
Sean McDuffie
**MARCH:**
Dale Fox,
Justin Clark

## THINKING OF MOVING YOUR INDOOR PLANTS OUTSIDE FOR THE SUMMER?

The process of gradually acclimating indoor-grown plants to outdoor conditions like direct sunlight, cold soil, strong winds, and pelting rain is called *hardening off*. About two (2) weeks before your area's last frost date, reduce water, giving your seedlings just enough to prevent wilting, and keep a fan on them at low speed, to toughen stems. After a week, place the plants outside for a few hours in a spot sheltered from sun and wind. Check their soil regularly for moisture taking care not to let it get too dry. Increase exposure incrementally, then plant out.

**Figure 1–9  Company Catalog**
Some companies follow up with clients by sending quarterly catalogs that offer maintenance advice and company updates. *(Photo courtesy of Good Earth, Inc., Charleston, SC.)*

# What to Get from A Client

## Trust

The client should feel comfortable with the designer. The client should feel confident that the designer's skills and decisions will meet their needs.

## Commitment

Get a firm commitment. Some designers like to use a simple **contract** to establish the terms of agreement. It is legally binding, but more than that it instills a sense of commitment to the project.

## Site Survey

A survey of the property will save time (covered in the next chapter). If a site survey cannot be obtained, be sure to include additional time in the project for the collection of necessary measurements.

## Photos

Take plenty of photos to avoid having to go back and check on details. Photos are great reminders of details that may have been overlooked or forgotten, like the color of the house or the position of a shed.

## Schedule the Next Meeting

If an agreement and commitment have been reached during the interview, then schedule the next meeting to present the preliminary plan. This depends on the designer's schedule and the size of the project, but a good time frame for many residential projects is about 7 to 10 days.

> *Tip Box*
> **Follow-Up Call**
> A good professional courtesy is to call the clients a few days after the initial interview and ask if there is anything they may want to add.

# Upon Arrival

## Arrive Early

Always be on time, and if possible five to ten minutes early. Showing up late never gives a good first impression. Being punctual gives the impression of trustworthiness. In fact, a good practice is to call in the morning or at least thirty minutes ahead of time to confirm the appointment. Arriving early creates an opportunity to drive around the neighborhood and assess the landscape styles and cost. This will impact the design for the prospective client.

If being late is unavoidable, call as soon as possible to inform the clients of the situation and when they can expect you to arrive.

## Small Talk

Allow several minutes of small talk with the clients. Talk to the kids if they are there and reach down to pet the dog. This will set a relaxed tone for the rest of the interview and will allow you to get familiar with your clients' personalities.

# Discussion of the Design Work

## Quiet Setting

Find a quiet place to sit down—the kitchen, living room, or even outside on the deck (Fig. 1–10) or anyplace that minimizes distractions like the television. Don't be shy to request a quiet, comfortable setting if you notice one. If the clients want to walk around and discuss the project, that's great. But there should also be time set aside to sit down and discuss services and compensation.

## Design Philosophy

Once the clients have had several minutes to discuss what they want, take a few minutes to talk about your design philosophy. This can include showing a portfolio and discussing low maintenance designs, flowing lines, or easy maintenance.

*Figure 1–10* **Sitting at a Table**
When discussing the design, find someplace to sit with clients that is free of distractions where notes can be taken and ideas discussed.

They should also be aware of the cost of the services. It wouldn't be prudent to spend an hour to interview only to find the clients shocked to hear what it will cost them. If they understand the price range of the design services and are agreeable to it, then the interview can proceed. However, if screened properly the clients will be familiar with the fees and services.

Once an understanding is reached on services and fees, begin discussing the project in detail.

## Opening the Discussion

Allow the clients to express what they want. Open the discussion by asking an open-ended question:

*"How can I help you?" or "What can I do for you?"*

This will give the clients an opportunity to discuss why they contacted the designer—if it's just to give them some ideas of what to do with the front yard or to create a design concept for the entire property. If calls are screened carefully, the designer should already be familiar with what they want and they should know how you do business. Regardless of how much the designer knows, the clients will feel more involved in the design if they're allowed to express their desires.

## Listen to the Client

Although the designer records observations and an analysis of the surroundings, the most important source of information is what the clients want. While they are talking, have a clipboard or note cards and take notes vigorously. Writing everything down achieves the following

- It will be a reminder of things later at the design table.
- It communicates to the clients that the designer is actively listening. Everything they say is jotted down and helps instill confidence that the designer is taking the project seriously.
- It can help remind clients of the discussion if there is a dispute later on in the project about what was discussed.

Give clients plenty of time to discuss what they want to do. Spend time listening and acknowledging their comments and wishes. If some things sound unreasonable or out of reach, then propose a suggestion and possible solution, otherwise just listen and take notes. Don't force your opinion over what they want.

### What Does the Client Want?

Oftentimes it becomes the job of the designer to help the clients know what they want. In some cases they may be requesting something that is in complete opposition to their living style. This would be the case with clients who have a formal living style and are requesting wildflower beds, or clients who want a specific plant that is wrong for the site or location. This requires some insightful, gentle discussion to determine what the client is really asking. Instead of wildflowers, do they really just want a lot of color? Instead of that particular plant, do they simply like the tropical characteristics?

# Project Cost

Design fees may have been discussed, but how much do they want to spend on the installation of the design? This will affect the extent of the design and bring the feasibility of their wishes into focus. If they want a large flagstone patio but only wish to spend a couple hundred dollars on it, then they should be aware of what it would cost to build it. Most clients will have a preset range of money in mind to spend on landscaping.

Here are some points to educate clients that landscaping is a good investment:

- Landscaping can add about 10 percent to a home's value (Gallup Organization).

- The cost of landscaping can be recovered by 100 percent to 200 percent (Clemson University).

- Landscaping can reduce energy costs by as much as 50 percent (American Public Power Association).

- More facts can be found on the American Nursery and Landscape Association Web site, http://www.anla.org/industry/facts/valueof.htm.

Some designers estimate that landscaping should cost about 10 percent of the value of the residence. For example, if a residence is valued at $100,000, then $10,000 should be earmarked for landscaping. Another rough estimate is to calculate $2 per square foot of the property. Both of these approaches would include all hardscaping as well as plants. In most cases either one of these estimates is much higher than the cost of most projects. The majority of clients want to spend about half as much as either one of these estimates.

---

### *Tip Box*
### Phasing-In

One solution to ease the sticker shock is to discuss **phasing-in** the design. Approach the design to be installed over the next three to five years. Do the front yard the first year, the deck the second year, backyard beds the third, and finish the side yards the fourth year. This makes the project reachable.

---

# Client Information

This discussion may take place at any time during the interview, not necessarily in the order it's laid out. In most cases these discussions will take place throughout the interview.

The following are some questions to ask the client and to record. These are certainly not the extent of the interview questions. In fact, many of these will often lead to other questions and conversations that will further define what the client wants.

## Family

How many family members?

*Ages?*

*Occupations?*

Are there any allergies to consider, such as bees or specific plants?

Are there any pets to consider?

*Dogs are often the most destructive on plant material. If they do have a dog, do they want to develop a dog run? If not, consider avoiding plants susceptible to being trampled, such as annuals and perennials.*

## Design Goals

Always give the clients the opportunity to address their design goals. This most likely will have already been addressed when the discussion was opened with "How can I help you?" However, during the course of the interview other concerns may arise.

## Lifestyle

Asking them questions about how they use their residence, or intend to use it, will help define the project needs as well as lead the client to other ideas. The following are sample questions.

What kind of things do you do in the:

Front yard?

Side yard?

Backyard?

*For instance, do you have outdoor hobbies or storage needs? Where do you spend time relaxing, entertaining, and recreating?*

### Hobbies

Do you have any outdoor hobbies, such as gardening?

*How about the children? Is there a need to develop an area for them to play?*

### Entertaining

Do you spend time entertaining guests?

*Large crowds? Small? Informal? Formal?*

*Is there a need for a deck or patio?*

*If there is an existing one, is it large enough?*

Do you need to develop an area for outdoor cooking and eating?

## Views

Are there views you would like to keep?

Are there views you would like to block?

*Are there any unpleasant items to be screened, such as a utility box, air-conditioning unit, nearby traffic.*

What about views from inside the house?

Is there any need for privacy from the neighbors?

# Client Preferences

Find out what their preferences are concerning plants, hardscapes, and other features.

Do you prefer informal, natural areas, or layouts that are more formal?

*This may be apparent by observing their living habits, the way their house is kept, and their taste in décor.*

What level of maintenance would you care to have?

*In the vast majority of cases, clients will stress low maintenance. They don't want to have to deal with it, or at least they want to spend less money to have someone else to maintain it. Rarely will the designer hear someone request a "high maintenance landscape." However, if a client would like to develop a rose garden make sure they are aware of the maintenance requirements.*

What are your favorites plants?

*There may be specific plants or just general characteristics.*

"I love lilacs."

"Anything that has fragrance."

"I like tropical-type plants (palms)."

What are your least favorite plants?

*Find out if there are plants they are allergic to or just don't care for.*

"Can't stand those mulberry trees. The birds eat the fruit and then leave it all over everything."

"Don't use any of those yucca plants."

"Don't use anything I have to spend a lot of time pruning."

---

### *Tip Box*
### Landscape Design Examples

Ask if there's a yard they've seen that they really like. If it's convenient, stop by to get an idea of what they like. Ask the client what it is they like about it.

---

Ask about other parts of a design they may be interested in looking at, such as water features, low-voltage lighting, and irrigation.

# Questionnaire

Prepare a handout that they can fill out ahead of the interview (if possible), leave it with them, or go over it with them during the interview (Fig. 1–11).

# Design Fees and Contract

Some designers prefer to talk about their design fees at the beginning of the interview to get it out of the way. It is a good idea for the clients to have some idea of fees to avoid having to complete an hour-long visit and then not agree with the fees.

# LANDSCAPE DESIGN QUESTIONNAIRE

NAME:_____

ADDRESS:_____

CITY, STATE, ZIP CODE:_____

PHONE:_____


## FAMILY

Name and age of family members



Are there any allergies? YES OR NO

Type of outdoor pets (please specify):

Time of day and season family most active in landscape:_____

Is there a need for handicap access? YES OR NO


## BUDGET

Will this design be installed by homeowner or contractor?  YES OR NO

Approximate budget allowed for the design and installation: $_____

       Or is it dependent upon consultation? YES OR NO

Would you consider implementing design over a few years to spread out cost? YES OR NO


## SOIL/DRAINAGE

Are there problems with standing water in the landscape? YES OR NO

Is soil extremely heavy (clay) or sandy?

Are there steep slopes on the property? YES OR NO


## VIEWS

Which rooms in the house offer the most common views to the outside?



Are there any views that need to be created, such as from an entertainment area? YES OR NO

Are there any unpleasant areas to be screened from view (utility box, traffic, A/C unit)?



Does there need to be more privacy in any areas?

**Figure 1–11  Questionnaire**
A questionnaire can be provided to the clients prior to the interview or downloaded from the Web site.

## MICROCLIMATES

*Answer any below that are applicable.*

Where are there areas of full shade or full sun:_____

Where is there a need for more shade:_____

Where is there a need for noise reduction:_____

Where are there areas that need overhead protection:_____

Where are there areas too windy:_____

Where are there problems with snow or ice:_____


## PLANT SELECTION

*Answer any below that are applicable.*

Name your favorite plants:_____

Any plants or materials you dislike:_____

Name your favorite colors:_____

Would you like to include: FRAGRANCE, ANNUAL FLOWERS, OR NATIVE PLANTS


## CIRCULATION

Does the driveway need to be expanded? YES OR NO

Does the front walk need to be improved? YES OR NO

Is there circulation to other parts of the yard that needs to be accessible or improved? YES OR NO


## ENTERTAINMENT

What is the average number of people you entertain:_____

Would you like to build or expand a deck or patio? YES OR NO


## SERVICE

Is there a need for storage space (boat, trailer)? YES OR NO

Are garbage cans:

      ☐ Accessible YES OR NO

      ☐ Unsightly YES OR NO

      ☐ Need to be relocated YES OR NO

Is there a need for: FIREWOOD STORAGE, COMPOSTING, VEGETABLE GARDEN, SHED


***Figure 1–11 Questionnaire—continued***
A questionnaire can be provided to the clients prior to the interview or downloaded from the Web site.

## ACTIVITY

*Please check any of the following to include in design:*

☐ Kid's playground

☐ Cooking and eating

☐ Privacy area

☐ Firepit

☐ Recreation (horseshoes, volleyball)

## MISCELLANEOUS CONSIDERATIONS

*Please check any of the following you would be interested in including in landscape design:*

☐ Water feature

☐ Low-voltage lighting

☐ Sculpture

☐ Butterfly garden

☐ Fence

☐ Energy efficiency

## ADDITIONAL COMMENTS

Are there any other areas or problems you would like to address that are not mentioned on this

questionnaire?

**Figure 1-11 Questionnaire—continued**
A questionnaire can be provided to the clients prior to the interview or downloaded from the Web site.

# Design Fees

There is a great variance in what designers charge, most of which depends on experience. Designer **fees** range anywhere from $20 to $100 per hour. Some designers do not charge per hour but by the project. For example, a typical residential design ranges from $100 to $500.

Designers who work for a design/installation firm will often, as an incentive to get the contract for installation and maintenance, take the price of the design out of the cost of installation.

As a beginning designer, be comfortable with your fees. Charging less may help you get started and develop a portfolio as well as confidence. But don't sell yourself short;

remember you are providing your expertise of plants and design. It can be pleasantly surprising to find out just how little most people know about plants.

The amount of time spent on a residential design project varies greatly between designers and the projects. Many designers expect to spend about 5 to 10 hours on an average project. They can expect to spend a various amount of time on the following phases of the design process:

**Measurements, inventory, and analysis –** 1 to 2 hours

**Preliminary design(s) and digital imagery –** 2 to 4 hours

**Presenting preliminary design(s) –** 1 hour

**Master plan –** 2 to 3 hours

## Contract

Once the interview is complete, estimate the amount of time it would take to complete the project and propose a design fee (Fig. 1–12). Some designers prefer to prepare a formal **proposal** and contract and send it to the clients a few days after the interview. Some prefer a verbal proposal and simple contract to be signed before they leave the interview. And there are others who simply work on the "gentleman's handshake," no legally binding document. However, it is a good idea to have a simple contract signed by the clients. In addition to the legal ramifications, it provides a sense of commitment between the designer and the client.

## Payment Schedule

A payment schedule is arranged in the contract so that part of the compensation is due before the project is complete. This can prevent a client from dropping the project after it has been started or nearly completed, with no payment. Some designers ask for a retainer fee, or money when the contract is signed to retain the designer's services. A **retainer fee** may be half of the design fee at the signing of the contract and the remainder  due upon completion; or one-third at signing, one-third at the preliminary, and the remaining one-third at the master.

Another typical payment schedule is as follows:

**Retainer fee upon signing the contract –** 20 percent

**Presentation of preliminary design(s) –** 60 percent

**Master plan –** 20 percent

# Make the Next Appointment

Once the fees and contract are completed, set the next appointment to present the preliminary design(s). This could be about seven to ten days after the interview, or dependant on mutual schedules. A designer should also consider asking the client for permission to return to the property, even if the client is not at home, to make observations or measurements.

# Pelican designs
### Landscape design solutions

## Proposal for Design Services
_____Residence

**Scope of Work.** Outlined below are the proposed tasks to be accomplished.

1. On-site measurement and development of the base map.
2. Analysis of existing on-site and immediate off-site conditions.
3. Development of a minimum of two Preliminary Diagrams.
4. Further refinement of one of the Preliminary Diagrams into a Master Plan.

**Drawings**. To be submitted according to the schedule outlined below.

1. Development of base map, site inventory, site analysis, and Concept Plans.
2. Two Preliminary Designs showing the location of all proposed site elements and existing site features that are to remain such as walks, driveway, fences, and plantings. These plans will be presented at your home for refinement and final approval.
3. One Master Plan showing the specific names of plant materials, other materials and patterns developed from the approved Preliminary Design, blackline, 24 x 36, for client retention.

**NOTE**: Scope of work does not include detailed construction or work drawings for any site structure, or actual construction and installation of the design. It is the client/installer's responsibility to determine the exact location of any buried utility services before digging.

### Fee Payment Schedule
I will prepare and execute the above noted drawings and design services for the sum of $_____, payment as follows:

$_____ submitted with signed contract.
$_____ paid upon completion and presentation of the Preliminary Design.
$_____ paid upon completion and presentation of the Master Plan.

### Contract Acceptance
Your signature below indicates your acceptance of the terms.

(Client)_____        Date_____

(Client)_____

**Figure 1–12  Contract**
A simple contract is a legally binding document that lays out a payment schedule and can be brought to the interview and signed upon completion of the interview or sent to the clients after the interview along with a proposal.

# Inventory and Analysis

After the interview, measurements and observations can be made for the inventory and analysis (discussed in the next chapter) or make a return visit.

# Other Considerations

Some other things you might do following the initial interview:

## Follow-Up Call

Two or three days after the interview, call the client(s) to touch base with them and see if there is anything they thought of since your visit.

## Thank-You Card

Send a card thanking them for the opportunity to discuss their design needs. This is another way to keep in touch between the interview and the next visit. It appears professional and may help you to find your next client.

For a closer examination of the interview process, see Appendix A, "The Design Process," for the Grant Residence Interview.

# Summary

The interview is an opportunity for the landscape designer to present services and fees to a prospective client in addition to learning their needs and goals. This generally takes an hour to complete. The designer should appear and conduct himself or herself professionally by dressing appropriately, arriving on time, and being organized. The designer may present a portfolio of past work to familiarize the clients with the designer's design philosophy and competence. If the services and fees are agreeable, then the clients should be given ample opportunity to discuss their wants and needs from the landscape while the designer takes notes. The designer may ask questions or a questionnaire may be made available for the clients to fill out so that the designer may accurately incorporate the needs of the family and their lifestyle into the design. When the discussion is completed, the interview is concluded with a signed contract and payment schedule or a commitment from the designer to send a proposal in a few days.

# Key Terms

**Brochures:** include several photos of design work, philosophy, and achievements

**Business card:** 2″ × 3.5″ card with business name, phone number, and other information

**Camera:** used to take photos on site, film or digital

**Catalogs:** news and tips about their landscapes sent to clients following their projects

**Compact disc:** contains business goals and services along with a digital portfolio

**Compass:** used to find magnetic north

**Contract:** legally binding document that the client signs and agrees to the services and fees outlined

**Door hanger:** small sign you can hang on a client's front door in case they are not present for appointment

**Fees:** designers charge anywhere from $20 to $100 per hour, or $150 to $500 a project

**Interview:** the initial meeting with the prospective client for whom you will provide the service of landscape design

**Laptop computer:** used to present a digital portfolio of past projects

**Payment schedule:** outlines when and how much of the fees will be paid to the designer

**Phasing-in:** installing the project over the next three to five years to spread out the cost

**Portfolio:** a collection of previous design projects to show to prospective clients

**Proposal:** a written document that outlines the services and fees of the designer

**Referral:** a previous client who has recommended your services to a potential client

**Retainer fee:** payment to reserve the designer's services.

**Screening:** asking a potential client questions so that they understand your services and fees to avoid wasting time

**Web site:** contains business goals and services along with a digital portfolio; the Web address can appear on your business card, brochure, and other items

# 2 | The Base Map

### Objectives

- Understand the terminology relating to a plat, or site survey
- Know the drafting tools used to draw a base map
- Understand how to interpret plat information
- Learn how to take site measurements
- Be able to draw a base map to scale

The next step after the analysis is to draw an accurate base map. To do so, there are a few definitions you should be aware of in order to understand a site survey and base map, as well as the techniques in taking measurements.

## Plan Drawing

A **plan drawing** is a two-dimensional drawing of an area that appears like a bird's-eye view looking from directly overhead, sometimes referred to as a "**plan view drawing**" (Fig. 2–1). It will be the plan, or map, on which the design will be illustrated.

## Drafting Tools

Before discussing the components of a base map, it is important to be familiar with some of the tools and materials required to draw a plan.

### Paper

**Tracing paper,** sometimes called **trash paper, onionskin,** or **bumwad,** is a thin translucent paper used to sketch ideas (Fig. 2–2). It is a *low-quality paper* that will be useful for sketching ideas such as the concept plan.

**Vellum paper,** or **rag vellum,** is a higher quality paper that is translucent and can be placed over previous drawings to trace. It is typically used for the final plan of lead drawings. **Mylar** is a high-quality paper that is actually drafting **film.** It can be used for the final plan but is often used when drawing with ink because ink can be easily erased from mylar.

The dimensions of the paper are dependant on the project. A **full sheet** is 24″ × 36″, which is typical for many projects (Fig. 2–3). This allows the designer to work in a comfortable scale that shows detail reasonably well. However, as the project permits, smaller sheets can be used. Typical sizes are:

**Full sheet:** 24″ × 36″

**Half sheet:** 18″ × 24″

**Quarter sheet:** 12″ × 18″

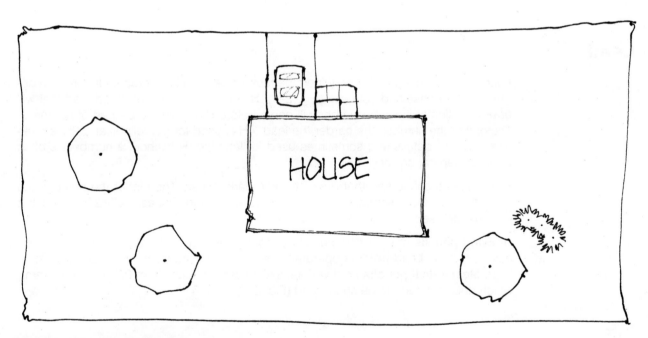

***Figure 2–1*** **Plan Drawing**
A plan drawing is a bird's-eye view looking directly from the site.

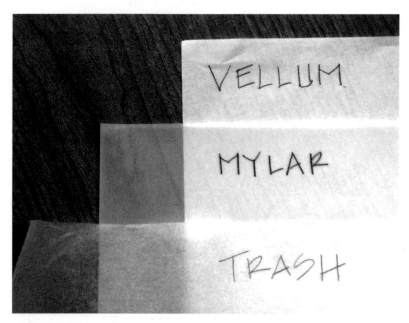

***Figure 2–2*  Paper**
Tracing paper (bottom) is used to sketch ideas, while vellum and mylar are commonly used for the final drawing because of higher quality and longevity.

# Lead

**Lead** is a good medium for beginners because it can be easily erased. It comes in degrees of hardness and softness (Fig. 2–4). **H** is used to designate hard lead that will draw thin, lighter lines. A number will come before H to give the degree of hardness. The higher the number, the harder the lead. 4H is used for guidelines and 2H is often used to draw details and sometimes used for lettering. H (without a number) is often used for general drawing.

**B** designates softer lead that draws thicker, darker lines. The higher the number, the softer the lead. HB is sometimes used for general drawing. Occasionally 2B is used, but it should be used with caution because it smudges easily.

**Drawing pencils** are wooden pencils without an eraser at the end; inexpensive and easy to handle. **Lead-holders** operate like a mechanical pencil but hold larger sticks of lead. **Mechanical pencils** hold various thicknesses of lead (from 0.5 mm to 0.9 mm), which does not need to be sharpened (Fig. 2–5).

# Ink

**Markers** and **ink** provide excellent line quality. The contrast of black lines on white paper creates a very clean and legible document. Ink will not erase from vellum. *Be sure the ink is dry before moving tools across the vellum.* Otherwise, it will smudge and ruin a drawing.

**Technical pens** have tips made of metal and an ink reservoir. Sets will have very narrow tips, such as 0.2 mm, and wider tips around 1.0 mm. They are relatively expensive. **Pigment liners** are fiber-tip markers that also have a variety of line widths. They are relatively inexpensive and disposable (Fig. 2–6).

**Figure 2–3  Paper Dimensions**
A full sheet is common for many projects, but smaller projects may be on a half or quarter sheet.

PENCIL 4H — INK 0.1 mm

PENCIL 2H — INK 0.3 mm

PENCIL H — INK 0.5 mm

PENCIL 2B — INK 0.7 mm

**Figure 2–4  Lead and Ink**
H leads (left) are harder leads that draw lighter lines; the higher the number the harder the lead. B leads are softer leads that draw thicker, darker lines; the higher the number the softer the lead. Various widths of ink tips (right) are used to get variations in line width. Tip widths are measured in millimeters.

**Figure 2–5 Lead**

Often used by beginning designers because it erases easily. (a) Drawing pencils, (b) lead holders, or (c) mechanical pencils.

(a)

(b)

***Figure 2–6*** **Ink**
Ink provides a higher quality line but can be difficult to work with. (a) Technical pens. (b) Pigment liners.

## Compass

A **compass** is used to draw large circles or strike arcs for base map preparation (Fig. 2–7). It consists of one leg that has a sharp point that sticks into the middle of the circle and another leg with lead at the end. When the compass is spun around on the point, the lead draws the circle.

## Scale

A **scale** is a ruler that has units to represent feet in the plan drawing (Fig. 2–8). It is used to draw the plan accurately. There are two types of scales: architect and engineer. An **architect scale** is based on units of an inch. For instance, the plan may be drawn so

*Figure 2–7* **Compass**
Used to draw circles or strike arcs in site plan preparation.

that every 1/4″ is equal to 1′. Many designs are drawn with an 1/8″ scale (every 1/8″ equals 1′), although it will depend on the scope of the project and size of the paper.

An architect scale can be confusing to use at first since it utilizes unit measurements running in both directions. The nice thing about working with increments of an inch is that a ruler can be used in case an architect scale is not available.

> ### *Tip Box*
> Landscape designers and architects commonly use the architect scale.

An **engineer scale** is based on *unit increments IN an inch*. The 10-scale has 10 evenly spaced increments per inch, the 20-scale has 20 increments per inch, and so on. So, if using the 10-scale, where every inch has 10 increments, the scale would be 1″ = 10′.

> ### *Tip Box*
> Surveyors commonly use the engineer scale. Therefore, any site survey obtained from clients or a city surveyor will most likely be drawn to an engineer scale.

(a)

(b)

(c)

***Figure 2–8*** **Scale**

(a) The architect scale (above) and engineer scale (below) are often used to draw accurate plans. (b) The engineer scale is a measure of units in an inch, such as the 20-scale that has 20 units in an inch, which would be used as 1″ = 20′, or each individual unit is equal to 1 foot. The above compass is adjusted to 20 feet. (c) The architect scale is a measure of units of an inch, such as every 1/8″ = 1′. The above compass is adjusted to 20 feet.

# Site Survey

The **site survey** contains the resident's lot with additional info. This is ideally the document you should obtain from the clients from which you will easily be able to design the plan drawing (Fig. 2–9). This survey is done by a registered land surveyor and shows the property lines and their length and bearings, the house located on the lot, and sometimes other objects like fences, driveway, sidewalks, and decks/patios. The site survey is commonly referred to as a **plat, mortgage plat,** or **closing survey**. This book will refer to this document as a site survey. Information in the survey is as follows: lot, bearings and distance of property lines, footprint, right-of-way, and easement. Setbacks and covenants may not be on the survey but are important to understand as well.

**Figure 2–9  Site Survey**

A site survey is a surveyor's map of the property, referred to as a plat, including the footprint of the house and other permanent objects such as driveway, deck, etc. It is usually obtained by the residents upon the closing of the house. It is important that the designer has a copy to draw an accurate plan to scale. (This survey has been altered to conceal the identity of resident and surveyor.)

**Figure 2–10  Lot**
A lot is a map of the resident's property. This plan includes all the lots in the subdivision.

# Lot

Lot refers to the residential property. It shows the **property lines,** which define the property boundaries (Fig. 2–10). Some residents may have a copy of the subdivision that shows the layout of lots.

# Property stakes

**Property stakes** locate the beginning and end of a property line (Fig. 2–11). Stakes are generally a metal bar (usually a 1/2" diameter rebar) buried vertically in the ground. The top of the stake is about 6 inches from the surface. Property corners may be identified by other permanent objects, such as a manhole cover, and would be indicated on the survey. You can locate the general vicinity of the stake by sighting along a fence line and 10' in from the curb (assuming the right-of-way is 50'; see section on right-of-way later in the chapter). Use a shovel to cut through the ground at an angle to hit the stake.

***Figure 2–11  Property Stakes***
Property corners are established with property stakes, or other permanent objects such as a manhole cover. Property stakes are metal rods that are vertically located about 6 inches below the surface.

***Figure 2–12  Bearings and Length***
Information on the property lines of a site plan provides the orientation of the property line (as it relates to north, south, east, west) and length.

# Bearings and Length of Property Lines

The property lines show the **bearings**, which provide the orientation and the distance, or length (Fig. 2–12). For instance, look at the property line on the left in Figure 2–12 between LOT 8 and LOT 9. The bearing is:

S 39° 42′ 29″ E 212.11′

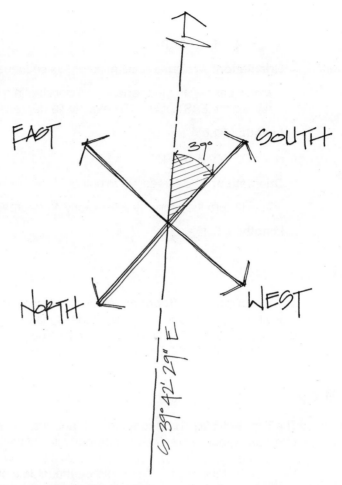

*Figure 2–13* **Bearing Orientation**
The orientation can be related to how many degrees from the north or south direction.

**Bearings:** The aforementioned property line is pointing in a direction that is 39 degrees, 42 minutes, and 29 seconds EAST of a SOUTHERN direction. (Although you are familiar with degrees, surveyors use minutes and seconds as smaller increments to more precisely measure angles.) In other words, if you draw a property line running directly NORTH-SOUTH, turn the property line as if it is stuck on a peg like a spinner exactly 39 degrees, 42 minutes, and 29 seconds in an EASTERLY direction (Fig. 2–13).

**Length:** The length of the property line is also indicated. In this case the property line is 212.11 feet long.

Let's continue around the property lines in a clockwise direction.

S 29° 50′ 39″ W 100.29′

**Orientation:** 29 degrees, 50 minutes, 39 seconds WEST (left) of SOUTH

Again, if the property line was mounted on a peg pointing in a NORTH-SOUTH direction, turn it toward a WESTERLY direction exactly 29 degrees, 50 minutes, 39 seconds.

**Length:** 100.29'

N 40° 54' 35" E 231.03'

**Orientation:** 40 degrees, 54 minutes, 35 seconds EAST (right) of NORTH

In this case, with the property line pointing in a NORTH-SOUTH direction, turn it toward the EAST of NORTH exactly 40 degrees, 54 minutes, 35 seconds.

**Length:** 231.03'

N 41° 00' 00" E 100.13'

**Orientation:** 41 degrees, 00 minutes, 00 seconds EAST (right) of NORTH

Finally, turn the property line exactly 41 degrees toward the EAST of NORTH.

**Length:** 100.13'

# Footprint

The **footprint,** or the **floorplan,** of the house will be located within the lot. The footprint may or may not include the dimensions of the outer walls. In some cases a floorplan is included separately with the survey and indicates the wall dimensions and the location of windows and doors (Fig. 2–14).

# Right-of-Way

The **Right-of-Way** (R/W) is a strip of land that is publicly owned, which includes the street and ground up to the front property line of the lot (Fig. 2–15). The width of the R/W varies, but it is often about 50 feet. Visualize the R/W by drawing an imaginary line down the middle of the street. This would be the middle of the R/W. Thus, the R/W would extend 25 feet in each direction of the line, a total of 50 feet wide.

***Figure 2–14*  Footprint**
An example of a house floorplan.

(a)

(b)

(c)

**Figure 2–15  Right-of-Way**

(a) The Right-of-Way (R/W) is the strip of land where the road and sidewalk are located. (b) The property line is usually located right at the edge of the sidewalk. (c) Where there is no sidewalk, the R/W is part of the front yard, usually 10 feet from the curb. Notice where the fence is located on the neighboring corner lot.

If there is a public sidewalk running parallel with the street, the front property line is normally located just before the sidewalk. The sidewalk would be located in the R/W. In neighborhoods with no public sidewalks, the R/W may not even be noticeable. It would be approximately 10 feet, depending on R/W width, of turf that runs from the curb and appears like the front yard.

Be aware that the site survey will not indicate the R/W and curb, but only the property lines of the lot. Do not make the mistake of identifying the front property line as the curb. If a sidewalk is not present, the curb is usually another 10 feet or so, depending on R/W from the front property line. If you draw the design using the front property line as the curb, the design will be misrepresented.

### Right-of-Way Access

Be aware that the city or county street department has access to the R/W and can excavate it for repairs or installations. It is a good idea to check with the local government before planting or making changes in this area. In most cases, they will ask that nothing be planted in it. At the least, do not plant anything of significant size or construct a permanent structure that cannot be relocated easily.

> ### *Tip Box*
>
> Include the Right-of-Way in the plan drawing. The site survey only shows the property line, while the front yard may actually extend another 10′ to the curb.

## Easement

An **easement** is a strip of land on the property that others have access to. This is primarily the case with utility companies that locate or install cable or drainage (Fig. 2–16).

## Setback

A **setback** is the minimum distance from a property line that any permanent construction can take place although this information does not typically appear on a site survey. Setbacks are included in the set of building ordinances that keep houses a specified distance from the front (front setback), side (side setback), and back property lines (back setback) (Fig. 2–17).

## Covenants

Although not found on the site survey, it is important to be aware of restrictions that may apply to the landscape within a subdivision. A **covenant,** sometimes referred to as a **restrictive covenant,** is a legal agreement created by the land developer that a homeowner enters into when purchasing a house within a subdivision. These agreements are meant to preserve the quality of living and value of the property. Such restrictions could

**Figure 2-16 Easement**

(a) An easement is an area along the property line that other authorities have legal access to, usually utility companies. Do not construct permanent objects in an easement, although fences are typically permitted. (b) An easement is located on this site survey along the back and right property lines.

**Figure 2-17   Setback**
A setback is the distance from the front, side, and back property lines where construction can take place. The house must be located within the setback.

include plants and how they are maintained, minimum cost of house, color of house (even the shingles), and parking spaces (no cars in the front yard). This could keep the pink flamingos out of the neighborhood (Fig. 2–18). Most states require the seller to inform the buyer of such covenants. It is important to be aware if any covenants apply to the site and what they are. The owners should be aware of these, if they are not then contact the builder of the house.

# Obtaining the Site Survey

Most residents are given a copy of the site survey upon closing of the house which is often required by the lender to verify the property, which is why this document is commonly referred to as a mortgage plat. Make every effort to obtain a copy of this document; otherwise, it will take additional time and effort for you to draw an accurate plan to design. If the client cannot locate a copy, the county surveyor will most likely have a copy on file.

***Figure 2–18* Covenant**
Covenants may restrict landscaping, such as the
use of pink flamingos or certain plants and colors.

*Tip Box*

**Locating the Site Survey**

Look at the following locations to find the site survey:

- Closing papers
- County surveyor
- Architect of the house
- General contractor who built the house
- Mortgage company

# Proofread the Site Survey

Take a few measurements to make sure that the site survey is accurate and up to date.
This could save hours of wasted time and embarrassment. Additions or renovations
since the last survey could change the accuracy of the site survey.

# Measurements

Measurements of the property will be needed to locate objects and lay out the ground
plan of the site. It's important to be accurate since the site survey will not always include
all the objects or areas on site.

To take measurements, the following items will be needed:

- Clipboard
- Measuring wheel: This is the most convenient way to take measurements, but it may
  not work if the terrain is extremely rough or objects are in the way (Fig. 2–19).

- Measuring tape: 100′ or 200′ long (Fig. 2–20)
- Screwdriver: To hold the tape in place

## Units of Measurement

Know what units your equipment is measuring. Tape measures and measuring wheels will measure in feet/inches or decimals of a foot. Most field measurements do not need to be this accurate, but be familiar with the difference. Some feel that recording measurements in decimals is easier than inches because it uses one unit of measurement, feet, instead of two units, feet and inches, although this is primarily preference.

(a)

(b)

**Figure 2–19   Measuring Wheel**
(a) Measuring wheel is a quick and easy way to get distance measurements. (b) A counter records the distance as the wheel turns.

(a)

(b)

(c)

**Figure 2–20 Tape Measure**
(a) A measuring tape can be used to get measurements, ideally a 200-foot tape. (b) Measurements might be in feet and inches or feet and decimals of a foot. Be sure you know which unit is used. (c) Hold tape tight for accurate measurement.

Converting the units is very simple. Since there are 12 inches in 1 foot, converting utilizes a factor of 12.

### Converting Inches to Decimals

Divide inches by 12

4" ÷ 12 = .33'

### Converting Decimals to Inches

Multiply decimal by 12

0.4 × 12 = 4.8"

# Pacing

If you find yourself without a measuring tape or wheel, train your pace to equal 3 feet (Fig. 2–21). For most people this is a stride that is a little longer than their normal pace. Practice **pacing** a few times to get an accurate feel for a 3-foot step. Measure off a 30-foot course and practice a pace that will complete it in ten 3-foot steps.

# Direct Measuring

**Direct measuring** is simply measuring from one point to another. If you are using a tape measurement, pull the tape tight. Any slack in the tape will skew the measurement (Fig. 2–20).

***Figure 2–21*  Pacing**
Pacing is a quick technique to get a rough estimate of distance. Each step should approximate 3 feet. Practice pacing on a 30-foot course until it takes ten steps to complete it.

# Baseline Measurement

**Baseline measurement** is the quickest way to obtain several measurements along one line (Fig. 2–22). It reduces the need to move the tape and minimizes compounding errors.

## Obtaining Measurements Using a Baseline

To obtain measurements using a baseline, start at one end of the line and pull the measuring tape tight to the end of the line. At each point along the line, locate and record the measurement on the tape. Laying down the tape measure once can avoid re-staking the tape measure and compounding errors from one measurement to the next. If using a measuring wheel, start at zero and stop at each point to record the measurement, although it can be difficult to hold the wheel and write at the same time. Do not re-zero the wheel. Continue to the next point and record. Repeat until the end of the line is reached.

A good example would be locating the windows and door along the front of the house. Stake the tape measure on one corner of the house and pull it tight to the other corner. Starting at zero, locate the first edge of the first window and record the measurement on the tape. Next, record the measurement of the second edge of the window. Continue along the tape measure until you mark everything to the opposite corner. If using a measuring wheel, start at zero and stop at the first edge to record the measurement and continue on without re-zeroing the wheel.

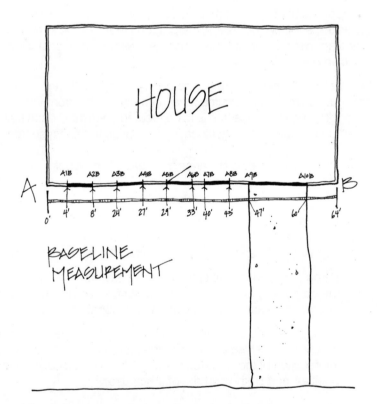

***Figure 2–22*** **Baseline Measurement**
Baseline measuring is taking measurements along a straight line starting at zero and recording each measurement without starting over at zero. It is more efficient and reduces errors from compounding when starting over at each point.

## Recording Baseline Measurements

To keep measurements orderly, record them as follows.

The beginning and end of the line can be labeled with letters.

**Zero mark:** A          **End mark:** B

If more than one baseline measurement is taken on site, the letters can continue with C, D, etc.

The measurements between line A–B are numbered in order (1, 2, 3 . . . ) as follows:

A1B = 4'               A6B = 33'

A2B = 8'               A7B = 40'

A3B = 24'              A8B = 43'

A4B = 27'              A9B = 47'

A5B = 29'              A10B = 60'

AB = 64' (Referring to the entire line)

# Triangulation

Triangulation is a very useful way of locating objects on the property. **Triangulation** is the application of locating an unknown point from two known points (Fig. 2–23). In most cases there will be a house on the property that has two known points that can be used. Any other permanent structure such as a fence, curb, or storage shed can be used as a known point (Fig. 2–24).

Let's use the corners of a house as point A and point B (the same two points used in the previous example for baseline measurement). In the front yard there is a tree, we'll call point T. (If more than one tree is to be located, then label each tree T1, T2, T3, etc.) Point T can be located in its exact location in relation to the house from corners A and B.

1. Direct measure the distance from each known point to the unknown point.

   AT = 32'

   BT = 43'

   Point T (tree) can now be located from the footprint of the house.

2. Using a compass, adjust the legs to equal 43' in the scale of the base map. Stick the compass point into corner B and strike an arc with the lead across the approximate area where point T will be located.

3. Next, adjust the compass to equal 32' in the same scale. Stick the point into corner A and strike an arc with the lead so that it *crosses the first arc*. Where the intersection of the two arcs occurs is the exact location of point T in relation to points A and B (the corners of the house).

## Triangulating a Curve

Triangulation can also be used to draw the curve of a curb or bed (Fig. 2–25). By randomly locating several points along the curve and triangulating them, the points can be drawn on the base map and then connected. Of course, the more points that are located, the more accurately the curve can be drawn.

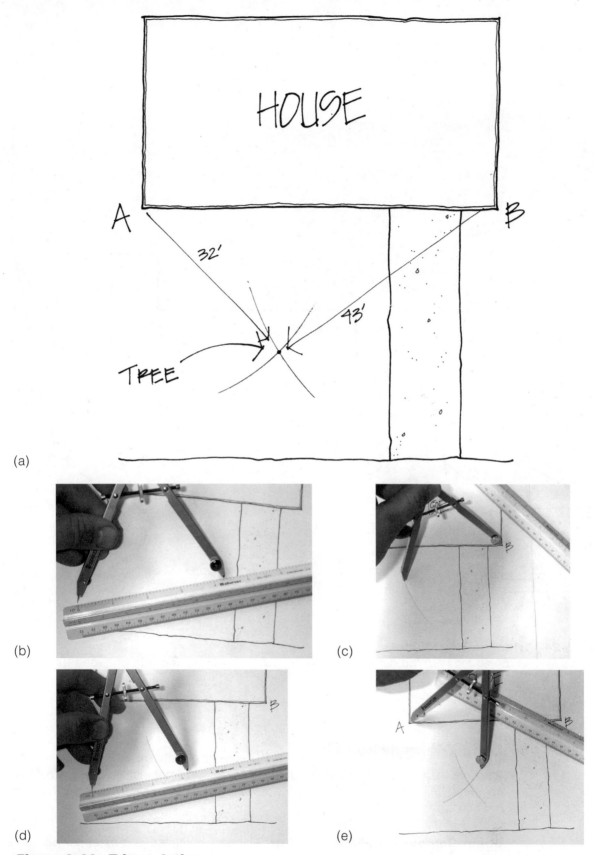

## Figure 2-23   Triangulation

(a) Triangulation is locating an unknown point from two known points. An example would be locating a tree from two corners of a house. Label the corners A and B and measure the distance to the tree from each corner. (b) A compass is adjusted to scale to equal 43 feet and (c) an arc is struck from point B. (d) The compass is adjusted to equal 32 feet and (e) an arc is struck from point A, and where those two arcs cross is the location of the tree.

***Figure 2-24  Triangulating Objects***
In addition to trees being located, the corners of objects, such as a shed and a hedge, can be located to orient.

## Long Triangulation Lines

Students may run into the problem of triangulation lines that exceed the span of their compass. Without larger equipment, the arcs cannot be accurately marked with a standard compass.

**Beam Compass or Extender Bar**   A beam compass and extender bar have much wider spans that can be used to strike long arcs (Fig. 2–26). A **beam compass** is a long rod that has a point and a lead that can be slid up and down to adjust the length of the radius. An **extender bar** can be inserted into the end of the compass to increase the radius.

(a)

(b)

**Figure 2–25  Triangulating a Curve**
(a) A curve can be located by triangulating random points and then (b) connecting the dots. Of course, the more points triangulated, the more accurate the curve.

# Grid

A **grid** can be useful to locate an object or accurately draw a ground plane area, such as the curving shape of existing beds (Fig. 2–27).

Use an existing form to measure parallel lines at measured intervals. The existing form can be a house, building, or curb. The length of parallel lines can be used to mark points along the curve and then connect them.

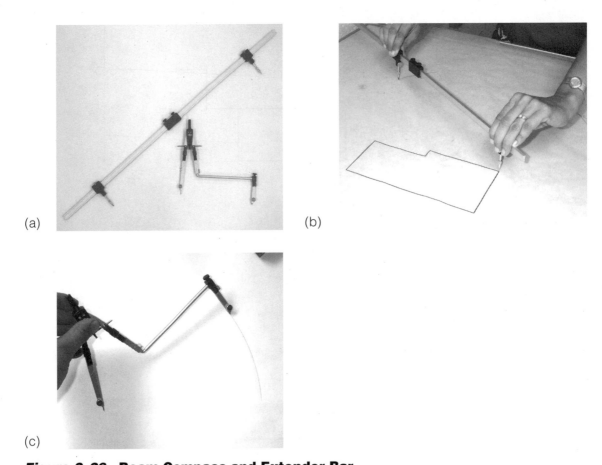

*Figure 2–26*  **Beam Compass and Extender Bar**
(a) For triangulating lines that exceed the capacity of the standard compass a beam compass (left) or extender bar attachment (right) can be used. (b) Beam compass. (c) Extender bar.

# What to Locate on Site

Items to be located on site:

**Existing trees, shrubs, and other objects** Method: Triangulation, grid

**Dimensions of additions, such as decks or storage sheds** Method: Direct measurement for dimensions; triangulating corners of additions that stand separate from house

**Windows and doors on house** Method: Baseline measurement

**Sidewalks, driveway, beds, or other permanent fixtures** Method: Triangulation, grid, and direct measurement

**Property stakes from house (to locate the footprint on the lot)** Method: Triangulation

# Creating the Base Map

With all the measurements and site survey, the **base map** can be drawn in a scale that will be appropriate for the plan drawing. The base map is a plan drawing that includes all pertinent objects and areas on the property that will impact the design not found on the site survey. Some refer to this plan as a **site plan.**

The site survey acquired from the client will most likely be on an 8.5″ × 11″ sheet of paper, or similar size. Typically, this scale will not be large enough to design because the details would be difficult to read.

Instead, increase the scale of the plan drawing. In most cases, a scale of 1/8″ = 1′ or larger will be appropriate. If using an engineer scale, 1″ = 10′ or less will be appropriate. A 24″ × 36″ sheet of tracing paper will serve as the initial drawing for the base map, which can be transferred to vellum later, although smaller sizes of paper can be used depending on the detail of the project and the size of the property.

> ### *Tip Box*
>
> Draw the base map in a scale large enough so that detail is adequate to read. Most commonly used scales are 1/8″ = 1′ (architect) and 1″ = 10′ (engineer).

**(a)**

### *Figure 2–27* **Grid Measurement**

Another approach to locating objects is grid measurement. (a) Measure perpendicular from a permanent object, such as house or curb, to an unknown object.

*(continues)*

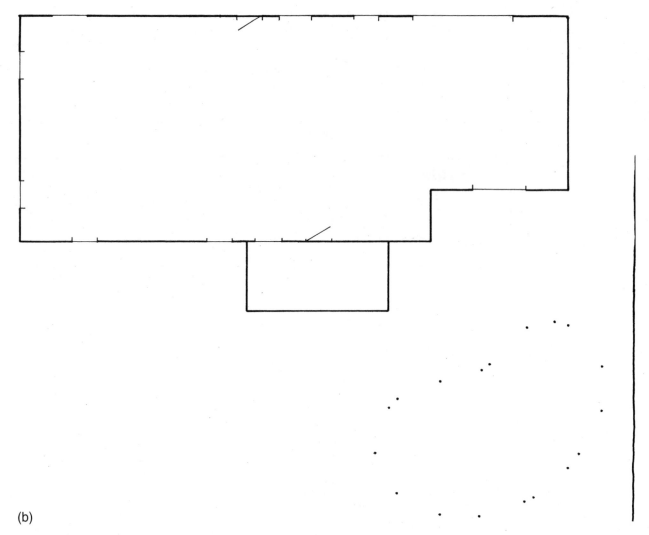

(b)

**Figure 2-27 Grid Measurement—continued**
Another approach to locating objects is grid measurement. (b) Locating a curve can be done by locating random points on the curve.

(c)

**Figure 2–27  Grid Measurement—continued**
Another approach to locating objects is grid measurement. (c) Connecting the dots.

# Printing Site Survey

One of the easiest ways to get the base map drawn to a larger scale is to have a blue-printer increase the size of the site survey (Fig. 2–28).

Every time the site survey is *doubled,* the scale is *reduced by half.* For instance, if the original scale is 1″ = 40′, then doubling it (200 percent) will make the scale 1″ = 20′. Having that survey doubled again (200 percent) would make the scale 1″ = 10′. (If the original survey were increased 400 percent, it would get the same result.)

> **Tip Box**
>
> Every time the site survey is doubled in size, the working scale will be reduced by half.

***Figure 2–28  Enlarging the Site Survey***
Having a printer enlarge the site survey (original size in the lower middle of the enlarged) is an easy way to enlarge the base map to scale. Every time the survey is doubled, the scale is reduced by half.

***Figure 2–29*  Scanning Survey**
Students are taping together an enlarged site survey after it was scanned and printed on an office printer.

## Scanning Site Survey

An inexpensive way to increase the size of the site survey is to scan the document and use a graphics program to double the size of the image. It can be printed on multiple pieces of paper then put together like a puzzle and traced (Fig. 2–29).

## Drawing the Base Map

If a printer is not available to increase the size of the site survey, it can be drawn to a larger scale (Fig. 2–30).

### Property Lines

Start by drawing the property lines. Use tracing paper to allow for notes and mistakes. It can be transferred to vellum later.

It is important to draw the corners at the correct angle because not all property corners are going to be 90 degrees. A simple approach to drawing the property lines is to slide the original site survey underneath the tracing paper and line up the corners. Once the angle of the line has been started, the entire length of the line can be drawn to scale. Continue this until all the property lines have been completed (Fig. 2–31).

### Footprint

On a separate piece of tracing paper, draw the footprint of the house. Include the location of the windows and doors.

In most cases, the corners of the footprint are square. Therefore, the 90-degree corner of a triangle can be used to draw them.

(a)

(b)

(c)

(d)

(e)

## *Figure 2–30*  **Drawing the Base Map**

(a) If the base map has to be drawn to a larger scale, start by drawing the property lines on one piece of paper (left) and the footprint (right) on another piece. The footprint should have the property stakes triangulated on it. (b) Slide the footprint and property stakes underneath the property lines. (c) Then, line up the property stakes (below) with the property corners (above) to orient the footprint on the property. (d) Transfer the footprint onto the above sheet with the property lines (e) to finish.

***Figure 2–31* Drawing Property Lines**

Many properties will not have square corners. A quick way to duplicate the angle is to slide the site survey underneath the paper and start the line, then it can be drawn to desired length.

**Figure 2–32 Locating Points to Center Footprint**

If property stakes cannot be located, measure to other permanent points to center the footprint. Examples include where the driveway meets the curb or to a fence (usually located close to the property line).

## Property Stakes

On the footprint, locate the property stakes that were triangulated from the house. If you cannot locate the property stakes, then triangulate to another permanent point, such as where the driveway meets the street (Fig. 2–32).

## Locate the Footprint on the Lot

With the sheet of property lines laying flat on the table, slide the sheet with the footprint underneath. Rotate the footprint until the property stakes on the footprint are located directly under the corners of the property lines. This will orient the footprint within the property lines. Trace the footprint on the sheet with the property lines.

## Add Other Objects and Areas

Any other objects or areas that were located on site can now be located on the base map (Fig. 2–33). This might include triangulating existing trees, the grid location of existing beds and driveway, or noting the location of windows and doors.

This completes the base map with property lines and footprint. This can now be slid underneath higher quality paper, such as vellum, to trace and begin designing.

***Figure 2–33  Locating Other Items on the Site Plan***
After the base map is drawn, locate other objects that will remain or have an impact on the design.

## Tip Box

Some designers, after transferring the base map to vellum, will add the border and title block (see Chapter 7) and make multiple copies on vellum for the preliminary design, master plan, or other plans. This is referred to as a **base sheet** (Fig. 2–34). This way the base map does not need to be redrawn multiple times.

**Figure 2–34   BaseSheet**
Make multiple copies of base map with border and title block so base map doesn't have to be redrawn.

# Summary

A plan drawing is a two-dimensional drawing of an area that appears like a bird's-eye view looking from directly overhead. It will be the map on which the design is illustrated. A lot is a plan drawing that includes the property lines, while a base map includes more information such as the location of the footprint, driveway, fences, deck, and other objects. Most clients will have a copy of a site survey of their property, which was included in the closing papers when the house was purchased. Site measurements will have to be taken to locate existing objects not included on the site survey. Tape measure or measure wheel can be used to take direct or baseline measurements, while triangulation or grid measurements can be used to locate objects on the base map. A site survey can be increased in size by a printer and kept to scale; each time it is doubled in size the scale is reduced by half. The base map can also be drawn to scale by selecting a working scale and drawing the property lines on one page and the footprint with property stakes on a separate page that can be slid under the property lines, lining up the property stakes with property corners to properly center the footprint.

# Key Terms

**Architect scale:** based on units of an inch

**B lead:** designates softer lead that draws thicker, darker lines; the higher the number, the softer the lead

**Base map:** a plan that includes all objects on site pertinent to the design

**Base sheet:** the base map with border and title block added to make multiple copies

**Baseline measurement:** obtains several measurements along one line; it reduces the need to move the tape and minimizes compounding errors

**Beam compass:** a long rod that has a point and a lead that can be slid up and down to adjust the length of the radius

**Bearings:** indicate the orientation of property lines

**Bumwad:** see tracing paper

**Compass:** used to draw large circles or strike arcs for site plan preparation

**Covenant:** a legal agreement created by the land developer that a homeowner enters into when purchasing a house within a subdivision; sometimes referred to as a restrictive covenant

**Direct measurement:** measuring from one point to another

**Drawing pencils:** wooden pencils without an eraser at the end; inexpensive and easy to handle

**Easement:** strip of land on the property that others have access to

**Engineer scale:** based on unit increments in an inch

**Extender bar:** inserted into the end of the compass to increase the radius

**Floorplan:** see footprint

**Footprint:** layout of the house plan

**Full sheet:** 24″ × 36″ dimensions; typical for most projects

**Grid:** use an existing form to measure parallel lines at measured intervals to locate points

**H lead:** designates hard lead that will draw thin, lighter lines; the higher the number, the harder the lead

**Half sheet:** 18″ × 24″ dimensions

**Ink:** provides excellent line quality

**Lead:** good medium for beginners because it can be easily erased

**Lead-holder:** operates like a mechanical pencil but holds larger sticks of lead

**Lot:** refers to a plan drawing of the property that includes property lines and bearings

**Markers:** used to draw with ink

**Mechanical pencil:** holds various thicknesses of lead (from 0.5 mm to 0.9 mm), which does not need to be sharpened

**Mylar:** high-quality paper that is actually drafting film used for the final plan; often used when drawing with ink

**Onionskin:** see tracing paper

**Pacing:** an estimation technique for measuring distance; each step is approximately equal to 3 feet

**Pigment liners:** fiber-tip markers that have a variety of line widths; relatively inexpensive and disposable

**Plan drawing:** two-dimensional drawing that appears like a bird's-eye view looking from directly overhead

**Plan view drawing:** see plan drawing

**Plat:** refers to a site survey of the resident's property

**Property lines:** define the site boundaries

**Property stakes:** locate the beginning and end of a property line

**Quarter sheet:** 12″ × 18″ dimensions

**Rag vellum:** see vellum paper

**Right-of-Way:** strip of land that is publicly owned, which includes the street and ground up to the front property line of the lot

**Scale:** ruler that has units to represent feet in the plan drawing

**Setback:** the minimum distance from a property line that any permanent construction can take place

**Site plan:** sometimes used to refer to base map

**Technical pen:** has a tip made of metal and an ink reservoir; relatively expensive

**Tracing paper:** thin translucent, low-quality paper used to sketch ideas.

**Trash paper:** see tracing paper

**Triangulation:** an unknown point that is located from two known points; a useful way of locating objects on the property

**Vellum paper:** high-quality, translucent paper used for the final plan

# 3 Inventory and Analysis

## Objectives

- Know the process of collecting and analyzing inventory
- Understand the role of analysis in the landscape design
- Learn the importance of circulation, views, and site conditions

Information about the site needs to be gathered and evaluated. This is the process of **inventory** and **analysis,** which some refer to as **needs assessment.** The interview revealed the clients' needs and wants and the next step for the designer is to study the site, assess the strengths and weaknesses, and while considering the clients' needs and wishes, develop a plan of action (Fig. 3–1).

Taking inventory of the site involves recording what already exists on site. This is similar to the storeowner who takes inventory of what is sitting on the shelves. There is no direction or possible solutions taken at this point, just collecting and recording information.

From the inventory, the analysis will develop. The inventory will be evaluated to determine what changes or actions need to be made. The analysis uncovers the problems and the potentials. The inventory is evaluated for areas that are problems and need to be corrected, as well as potentials that can be utilized in the design. This, as mentioned, will be the basis for a plan of action to develop a functional, aesthetic landscape design.

> ### Tip Box
>
> *Inventory* is fact.
>
> *Analysis* is evaluation and action.

## Items Needed

- Site survey
- Clipboard

Use the site survey to take notes (Fig. 3–2). It's often much easier to take inventory on the map than with written notes. Taking data in the backyard can be quickly noted on that part of the map as opposed to the front yard. If a site survey is not available at the time of the inventory, then rough sketch the site. Although it's not to scale, the notes will make sense.

## Inventory and Analysis

The following are areas and situations to make note of for inventory and analysis.

**Figure 3–1   Inventory and Analysis**
(a) Inventory is recording what is present on site, or observing problem areas such as poor views. (b) Analysis is taking action in response to the inventory.

(a)

(b)

**Figure 3–2  Observations**
(a) Using a clipboard, take the inventory and notes concerning the analysis while on site. (b) Using the site survey makes it easier to take notes.

(a)

(b)

***Figure 3–3*** **Window Height**
Make observations of window height to avoid plants that will block views (a); use plants that are low growing (b).


# House

### Color of the House and Materials

This may have a large impact on the color of paving material, such as repeating the bricks used in the foundation as a border along the flagstone entry walk.

### Locate Doors and Windows

• Doors will impact circulation patterns

• Windows will have an effect on the plant size. Avoid placing large shrubs in front of windows which will screen the view as well as create a security hazard (Fig. 3–3). Measuring from the ground to the bottom of the window will facilitate plant selection.

### Identify Rooms (Fig. 3–4)

• Bathrooms and bedrooms will be more private with views through windows.

• Kitchen and living room will utilize views to outdoors.

# Circulation

### Parking

Assess whether there is enough room to accommodate the clients' parking needs (Fig. 3–5).

### Primary Paths

Identify the major routes of foot traffic, such as the entry walk (Fig. 3–6). Note how guests would comfortably approach the house from the road.

### Secondary Paths

Identify areas of infrequent foot traffic, such as around the side of the house or to the back door.

DINING ROOM

OFFICE

BEDROOM

KITCHEN

BEDROOM

WINDOW 4' FROM GROUND

**Figure 3-4** **Identify Rooms**
Make note of rooms on the floor plan that will impact views and circulation.

**Figure 3-5** **Parking**
Observe if parking space meets needs.

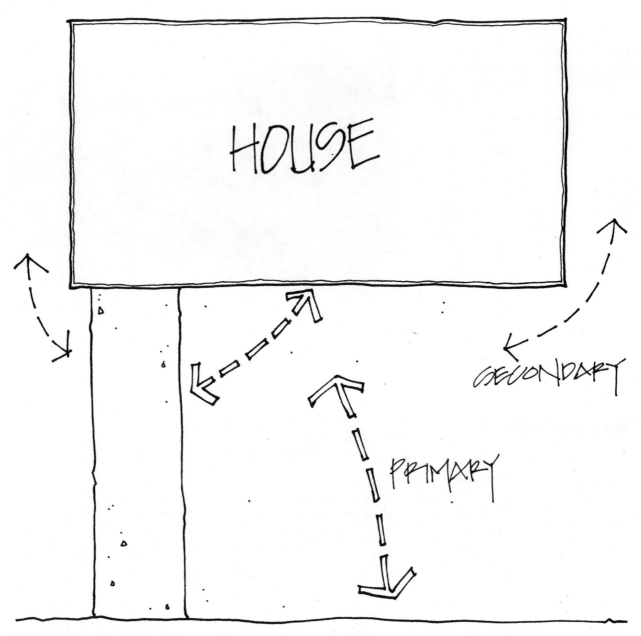

***Figure 3–6*** **Circulation**
Observe path of circulation, or foot traffic. Make note of paths that are primary, frequently traveled (large arrows) and secondary, infrequently used (small arrows).

### Pavement

Note whether the pavement for vehicular and pedestrian traffic is sufficient for the purpose. Areas of worn grass may indicate a need for a harder, more permanent surface (Fig. 3–7).

## Utilities (Fig. 3–8)

### Septic Tanks

A **septic tank** is a private sewage treatment plant for an individual residence, often found in rural areas where houses are far enough apart that a public sewer system

### *Figure 3–7*  **Worn Areas**

Take note of areas of turf that are worn down from foot traffic which may indicate a need for a harder, more permanent surface.

### *Figure 3–8*  **Utilities**

Note the location of utilities and other objects that may need to be screened from view or carefully avoided.

***Figure 3–9*  Septic Tank**
Avoid planting trees near a septic tank, which would clog it with roots.

would be too expensive (Fig. 3–9). If the clients have a septic tank, then note the location. Large trees can rapidly plug a septic tank with roots and prevent it from draining, especially trees that love water like willows!

## Overhead Lines

Note the location and approximate height of **overhead lines,** or power lines, that run to the house or along the road to avoid planting large trees under them (Fig. 3–10).

## Utilities

**Air-conditioning units** are often noisy and unsightly (Fig. 3–11). Note their location to visually screen and allow space for ventilation. Other utilities include electrical boxes, pumps, gas meters, or cable boxes.

## Trash Cans

**Trash cans** are also unsightly but need to have adequate access from the house and to the curb for pickup (Fig. 3–12). Note where trash cans are stored and the path used to access and move them.

***Figure 3–10*** **Overhead Lines**
Avoid planting trees that will grow into overhead power lines.

***Figure 3–11*** **Air Conditioner and Other Utilities**
The A/C unit can often be a noisy, visual problem in the side or backyard. In this case, the A/C is conveniently located in the side yard out of sight, along with the compost pile.

## Storage Areas

Like trash cans, **storage areas** can be unsightly but accessible. Locate areas used to store materials or equipment, whether it's a shed or out in the open (Fig. 3–13).

***Figure 3-12*** **Trash Can**
Trash should be located so that it is easily accessible from the house but avoids being a visual problem.

***Figure 3-13*** **Storage**
Storage area is important; it is often a place where equipment is stored and locked. It should be accessible but not become a visual problem.

# Views (Fig. 3–14)

## Poor Views

Note distasteful views. They could include

- Objects, such as utility boxes and air conditioners (Fig. 3–15)
- Lack of privacy from neighbors
- Unsightly areas of the yard, such as storage

### Figure 3-14 Views

Three important types of views should be studied: poor views that will need to be blocked, good views that need to be maintained, and potential views that are locations where a good view should be created.

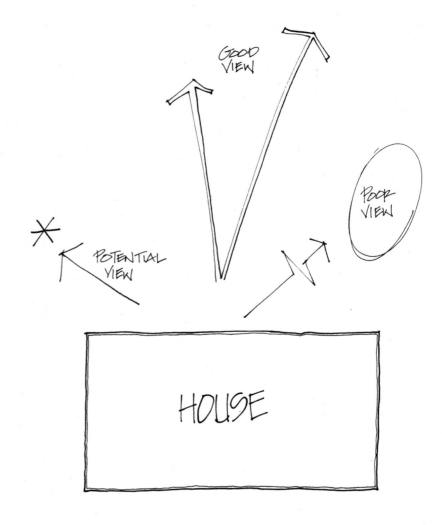

### Figure 3-15 Poor View

Utilities are items that are often eyesores.

***Figure 3–16*** **Good View**
(a) Water is often a preferable view that needs to be preserved from the house or entertainment area. (b) The view of the mountain range can raise the value of the residence considerably.

(a)

(b)

## Good Views

Note attractive views that already exist (Fig. 3–16) such as a:

- Golf course
- Lake
- Wooded area

## Potential Views

Note areas that would utilize and appreciate an interesting view (Fig. 3–17) such as:

- Entertainment area
- Views from inside the house

*Tip Box*
### Views From Inside the House

Take the time to go inside the house and look through all the windows to see the views from inside. Time spent in the family room and dining room may utilize the views more than the bedrooms and bathrooms.

***Figure 3–17*** **Potential View**
Views from inside the house or from the entertainment area (deck below window) should be enhanced with landscaping.

# Exposure

Verify magnetic north with a compass (Fig. 3–18). North, south, east and west exposures have different impacts on the environmental conditions, how these areas can be used, and plant selection.

## Light and Temperature

In the Northern Hemisphere, the sun always shines from the south (Fig. 3–19). This will have an effect on sunlight intensity, temperature, and moisture/humidity around the house and site.

**Northern exposure** receives full shade most of the day. It stays cooler and remains the dampest. This is why in an open, temperate forest moss only grows on the north side of a tree (Fig. 3–20).

**Southern exposure** receives full sun and gets hotter than the northern exposure. This is why snow melts off the south side of a hill before the north side (Fig. 3–21a).

**Eastern exposure** receives full sun in the morning when temperatures are cool and shade in the afternoon when temperatures are hot. These areas stay cooler and damper than the western exposure.

---

***Tip Box***
### Take Advantage of the Eastern Exposure

Locate an entertainment area for optimal comfort; or locate plants that need protection from high temperatures.

---

**Western exposure** gets morning shade and the hot afternoon sun. It tends to be warmer and drier.

**Figure 3-18  Exposure**
Make note of magnetic north, which will impact the temperature, moisture, and prevailing wind around the house.

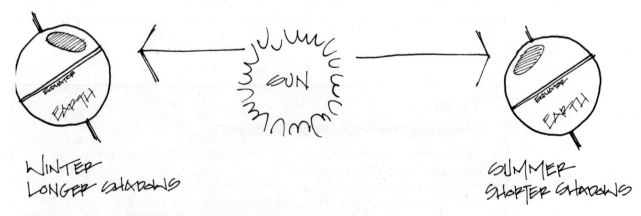

**Figure 3-19  Northern Hemisphere**
In the Northern Hemisphere, sunlight enters the atmosphere from the south.

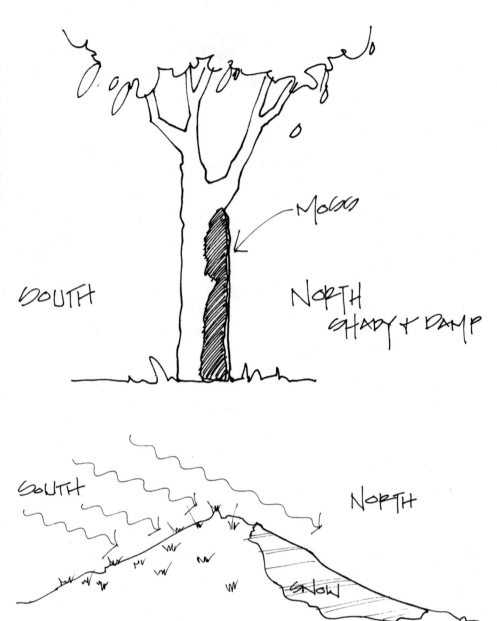

***Figure 3–20***
**Northern Exposure**
Since sunlight enters from the south, the north side of objects, such as a house or trees, is shaded throughout most of the day. This is why moss grows on the north side of a tree because it is more shady and moist.

**Figure 3–21a   Southern Exposure**
Since sunlight enters from the south, the south side of objects or areas warms quicker because sunlight is more intense. This is why snow melts first on the south side of a hill.

***Tip Box***
**Screening the Southwest Exposure**

It is more environmentally responsible to screen the house from the **southwest exposure.** This will help keep the house cooler by keeping the hot afternoon sun off of it. By using deciduous trees to screen, the leaves will fall in the autumn and allow the southwest exposure to warm the house in the winter months (Fig. 3–21b).

SOUTHERN
EXPOSURE

SUMMER

HOUSE

(Top)

SOUTHERN
EXPOSURE

WINTER

HOUSE

(Bottom)

**Figure 3–21b  Screening Southwest Exposure**
Using deciduous trees to screen the southwest exposure (Top) blocks the summer sun to cool and (Bottom) allows the winter sun to warm.

*Figure 3–22*  **Seasonal Sun**
Beware that the angle of the sun changes with the season. During the winter, the sun is lower in the sky and creates longer shadows while the opposite is true during the summer. Make note that observations of shady areas during the winter may be in full sun in the summer.

# Seasonal Impact on Light and Temperature (Fig. 3–22)

## Shorter Shadows in the Summer

In the summer the orientation of the earth makes a shorter, more direct path for the rays of the sun. This makes the sun appear higher in the sky and also results in warmer temperatures than winter. Therefore, in the summertime the shadows are shorter.

## Longer Shadows in the Winter

Winter is the result of a longer path for the sun's rays to reach the earth and therefore there are longer shadows. As a result, it is important to note the time of the year that you make observations of where shadows are falling. If you are on site during the winter months and plan to select shade plants in an area of shade, it may be in full sun come the summer months, which will cause the plants to burn.

# Wind

The **prevailing wind** comes from the west (Fig. 3–23a). Colder prevailing winds come from the northwest during winter months and warmer winds during the summer come from the southwest (Fig. 3–23b).

---

### *Tip Box*

### Blocking the Winter Wind

Screen the NW wind to reduce the impact of the cold winter wind on the house.

### Allowing the Summer Breeze

During the summer months, consider screens that will allow the prevailing wind to cool areas outdoors, such as playgrounds or entertainment areas.

---

(a)

BLOCK WINTER WIND

NORTHWEST EXPOSURE

BLOCK SUMMER HEAT

ALLOW SUMMER BREEZE

(b) SOUTHWEST EXPOSURE

**Figure 3–23  NW and SW Wind**
(a) Screen the prevailing winter wind from the Northwest to make the house more energy efficient. (b) During the summer allow the prevailing wind from the Southwest to cool the summer heat.

# Existing Landscapes

There will be variation from project to project on how many existing plants will remain (Fig. 3–24). Some clients may request that all existing plants be relocated or removed for a new design, while others will want to expand on what is already present. Existing plants may provide important roles already, such as screens, while some may be potential specimen plants or focal points (Fig. 3–25). In many cases, large trees will remain because of their value or because local laws prohibit their removal. Some designs

**Figure 3–24  Existing Plants**
Note existing plants, their condition, size, location, and whether they need to be removed or included in the design.

**Figure 3–25  Existing Plant Value**
From the back porch, the live oak in the neighbor's yard is an exceptional specimen that should be preserved for view.

**Figure 3–26  Remove, Relocate, or Remain**

Existing plants are often located on a plan and noted whether they are to be removed, relocated, or remain so the contractor knows what to do with them.

will locate all existing plants and indicate whether the plant is to be removed, relocated, or remain so the contractor knows what to do with it (Fig. 3–26).

For all existing plants, note the following:

- Identification
- Location
- Height and spread of canopy
  - For large trees, note the diameter of the trunk
- Condition
  - Note apparent damage or disease

## Soil

Collect a soil sample to determine texture, structure, pH, and other nutritional status (Fig. 3–27). Collect a small handful of soil 6 inches deep from several spots on the residence using a **soil probe,** a t-handle instrument with a hollow core. This is used to pull a soil sample at the correct depth (Fig. 3–28). Remove any debris and place in a plastic bag or jar. Submit a sample for a **soil test.** Most extension agencies of state universities provide a soil test for a nominal fee.

## Figure 3–27 Soil Test

(a) Collecting a soil sample 6 inches deep from several places can assess the soil texture and structure (b) as well as submitting for a soil test to analyze the nutritional status and pH.

(a)

(b)

| Test | Results | SOIL TEST RATINGS | | | | | Calculated Cation Exchange Capacity |
|------|---------|---------|-----|--------|---------|-----------|------|
| | | Very Low | Low | Medium | Optimum | Very High | |
| Soil pH | 5.8 | | | | | | **14.5** |
| Buffer pH | 7.69 | | | | | | meq/100g |
| Phosphorus (P) | 216 ppm | | | | | | **Calculated Cation Saturation** |
| Potassium (K) | 59 ppm | | | | | | |
| Calcium (Ca) | 2071 ppm | | | | | | %K     1.0 |
| Magnesium (Mg) | 161 ppm | | | | | | %Ca    71.4 |
| Sulphur (S) | 47 ppm | | | | | | %Mg    9.3 |
| Boron (B) | 1.9 ppm | | | | | | %H    17.1 |
| Copper (Cu) | 3.8 ppm | | | | | | %Na    0.9 |
| Iron (Fe) | 150 ppm | | | | | | |
| Manganese (Mn) | 21 ppm | | | | | | **K : Mg Ratio** |
| Zinc (Zn) | 25.9 ppm | | | | | | 0.11  ⬛ |
| Sodium (Na) | 31 ppm | | | | | | |
| Soluble Salts | 0.13 mmho/cm | | | | | | |
| Organic Matter | 3.9 %    ENR 122 | | | | | | |
| NO3-N | | | | | | | |

## Figure 3–28 Soil Probe

A t-handle instrument that is used to pull soil samples 6 inches deep.

**Figure 3–29   Soil Texture**
Soil texture is the proportion of sand, silt, and clay that makes up the soil.

## Texture

The **soil texture** is the proportion of sand, silt, and clay (Fig. 3–29). This will have an impact on plant material and the extent of renovation. For instance, palms grow well in sandy soil but not in clay.

**Sandy Soil**   **Sand** is the largest soil particle of the three. It is a solid particle of silica that resists compaction. Sandy soil contains 70 percent sand. It drains well, but is susceptible to drying out too quickly and has low fertility.

**Clay Soil**   **Clay** is the smallest soil particle and is very porous and plastic in nature. It compacts easier than sand. Clay soil contains at least 40 percent clay. It holds nutrients and water very well but tends to remain too moist and often has low aeration.

Clay may be a problem when the building contractor has removed the topsoil and left a clayey subsoil. Check the soil near the foundation of the house as well as out in the yard to determine if clay has been left from construction.

**Silt Soil**   **Silt** is a particle that is in between sand and clay in size and porosity. It is not as dry and infertile as sand, and it drains better than clay.

**Loamy Soil**   The ideal soil is referred to as **loam,** which is an intermediate mixture of sand, silt, and clay.

Take a look at the soil in several areas around the property several inches deep. Be sure to check around the foundation as well as out in the yard. Special planting instructions will need to be specified for the contractor if soil texture problems exist.

---

### *Tip Box*
### Texture Analysis

*Ribbon test.* Roll a handful of moist soil and squeeze between your thumb and fingers in your palm (Fig. 3–30). Roughly classify the soil texture based on the length of the ribbon formed:

> **No ribbon:** at least 50 percent sand
>
> **Less than 2 inches:** roughly 25 percent clay
>
> **Between 2 and 3 1/2 inches:** roughly 40 percent clay
>
> **Greater than 3 1/2 inches:** 50 percent clay

**Figure 3–30 Ribbon Test**
Squeeze a handful of moist soil in the palm of your hand and measure the length of ribbon that can be formed without breaking to roughly determine soil texture.

---

### *Tip Box*
### Jar Test (Fig. 3–31)

1. Fill a quart jar half full with soil, then add enough water to bring the jar 3/4 full.

2. Shake vigorously until all the soil breaks apart and suspends in the water.

3. When set down on the table, the sand will settle out within minutes, the silt will settle over the next few hours, and the clay will require 24 hours to settle.

4. After a day, there will be three distinct layers: sand on the bottom, silt in the middle; and clay on the top. Measure the height of each layer in millimeters and divide each layer by the total height of the whole soil sample to get the percentage of each layer.

5. Use a texture triangle to classify the soil texture.

(a)

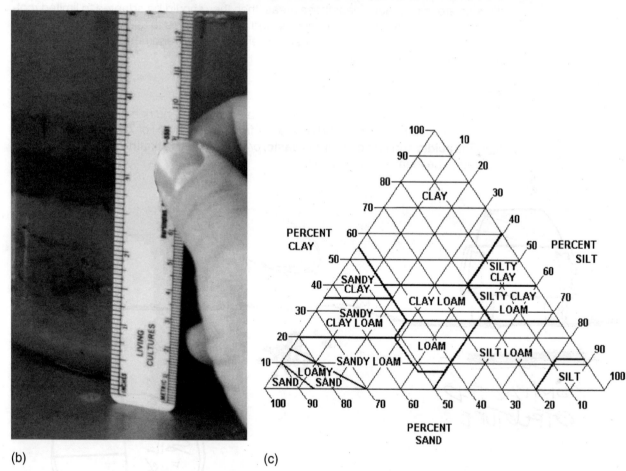

(b)                                    (c)

**Figure 3–31  Jar Test**
Fill a quart jar half full with soil and 3/4 to the top with water and shake vigorously; (a) after 24 hours, soil will settle out into distinct layers: sand on bottom, silt in middle, and clay on top; (b) measure each layer in millimeters and divide each layer by the total height of the whole soil sample to get the percentage of each layer; (c) the texture chart can be used to classify the soil texture by connecting the lines of the particle sizes. If the sample has 50% sand, 10% clay, and 40% silt, connecting the lines and the points classifies the sample as a loam soil.

Depending on the soil, the plant selection will have to be adapted to such texture as determined on site if the soil is not amended.

**Amending Soil**  Sandy soil can be amended with 2 to 3 inches of organic matter, such as compost or hardwood mulch, tilled into the soil. This is often limited to planting beds with flowers, shrubs, and trees since it can be expensive. Clay soils can be amended or even replaced at considerable cost.

## Structure

**Structure** is the arrangement of the soil particles (Fig. 3–32). Ideally, the structure of the soil should provide enough pore space to be well aerated with oxygen and to drain well. The condition of most concern regarding structure is compaction. With compaction, structure lacks adequate pore space, reducing aeration and drainage that will directly impact the health of the roots.

Look for causes of compaction, whether it was due to an earlier construction or ongoing traffic. Areas of high foot or vehicular traffic will be susceptible to compaction, and if plants are to be placed near these areas, then they should be adapted to limited rooting space. These areas may be more suited to hardscapes to tolerate the traffic. If the causes of compaction are no longer present, consider recommending cultivation or aeration to prepare the soil.

## pH

The **pH** of the soil affects the ability of the plants to uptake nutrients, primarily micronutrients (Fig. 3–33). It is measured on a scale from 0 to 14. A pH of 7 is **neutral;** pH lower than 7 is **acidic** and higher than 7 is **basic,** or referred to as **alkaline.** A pH of 6.5 is considered to be ideal for most plants.

**Figure 3–32  Soil Structure**
Soil structure is how soil particles are arranged to make up the pore space where water and air are stored for healthy roots. Soils tilled with compost have good soil structure. Compacted soils have poor structure that lacks pore space.

**Figure 3–33** **Soil pH**
The pH of soil is a measure of the acidity and has a large impact on nutrient availability.

**Changing Soil pH** If one of these conditions is present on site, the pH can sometimes be corrected if it's not too extreme. The pH can be easily raised with an application of **lime.** To lower pH, elemental **sulfur** can be used, although with less success because soil has a high buffering capacity against lowering pH. How much of either lime or sulfur will be needed is told on a soil test.

If correcting the soil is not feasible, then select plants that are adapted to those conditions. One example is **acid-loving plants** such as azaleas, begonias, gardenias, and hydrangeas.

**pH Meter** An inexpensive **pH meter** can be used without having to get a soil test (Fig. 3–34). Mix a cup of soil with a cup of water and stir until the soil is completely suspended. Allow it to sit for a day and then dip the pH meter into the water. This is not as accurate as a soil test, but it is accurate enough to uncover pH problems.

**Figure 3–34** **pH Meter**
An inexpensive pH meter can be used to assess the soil pH.

### Fertility

A soil analysis will reveal any nutrient deficiencies that will need to be amended before installation. Phosphorus and potassium are major nutrients that are immobile in the soil and are best corrected before installation by cultivating the nutrients in the upper 6 to 12 inches of the soil.

## Drainage

Note any areas where water is standing (Fig. 3–35). If you're on site during a dry period, ask the clients if there are any areas where water stands after it rains. This can especially be a problem in the path of circulation, making it difficult to walk without getting muddy or wet.

### Foundation

Look at the grade around the foundation of the house. It is imperative that water drains on the surface away from the house, especially when it is built on a basement or crawl space. Water that drains under the house can cause mildew and rot.

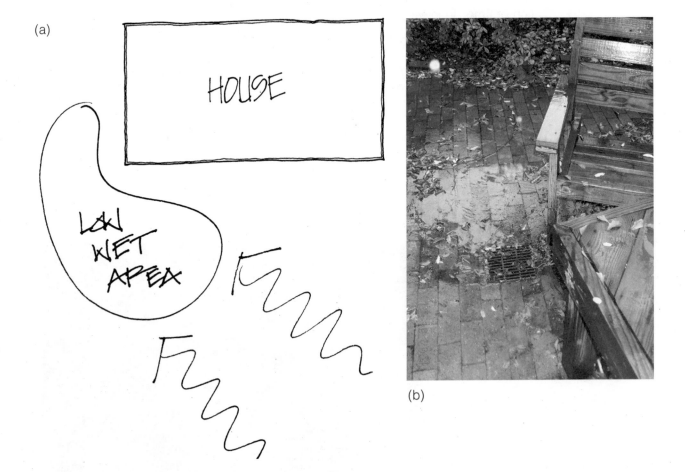

(a)

(b)

***Figure 3–35  Wet Areas***
(a) Make note of areas that are holding water. If the weather is dry, ask the residents if they notice areas that hold water. (b) This patio would flood until drainage was installed.

## Surface Drainage

Make note of the topography and any obvious signs of low spots that hold water due to improper grading (Fig. 3–36).

## Downspouts and Gutters

Note the location of **downspouts** from gutters. These should extend away from the house to avoid foundation problems. Also, these areas will be the wettest and could have a negative impact on some plants (Fig. 3–37).

*Figure 3–36* **Drainage**
Water should drain readily away from the foundation of the house. Any changes to the landscape should not affect this.

*Figure 3–37* **Downspout Location**
Make note of downspouts from gutters that will need to be re-routed or select plants that can not tolerate wet conditions.

(a)

PRIMARY CIRCULATION

SECONDARY CIRCULATION

MAJOR VIEW

BLOCKED VIEW

SCREEN

FOCAL POINT

SCREEN

FOCUSED VIEW

PANORAMIC VIEW

(b)

### Figure 3–38 Analysis Graphics

(a) Some simple ways to graphically illustrate the analysis. (b) Analysis is sketched on tracing paper with soft lead.

88

# Drawing the Analysis

An effective approach to developing the analysis is done with graphics and short descriptions (Fig. 3–38). From the analysis, other phases of the design process will be built. If the analysis is graphically drawn on the base map, then the next phase of the plan drawing can be done right over the top of it.

It is important to keep in mind the analytical approach. Every statement and graphic should express doing something and not the situation (which is the inventory), regardless of how vague the action may be. This will include statements or terms such as

- Needs to be . . .
- Create . . .
- Allow for . . .
- Develop . . .
- Improve . . .

Not every point on the inventory will have an analytical statement. Some inventory will be good information that is not a particular strength or weakness. For instance, if the inventory of the soil is "good loamy soil," then this would not necessarily require an analytical assessment. It's good soil.

Develop the analysis with bold graphics and brief statements on the base map (Fig. 3–39). These graphics are not only valuable for the designer's thought process; they will also be referred back to in the next phase of the design. Some designers graphically develop the analysis so it can be presented along with the preliminary or master plan to support the design.

For a closer look at Inventory and Analysis, see Appendix A, "The Design Process," for the Grant Residence Inventory and Analysis.

# Summary

The inventory and analysis follow the interview and, by using the information from the interview, the designer develops a "needs assessment," or a plan of action to guide the design. This is critical to the functional, or useful, aspect of the design. The inventory is observing the site conditions and elements, and the analysis takes the inventory to determine the problems and potentials that will make up the plan of action. Areas that are analyzed include the house, circulation, views, utilities, exposure, soil, and drainage. The analysis can be illustrated graphically with short verbal descriptions that can be used in the next phase of the design process. The graphical analysis can also be used during the presentation to the client to support the design.

**Figure 3–39**
**Graphical Analysis of**
**Grant Residence**
This is a graphical analysis
of the Grant residence.

# Key Terms

**Acid:** pH lower than 7

**Acid-loving plants:** tolerate low soil pH; examples include azaleas, begonias, gardenias, and hydrangeas

**Air-conditioning units:** often noisy and unsightly and need screening and ventilation

**Alkaline:** pH higher than 7

**Analysis:** based on the inventory, determines the problems and the potentials

**Basic:** see alkaline

**Clay:** the smallest soil particle, which is very porous and plastic in nature

**Downspouts:** extensions from gutters

**Eastern exposure:** receives morning sun when it's cooler and afternoon shade when it's hotter

**Good views:** areas or objects that already exist and can be accentuated in the design

**Inventory:** observing and recording what already exists on site

**Jar test:** determining soil texture by mixing a soil sample in a jar with water, which separates soil into three distinct layers of sand, silt and clay

**Lime:** used to raise soil pH

**Loamy soil:** ideal soil is referred to as loam, an intermediate mixture of sand, silt, and clay

**Needs assessment:** another term for "inventory and analysis"

**Neutral:** pH of 7

**Northern exposure:** receives full shade most of the day

**Overhead lines:** avoid planting tall trees under power lines

**pH:** affects the ability of plants to uptake nutrients

**pH meter:** used to obtain pH of soil

**Poor views:** unsightly areas or objects that need to be removed or screened

**Potential views:** areas that would utilize and appreciate an interesting view

**Prevailing wind:** comes from the west; colder prevailing winds come from the northwest during winter months and warmer winds during the summer come from the southwest

**Ribbon test:** quick test to roughly determine the soil texture by squeezing soil in the palm of the hand

**Sand:** the largest soil particle of the three

**Septic tank:** a private sewage treatment plant for an individual residence

**Silt:** particle that is in between sand and clay in size and porosity, not as dry and in-fertile as sand and drains better than clay

**Soil probe:** t-handle instrument with a hollow core used to obtain a soil sample

**Soil test:** analysis of soil that reveals pH and nutritional status

**Soil texture:** the proportion of sand, silt, and clay

**Southern exposure:** receives full sun and gets hotter than the northern exposure

**Storage areas:** can be unsightly areas but need to be accessible

**Structure:** the arrangement of the soil particles

**Sulfur:** used to lower pH

**Surface drainage:** study of water draining across the top of the ground

**Southwest exposure:** often screened to provide shade for relief from the hottest part of the day

**Trash cans:** unsightly but need to have adequate access from the house and to the curb for pickup

**Western exposure:** gets morning shade and the hot afternoon sun; tends to be hotter and drier

# 4 Functional Principles

### Objectives

- Know the basic functions of the landscape
- Understand the functional aspects of the front, side, and backyard
- Learn how to incorporate functionality into landscape design

The landscape should be more than just window-dressing for the house. The fundamental purpose of residential design should be to make the landscape useful. To achieve an order of usable space, an understanding of the **functional** aspects of a residence is important.

The landscape should support the activities of the residents. It could be compared with the floor plan of the home, which supports various activities such as cooking in the kitchen, sleeping in the bedroom, eating in the dining room, etc. In this way, the property is organized to improve the quality and comfort of outdoor living.

# Basic Functions

The residential property can be divided into three general-use areas: public, private, and utility (Fig. 4–1). **Public areas** of the residence are within view and open to the public. This area would serve to present an appealing appearance to the neighborhood, facilitate a safe, interesting approach onto the property, and occasionally entertain guests. The public area is typically regarded as the front yard and occasionally the side yard (depending on the lot).

**Private areas** are screened from the public view and used to entertain guests, for recreation and hobbies, or for the family to relax. This is typically in the backyard and occasionally the side yard (like the public area, it depends on the lot).

The **utility areas,** sometimes referred to as the **service areas,** are sections of the residence typically kept out of sight. They function as areas for storage, gardening, trash, compost, or other items that are functional but often unsightly, noisy, or odorous.

This chapter will look at the primary functions of the landscape in three areas: front yard, side yard, and backyard.

# Front Yard

The front yard is considered the public area, although there are exceptions where the front yard can be more private and enclosed. Many designers look at the front yard as having one purpose: getting people from the street to the front door. Although this is a major function of the front yard, let's look at other major components of the front, their function, and how they can be addressed in the design.

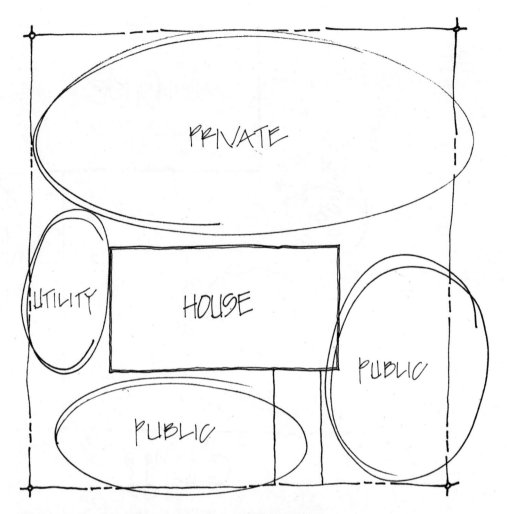

***Figure 4–1  Functional Aspects of Residence***
The residence is usually divided into public, private, and utility areas. The front yard is public, the backyard is private, while the side yard may be public or private depending on the property. Utility areas are typically in the side and/or backyard.

***Tip Box***

Many designers believe the main purpose of the front yard is to get people to the front door.

# Curb Appeal

**Curb appeal** is how the front of the house looks from the road, either driving by or walking. Curb appeal is what most people want from a design, whether it's to increase the value of their property, to take pride in their landscape, or to "keep up with the Joneses" (Fig. 4–2).

***Figure 4–2  Curb Appeal***
One thing that most residents are interested in is improving the curb appeal of their front yard.

**Traditional landscaping** primarily dealt with foundation planting (Fig. 4–3). This usually consisted of an evergreen hedge across the front of the house to hide the foundation. This hedge was often sheared into a box or other geometric forms.

The hedge was often punctuated with a large evergreen shrub planted at each corner and sometimes at both sides of the front door. Corner plantings were done to blend the sharp corners of the house with the ground and surroundings. Although the traditional landscaping was better than a barren landscape, it was often an unchanging green wall that lacked interest.

Ideally, the landscape should generate visual interest from the curb. It should contain an element of uniqueness, balance, and color. If done skillfully, the landscape will continually draw interest as it changes throughout the year with various flower colors, fall color, and winter characteristics.

(a)

(b)

**Figure 4–3  Traditional Landscaping**
(a) Traditional landscaping consists of green hedges that are sheared into boxes and have corners punctuated with taller shrubs. (b) Lacks color and interest.

## Framing the House

A common approach to creating curb appeal is using the landscape as a frame for the house (Fig. 4–4A). This is often done by planting large trees or shrubs on both sides of the house to focus an observer's attention within its boundaries.

## Draw Attention to the Front Door

Framing the house helps to draw attention to the front door as well as the approach. Some designers use a **funneling effect,** planting larger items on the outside and

*Figure 4–4A* **Framing**
To create curb appeal, the landscape should act as a frame for the house.

*Figure 4–4B* **Funneling Effect**
Designers sometimes funnel the attention of a visitor to the front door by planting larger items on the outside and placing progressively smaller plants closer to the door.

placing progressively smaller plants closer to the door so that attention is naturally drawn to the door (fig. 4–4B).

It is also important to avoid hiding the entrance or causing confusion on how to get there (fig. 4–5). A person should be able to identify the front door and how to get there. If the entrance is visually screened, it blocks the view from the street, not to mention the views from the inside of the house.

(a)

(b)                                                                 (c)

### *Figure 4–5*  **Hidden Door**
(a) Avoid tall plantings that screen the front door. (b) The front door is easy to find. (c) Where is the front door now? (digitally enhanced)

(a)                                                          (b)

**_Figure 4–6_  Blending of House with Environment**
(a) The house appears out of place with its surroundings. (b) Landscaping helps integrate the home with its surroundings by softening corners and edges.*(Photo courtesy of Visual Impact software.)*

(a)

(b)

**_Figure 4–7_  Front Yard Definition**
(a) Neighborhoods typically lack defining borders between front yards. (b) Landscape beds and plantings can help define the front yard and draw attention to the house.

### Blend the House with Its Surroundings

Houses have corners and angles in stark contrast to the natural landscape of trees, shrubs, and turf (Fig. 4–6). This is evident in new subdivisions where there are few large plants helping to balance the houses and integrate them with their surroundings. To some people, these neighborhoods feel too harsh.

Landscaping helps tie the house to the ground and blend it into the surroundings. Plants help to balance the structures with the landscape and *soften* the sharp corners of the house.

## Defined Borders

Some front yards focus most of the landscaping directly in front of the house and don't come out much farther than a few feet (Fig. 4–7). This leaves ill-defined space that blends front yards of the entire neighborhood together, separated only by the driveways (Fig. 4–8). This can create a sense of disconnection between the front of the house and the rest of the lawn, in addition to lacking distinction from the neighbors.

Even a simple extension of the foundation bed can be effective in defining the front yard (Fig. 4–9). This also helps integrate the front lawn with the foundation planting. The bed doesn't have to come all the way to the curb, but simply pulling out into the yard several feet can imply some separation. The beds may include trees and shrubs, or simply groundcover to imply separation.

## Driveway

The driveway's primary purpose is obviously to park vehicles. Review the residence analysis to determine whether it serves its purpose adequately. Consider if there is a need to expand the parking area (Fig. 4–10).

(a)                                                                                    (b)

***Figure 4–8*  Defining Borders**
(a) From the front yard there is little definition or interest except for driveways for several houses. (b) Beds and plantings help define the area and add visual interest. (digitally enhanced).

EXTENDING BED

**Figure 4–9   Defining Borders**
A simple extension of the landscape bed with low plantings can visually help define the front yard.

## Driveway Serving as a Sidewalk

Oftentimes the driveway serves as the walk from the road to the entry walk that continues up to the front door (Fig. 4–11). Most one-car garage driveways are about 10 to 12 feet wide to accommodate one car. When the car is parked in the driveway it often leaves little room for approaching guests to walk on the concrete. What often results is people walking around the car and in the grass.

Consider widening the driveway for a walking lane (Fig. 4–12). Using a paving material other than concrete helps to visually separate it from the driveway. This extension will accommodate the approach as well as provide a landing area for getting in and out of the car.

## Avoid Screening Driveway View

Avoid planting on the corners of the driveway where it meets the road, which will hinder the driver's view when backing out (Fig. 4–13).

(a)

(b)

(c)

**Figure 4-10   Driveway**
(a) The driveway is a visually dominant feature because it is so large. The warm, tan color and aggregate texture creates a more appealing feature than gray concrete. (b) Assess whether there is enough room to park
all cars. (c) Widening the end of the driveway can be an inexpensive solution. Paving is expensive but very
appealing. *(Photo (c) courtesy of Blue Ribbon LLC, Maryland. www.blueribbonllc.com)*

# Entry Walk

The **entry walk** provides access from the road or from the driveway to the front door. It
has the following functions:

• Provides a safe approach

• Guides people through the landscape

• Influences their views

## Common Shortcomings of Entry Walk

Many entry walks are poorly done (Fig. 4–14). They are often the result of the building
contractor pouring an inexpensive slab of concrete.

(a)

(b)

**Figure 4–11  Driveway Approach**
(a) The driveway often serves as the approach to the entry walk and front door. (b) This can often be obstructed by a parked car, which does not allow room for foot traffic.

***Figure 4–12*** **Approach Walk**

A simple widening of the driveway with a material other than that used for the driveway can help facilitate foot traffic to the entry walk around parked vehicles.

*(continues)*

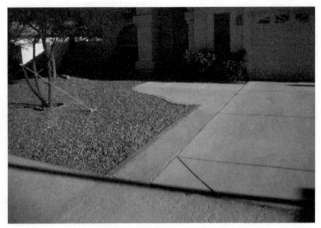

***Figure 4–12  Approach Walk—continued***
A simple widening of the driveway with a material other than that used for the driveway can help facilitate foot traffic to the entry walk around parked vehicles.

(a)

(b)

***Figure 4–13  Screen Driveway***
(a) Avoid screening the view of a car backing out of the driveway. (b) An obstructed view from a driveway can be hazardous.

***Figure 4–14  Poor Entry Walk***
This entry walk is a square corner that does not facilitate approaching foot traffic. It is too narrow to allow more than one person to approach, and shrubs (recently cut) were allowed to cover half the sidewalk, leaving about only 1 1/2 feet open.

***Figure 4–15  Poor Route***
The 90-degree turn is common because it is the easiest poured design for the building contractor, but it is prone to shortcuts at the corner because it is not convenient.

**Poor Route**   Many entry walks have two 90-degree turns from the driveway to the front door (Fig. 4–15). This results in an awkward approach and shortcuts across the corner. The reason for this shape is because it is the easiest and quickest way for a contractor to pour the sidewalk.

**Narrow Approach**    The width of most sidewalks is 3 feet, which is wide enough to accommodate one person comfortably (Fig. 4–16). If two or more people approach the house they will have to line up single file or walk in the grass.

**Overgrown Walk**    Shrubs planted too close to the walk eventually grow over it leaving even less room (Fig. 4–17).

**Figure 4–16   Narrow Walk**
Most walks are only 3 feet wide, forcing two or more people to approach single file.

**Figure 4–17   Overgrown Walk**
Close plantings or wrong plant selection eat up more of the already small entry walk, making it nearly irrelevant.

## Effective Entry Walks

If the designer has the opportunity to design and build the entry walk, the designer can ensure a comfortable, safe, and interesting path with the following approaches (Fig. 4–18).

(a)

(b)

(c)

(d)

***Figure 4–18*** **Effective Entry Walk**
(a) This entry offers a wide opening and proper route to the front door, as well as unique material, to make the approach safe and interesting. (b) This entry has been expanded with flagstone from the original concrete sidewalk. (c) Steps, materials, width, and landscaping make this entry walk effective. (*Photo courtesy of Decks by JRW Portland, Oregon. www.deckbyjrw.com*) (d) A wide, sweeping entry is simple but effective visually and functionally. (*Photo courtesy of Big Sky Landscaping, Inc., Clackamas, OR. www.bigskylandscaping.com*)

***Figure 4-19* Good Route**
The entry walk should be a convenient route that aids most commonly traveled paths.

**Facilitate Circulation**   Study the most common walking routes and lay out the walk accordingly (Fig. 4–19). If the majority of traffic comes up the driveway, then allow for someone to enter the walk smoothly. People feel more comfortable rounding corners rather than turning at an abrupt 90-degree turn. However, the walk does not necessarily need to be a straight line between two points. That can be mundane. Instead, a few slight bends in the walk are more interesting.

Also consider if access to other parts of the front besides the front door needs to be addressed. This may include a common path to one side of the house, or both sides. Also allow for access to the lawn from the front door (Fig. 4–20). This may just be allowing for space to walk through a bed with stepping stones and not necessarily a concrete path.

**Wide Approach**   Create a wide entrance to the entry walk that acts like a funnel to approaching traffic (Fig. 4–21). Once past the opening, the narrowest portion of the walk should be a minimum of 4 feet.

**Create Multiple Views**   Take advantage of turns along the entry walk to develop different views and to create an interesting, varied approach (Fig. 4–22).

(a)                                                              (b)

(c)

## *Figure 4–20*  **Secondary Access**

(a) Avoid blocking access to other parts of the yard, such as isolating the entry walk from the front. (b) Leaving a simple opening or path is often sufficient. (c) The door is isolated from the yard unless cutting through the plants or walking up the driveway.

***Figure 4–21   Wide Opening***
A wide opening helps funnel approaching traffic toward the front door.

# Greeting Area

The greeting area refers to the area, such as a porch, where guests stand at the front door.

## Size

The greeting area should be large enough so that at least two or three people can comfortably stand near the front door (Fig. 4–23). **Stoops** are usually small concrete pads that hold only a few people. If there is a door that opens out, the guests will have to step off the stoop to allow the door to open.

(a)

(b)

## *Figure 4–22* **Multiple Approaching Views**

Consider the various views as one approaches the front door. (a) The beginning approach views the front of the bed; (b) then overlooks the yard toward the corner planting;

*(continues)*

(c)

(d1)

(d2)

(e)

***Figure 4–22***  **Multiple Approaching Views—continued**
(c) then sees the planting near the entry opening; (d) then the entry walk #4 (close-up) planting at entry steps and (e) finally overlooks the yard again near the steps toward the planting near the curb.

## Protection

The greeting area should have some protection from the elements (Fig. 4–24). Overhead protection helps get guests out of the rain. A porch does that easily with the extension of a roof. Stoops, on the other hand, may provide little overhead protection.

Also, protection should provide a sense of **enclosure.** This will create a feeling of semi privacy when at the front door. Front doors that have a stoop completely exposed to the street make guests feel uncomfortable, like they are standing on a stage. By planting along the sides and perhaps the overhead of a tree canopy will make guests feel more comfortable as well as more protected from the elements like wind, rain, and sun. However, do not make the mistake of screening the front door so that the door is not visible from the road.

(a)                                                                (b)

(c)                                                                (d)

**Figure 4–23  Greeting Area**
(a) The greeting area, which is a stoop or porch, is often too small and exposed to the elements. (b) This stoop is large enough so that visitors can remain while the front door opens. (c) This stoop is too small to allow guests to be greeted at the front porch, but (d) is expanded with a warm material to be more welcoming. *(Photos courtesy of Robert J. Kleinberg Landscaping, East Lansdowne, PA. www.kleinberg.com)*

## Sitting Area

Although entertaining guests often takes place in the privacy of the backyard, some people like a sitting area in the front yard. This may be the front porch or a separate paved space (Fig. 4–25). This provides a nice greeting area for brief, semi private visits as well as neighborhood activities. Planning for some enclosure with trees and shrubs allows for protection from the sun and wind and creates a degree of privacy and comfort.

***Figure 4–24* Enclosing the Greeting Area**
Enclosure of the greeting area adds an element of comfort and semi privacy without screening the front door.

# Side Yard

There's a great deal of variation in the side yard, depending on the size and shape of the lot as well as the orientation of the house. Side yards are generally narrow and shady, primarily used to get people from the front to the backyard (Fig. 4–26). They are often used as the utility area.

> ### *Tip Box*
> The side yards of a typical residence have little more function than to connect the front yard with the backyard.

## Circulation

Because the main purpose of a side yard is often to **circulate** traffic to the backyard, creating a path that guides people is useful (Fig. 4–27). Allow for space to comfortably get to the backyard, and consider if there needs to be enough room to get equipment, like a riding mower, through the area. Although a concrete or a paved path would be ideal, many clients may not want to spend money on a secondary path where turf would function just as well.

## Storage Area

In some cases the side yard is considered dead space and used for **storage** (Fig. 4–28). Many residents will park a seldom-used camper or boat there, as well as other items such as firewood, garbage cans, or construction material.

(a)

(b)

(c)

(d)

**Figure 4–25  Entertaining at the Greeting Area**

(a) The front porch or (b) other area can serve as an area to entertain guests. (c) Partial enclosure of front porch creates a comfortable atmosphere. (d) Greeting area is expanded to casually host guests.

*(Photo (a) courtesy of King's Material, Inc. Cedar Rapids, IA. www.kingsmaterial.com; Photo (d) courtesy of Blue Ribbon LLC, Maryland. www.blueribbonllc.com)*

**Figure 4-26  Side Yard**
Most side yards are narrow, shady spaces that simply connect the front to the back-yard, as well as store utility items such as garbage.

**Figure 4-27  Circulation**
Circulation patterns throughout the residence should facilitate foot traffic.

(a)

(b)

**Figure 4-28  Storage**
(a) Locate areas of storage in less visible areas. (b) Storage areas screened with plants.

(a)

(b)

***Figure 4–29* Screening Side Yard**
(a) Often objectionable objects are located in the side yard. (b) Plantings and fences can reduce them from being visible.

## Screening

Consider the unslightly items that are along the side (Fig. 4–29). If an air-conditioning unit is there, consider screening it with a low lattice fence or small shrubs (Fig. 4–30). However, be careful not to smother the unit, preventing airflow and operation.

(a)                                    (b)

***Figure 4-30  Screening the Air-Conditioning Unit***
(a) These a/c units located in the side yard are screened from (b) the front yard with a small lattice fence panel.

***Figure 4-31  View From the Neighbor***
Because side yards are narrow, views may need to be screened so that the neighbor is not looking directly into the client's home.

If garbage cans are stored there, then create a screen that would hide them but still leave adequate access to them.

Look at whether views from the neighbor's house need to be screened from seeing into the client's house (Fig. 4-31).

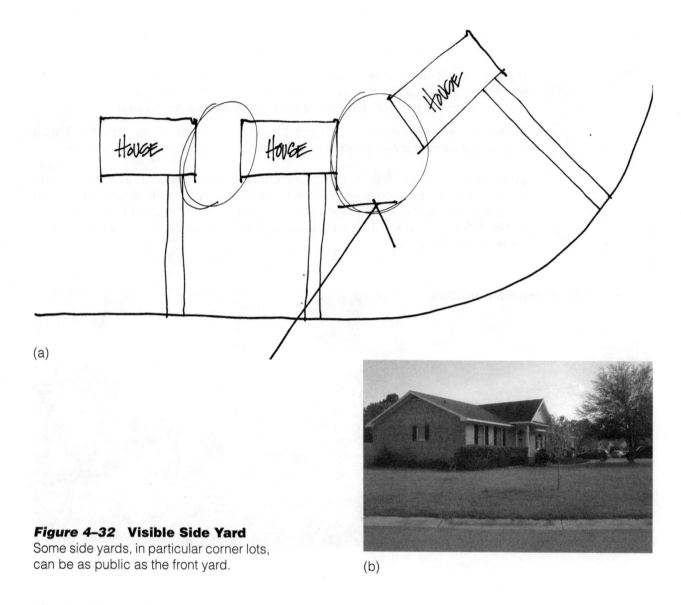

(a)

***Figure 4–32* Visible Side Yard**
Some side yards, in particular corner lots,
can be as public as the front yard.

(b)

## Curb Appeal

Some side yards can be large and in view of the public (Fig. 4–32). In this case, the side
yard would be part of the curb appeal that the front yard addresses.

# Backyard

The backyard is generally the private area. It's primarily used for entertaining guests,
eating, relaxing, recreation, and hobbies.

## Developing the Backyard

### Entertainment

An **entertainment area** may just be a simple place that two people can go to relax and
look out over the backyard, or as complex as an area for parties and various functions.
Typically, the entertainment area is a 10′ × 10′ concrete slab that comes off the back

door, which is too small for most activities (Fig. 4–33). As a result, the slab is usually crowded with chairs, table, and grill, leaving little room to circulate to the back door.

The slab has little enclosure or protection from the elements. With no overhead protection, the sun creates an extremely bright and hot area. With nothing planted on the side there is little protection from wind and the views of neighboring houses.

Develop the entertainment area to match the needs of the residents. This may just be an area to accommodate the family or large enough to host parties of 20 people.

**Size**   The size of the entertainment area should be large enough to allow room for seating and room for circulation through it. Complex entertainment areas can develop subspaces for smaller entertainment such as eating, sunbathing, reading, or just general intimacy (Fig. 4–34). This can be achieved with multilevel decks or separating areas with plantings.

*Figure 4–33*  **Entertainment Slab**
A common entertainment area is the 10′ × 10′ concrete slab installed by the contractor which is open to the elements and too small.

(a)

(b)

*Figure 4–34*  **Entertainment Size**
The size of the entertainment area should correspond to the client needs. (a) Simple, single level decks are suitable for small gatherings while (b) large, multi-level decks can host larger crowds.
*(Photo (a) courtesy of JRW Decks in Seattle. www.jrwdecks.com)*

(a)

(b)

(c)

***Figure 4–35  Patio Material***
(a and b) Pavers, (c) flagstone, or concrete are common patio materials. *(Photo (a) courtesy of Robert J. Kleinberg Landscaping, East Lansdowne, PA, www.kleinberg.com; Photo (b) courtesy of King's Material, Inc., Cedar Rapids, IA. www.kingsmaterial.com)*

**Materials**  Entertainment areas are often developed with a hardscape material to provide a solid footing as well as to separate them from the lawn. The most common types of materials used to develop entertainment areas are wood decks and patios. Patios can be constructed with pavers, flagstone, or concrete (Fig. 4–35).

**Enclosure**  Entertainment areas are generally for intimate to semi-intimate gatherings (Fig. 4–36). Creating a sense of enclosure provides a comfortable setting for gathering. This can be any degree of enclosure, ranging from complete screening to implied enclosure.

   **Overhead:** Develop an overhead plane with the canopy of a tree or the wooden structure of an arbor intertwined with vines (Fig. 4–37).

   **Sides:** Trees and shrubs can be used to create any degree of enclosure (Fig. 4–38). Dense shrubs that are 6 feet tall have a high degree of enclosure, where lower shrubs have more of an implied enclosure. The lower the shrub, the more the separation is implied. In fact, a simple bed of groundcover can be a nice separation that creates no visual separation.

**Cooking**  Many people like an area for grilling (Fig. 4–39). Consider whether this will be integrated into the sitting area or set as a separate BBQ pit. This area should have adequate proximity to the back door of the house to facilitate trips back and forth to the kitchen.

(a)

**Figure 4–36  Entertainment Enclosure**
(a) Partially enclosing the entertainment area overhead and along the sides adds to the comfort level and provides shade, protection, and privacy. (b) A large deck that has little protection from the sun and wind and provides no privacy from neighbors.

(b)

(a)                                          (b)

**Figure 4–37  Overhead Enclosure**
(a) This arbor provides a sense of overhead enclosure and comfort and provides a structure for fragrant vines to cover. (b) The canopy of the trees provides the overhead enclosure over this breakfast nook.

(a)

IMPLIED

PARTIAL OR COMPLETE

(b)

**Figure 4–38** Side Enclosure

(a) Shrubs provide more enclosure from other areas, while ground cover implies separation without screening. (b) Lattice walls enclose the hot tub for semi-privacy, allowing light and wind to pass through. *(Photo courtesy of Decks by JRW Portland, Oregon. www.decksbyjrw.com)*

(a)

(b)

**Figure 4–39** Cooking Area

An area designated for outdoor cooking should be close enough to the house to make convenient trips to the kitchen. *(Photo (b) courtesy of Decks by JRW Portland, Oregon. www.decksbyjrw.com)*

**Eating**   Will there be a permanent outdoor area developed for eating outside or will this be integrated into the entertainment area? Eating areas ideally should have some protection from the wind and sun, even rain if possible.

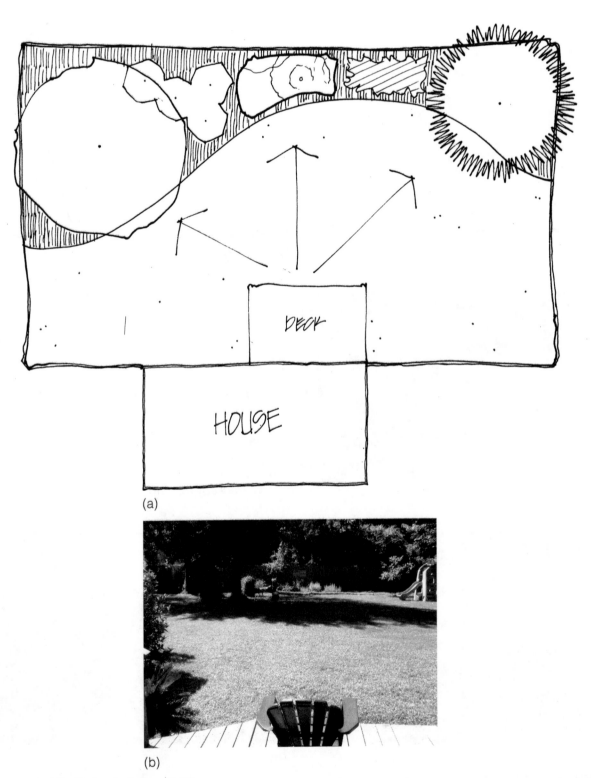

(a)

(b)

**Figure 4–40   Entertainment Views**
(a) Plantings can break up the long, monotonous run of privacy fence and provide interesting views. (b) From this deck, landscaping would help create an interesting view while entertaining.

**Views and Other Elements of Interest**   It is important to include elements of interest, in particular, views from the entertainment area to improve the comfort and appeal. Oftentimes there is little to break up the monotonous rhythm of the fence that runs the entire length of the backyard (Fig. 4–40). This creates very few interesting views looking out into the backyard. Also, make note of views that are unsightly and that need to be blocked. Pay attention to views from neighbors coming into the backyard (Fig. 4–41). Neighboring two-story houses look right down into the privacy of the backyard.

Other elements of interest include sound and fragrance. Water features add the dimension of a splashing sound and, sometimes, fish (Fig. 4–42). There are many plants that can add delightful fragrance when blooming.

(a)

(b)

(c)

***Figure 4–41 Screening Views Into the Backyard***

(a) A common problem is screening views that come over a 6′ privacy fence from neighboring two-story houses. (b) This backyard has little privacy, however (c) trees could enclose and screen the views from the tall neighboring homes.

ACCENT

FRAGRANCE

SOUND

HOUSE

(a)

(b)

***Figure 4–42* Entertainment Interest**
(a) Accent plantings, fragrance, and sound
offer interesting elements to the entertainment
area. (b) A small pond provides trickling water and goldfish.

## Recreation

The other major activity in the backyard is recreation (Fig. 4–43). This can take many forms, depending on the needs of the residents.

**Open Area**   A considerable amount of open area is needed for outdoor games, especially if there are children. It should be a continuous stretch of turf. However, the amount of open area is based on the client's wants.

**Playground**   If the residents have small children, it may be important to develop an area for a playground, which could include a swing set and sandbox (Fig. 4–44). Be sure that this area is in good view from inside the house as well as out since parents will want to keep an occasional eye on small children.

## Hobbies

There are many **hobbies** that can be addressed with the landscape. Gardening is one of the most common outdoor hobbies (fig. 4–45). This may include flowers as well as vegetables. Although the resident may have many ideas to develop this area, there are a few things to consider:

***Figure 4–43  Backyard Activities***
Several activities besides entertainment should be considered: open area for recreation, play area for children, quiet area, and screening views.

(a)

(b)

**Figure 4–44 Playground**
The playground for children should be in view of the house (a) or entertainment area (b) so that the playground (in back) can be easily monitored. *(Photo (b) courtesy of Blue Ribbon LLC, Maryland. www.blueribbonllc.com)*

**Figure 4–45 Garden**
Gardening, a popular hobby, should be in full sun with easy access to water. This garden is placed in an area out of view from the house and entertainment area.

**Water source:** If this is a vegetable garden, will there be adequate availability to water? It would be inconvenient to drag the hose across the yard.

**Exposure:** Is it shade or full sun? Vegetables require a lot of sun to grow successfully. Water gardens require at least 8 hours of sun for many aquatic plants to bloom.

# Summary

The landscape should be more than a pretty picture; it should be useful as well. The basic areas of the landscape are public (in view of neighbors and passersby), private (entertainment, recreation), and utility (storage, garbage cans, air conditioner). These basic areas are found throughout the landscape, but typically the public area is the front yard and the private and utility areas are in the back. The side yard varies depending on the lot and can be public, private, or utility.

The front yard is primarily developed to facilitate a safe and interesting approach for guests to the front door, in addition to improving curb appeal. The front door should be easy to find from the street, and the entry walk should comfortably facilitate walking. The driveway, in addition to having adequate space for parking cars, often serves as the approach walk from the street to the entry walk. There should be enough room to comfortably walk with cars parked. The front porch should be large enough and sufficiently protected to greet a few guests at the front door; it sometimes serves as a semi private entertainment area.

The side yard is typically narrow and shady, primarily used to connect the front yard to the backyard. Often times it is used as a storage area and should sufficiently screen unsightly items.

The backyard is often the site for recreation, entertainment, or hobbies that include playground, gardening, swimming, cooking, and eating. Areas should be developed to support the resident's activities, for children, pets, adults, or parties. Comfortable areas to sit and interesting views improve quality of life in the backyard. It is often a private area that is screened from the surrounding area.

# Key Terms

**Circulation:** paths commonly used to walk through the landscape

**Curb appeal:** how the front of the house looks from the road

**Enclosure:** plantings or construction that provides a sense of protection and privacy

**Entertainment area:** place where two people can go to relax or host parties and other various functions

**Entry walk:** provides access from the road or from the driveway to the front door

**Functional:** landscape supports the activities of the residents

**Funneling effect:** planting larger items on the outside and placing progressively smaller plants closer to the door to draw attention to the front door

**Hobbies:** outdoor activities; gardening is common

**Private area:** an area screened from the public view and used to entertain guests, recreation and for hobbies, or for the family to relax; often the backyard and occasionally the side yard

**Public areas:** within view and open to the public; often the front yard and occasionally the side yard

**Service area:** see utility area

**Stoops:** small concrete pads that hold only a few people

**Storage:** areas to keep belongings and materials such as camper or boat, firewood, garbage cans, or lumber

**Traditional landscaping:** primarily dealt with foundation planting that consisted of an evergreen hedge across the front of the house

**Utility area:** an area for storage, gardening, trash, compost, or other items that are functional but often unsightly or odorous; kept out of sight

# 5 | The Concept Plan

## Objectives

- Understand the components and function of the concept plan in the design process
- Learn the materials and techniques to draw the concept plan
- Know the concept plan graphics

The functional aspects of the landscape design in the previous chapter come together to form the **concept plan,** sometimes referred to as a **functional diagram** or **bubble diagram.** The concept plan is an organization of the ground plane to create functionality in the design. Looking at the base map, the concept plan organizes the space of the ground plane into lawn, planting beds, concrete, work area, and so forth. It is important to start with a good concept upon which to build the details of the design. Thus, the concept plan acts as the bones, or blueprint, on which the design is built. If the framework of the design is ill conceived, then the design is doomed from the start.

---

### Tip Box

If the framework of the design is ill conceived, then the design is doomed from the start.

---

This phase of the design will involve loose sketching of ideas and concepts (Fig. 5–1). Materials include tracing paper, soft lead (HB or 2B), and the site analysis. These sketches are an exercise for the purpose of organizing thoughts and generating design ideas at the fundamental level. In some cases, a designer may draw the concept plan for presentation to support the analysis and solutions of the final plan.

*Figure 5–1* **Sketching Concept Plan**
A loose approach to developing the concept plan.

*Analysis* ——→ *Concept Plan*

As the design process unfolds in later chapters it becomes apparent that each step becomes more detailed. The concept plan, fundamental in nature, is very general. It utilizes amorphous **bubbles** drawn on the plan to designate areas. It is important that the concept plan stays general and not become bogged down in any detail of plant material or hardscape.

Be loose. Make mistakes. And uncover new, fresh approaches to the design!

# Space

The concept plan uses bubbles to fill the entire space of the site. A bubble accounts for all the space. This avoids leaving any area up to speculation (Fig. 5–2).

# Analysis

It is imperative that the concept plan addresses the analysis. The concept plan is built right over the top of the analysis. In fact, some designers tape a sheet of tracing paper over the top of the analysis to draw the concept plan (Fig. 5–3). Good organization should always address strong and weak points of the analysis (Fig. 5–4).

# Activities and Materials

Using bubbles, the base map will begin to be divided into various activities, effects, and/or general materials (Fig. 5–5). The following is a basic list of areas, not all-inclusive, that can be used in any combination. Of course, the selection and arrangement of bubbles in a concept plan will depend on the needs of the client.

**Beds:** This can be as general as "planting areas" or "mulched beds" or can be as specific as "low shrubs, screen, large deciduous trees."

**Lawn:** An important component of most designs because it is inexpensive and supports many activities.

**Hardscape:** This refers to any hard surface such as a driveway, sidewalk, patio, or deck.

**Screen:** Areas that will block unpleasant sites from view or wind/sun exposure.

**Focal points:** Suggested development of an accent for view.

**Activities:** Designating areas for various activities. These include, but are not limited to

Garden

Work

Eating

Relaxation

Play

Entertainment

**Figure 5–2 Concept Plan and Bubbles**
(a) All areas are designated with bubbles to organize the ground plane. (b) Smaller bubbles leave too much open space that is undefined.

**Figure 5–3 Concept Drawing**
In order to address the analysis, some designers prefer to lay the concept drawing over the analysis, while some simply refer back to the analysis lying to the side.

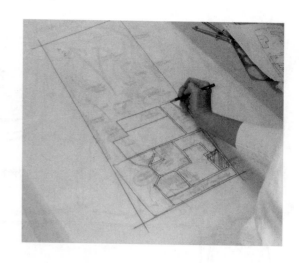

**Figure 5–4 Concept and Analysis**
(a) The concept plan will address the analysis; (b) if not, the concept plan and, ultimately, the design will be much less functional.

# Concepts

What is being defined in the concept plan by these bubbles? Besides establishing materials and activities in these bubbles, size, location, circulation, views, and exposure are also considered in their development and placement.

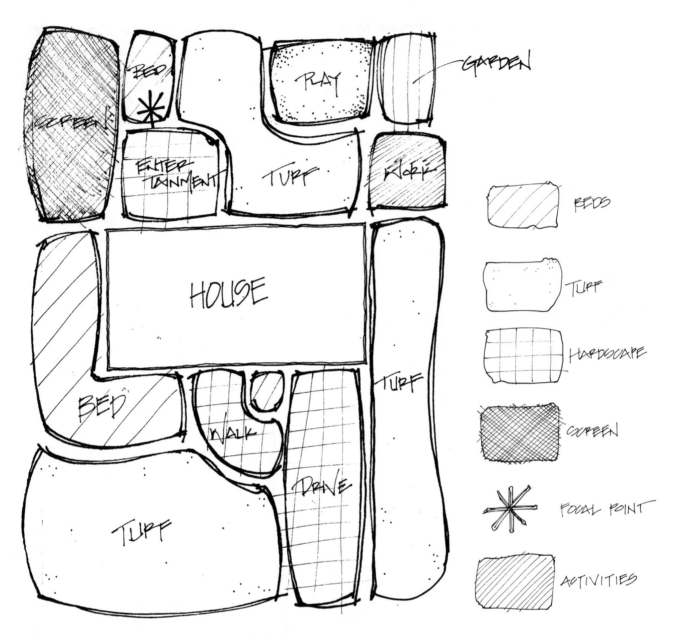

**Figure 5–5  Activities and Materials**
Each bubble represents a different function, or concept, on the plan.

# Size

The bubbles in the concept are generally rough sketches but should approximate the size of each designated area. The size of the area is often dictated by the client's needs.

## Entertainment

How large of an entertainment area is needed (Fig. 5–6)? If the client will host large parties, then the area may need to be as large as several hundred square feet. However, if the entertainment consists of an area where the family can sit and relax, then it may only be a couple of hundred square feet.

**Figure 5-6  Entertainment Size**
The size of the bubble is defined by the function of the entertainment area.

***Figure 5–7*  Lawn Size**
The size of the lawn and bed bubbles is relevant to level of mowing, as well as the activities that would require turf (recreation) or beds (plantings).

## Lawn and Beds

How much lawn will be required? Is there a need for play and recreation areas? Some residents like to have a good size lawn to maintain while others like bed space for trees, shrubs, and flowers (Fig. 5–7).

What kind of maintenance do the clients want? Lawns need to be mowed weekly during the summer. Planting beds need to be mulched, weeded, and occasionally pruned. However, the maintenance demands of planting beds, although higher during the first few years of establishment, eventually reduce if planting beds are designed properly for trees, shrubs, and groundcover to grow and smother most weeds and reduce mulching needs.

## Entry Walk and Other Paths

The width of primary sidewalks, which is generally the entry walk going to the front door, should be no less than 4 feet wide (Fig. 5–8). Secondary walks where traffic is much lighter can be as narrow as 2 to 3 feet.

# Location

The size of the bubbles allows for adequate space, but the bubbles also need to be located appropriately on the site.

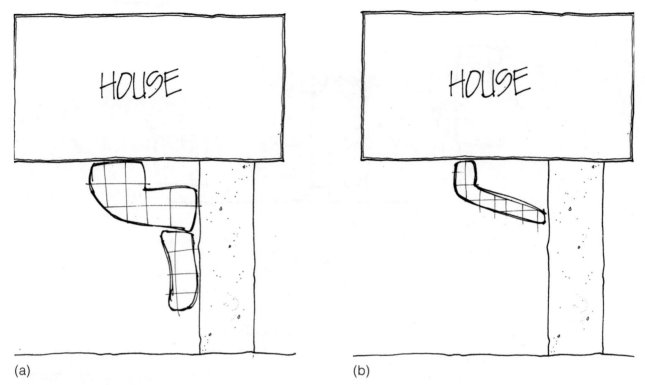

(a)                                                                                    (b)

***Figure 5–8  Entry Size***
The size of the bubble should be roughly equal to the dimensions of the entry walk. (a) Represents a wide, welcome walk, while (b) represents a narrow walk.

### Access

Make sure there is adequate access for each activity, as it requires.

- Gardening should be accessible to a water source (Fig. 5–9).
- Cooking should have close accessibility to the house kitchen.
- Work areas should be conveniently located near the garage or shed or at least a power source.

### Visibility

- Playgrounds should be in a visible location so parents can watch children easily (Fig. 5–10).
- Storage areas should be accessible, but not so that they are a visual problem.

## Circulation

The concept plan should address the circulation patterns observed in the analysis. Good circulation throughout the property makes a comfortable setting that is easy to navigate as well as facilitates safety (Fig. 5–11).

### Primary Circulation

This pertains to major paths. The most common, and most important in many cases, is the front walk which facilitates pedestrians from the street or the driveway to the front door. These paths should be wide enough to allow two people to walk side by side. At a minimum they should be 4 feet wide.

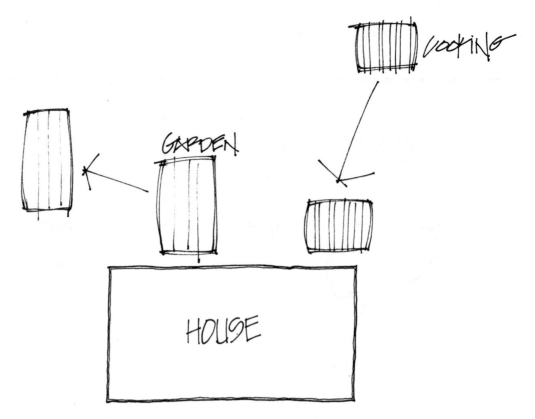

**Figure 5–9** **Access**

The concept plan should locate activities and areas appropriately. Cooking should be closer to the house while the garden is often away from the house in full sun and accessible to water.

**Figure 5–10** **Visibility**

Locate areas for appropriate exposure. Playgrounds should be within view of the house while storage areas are away from view.

***Figure 5–11*  Circulation**
Study the circulation patterns and layout bubbles in order to facilitate flow. Large arrows indicate primary circulation while smaller arrows indicate secondary circulation.

## Secondary Circulation

These are paths that are infrequently taken. They are usually taken by one or two people at any given time. Most common secondary paths are from the front or side of the house to the backyard. Other paths may include traffic around work areas and entertainment areas.

# View

Concept plans address the various views analysized on site. These views may be existing views (good and poor) and potential views (Fig. 5–12).

## Good Views

There are good existing views that should be preserved. These are often addressed by keeping the view open or framing.

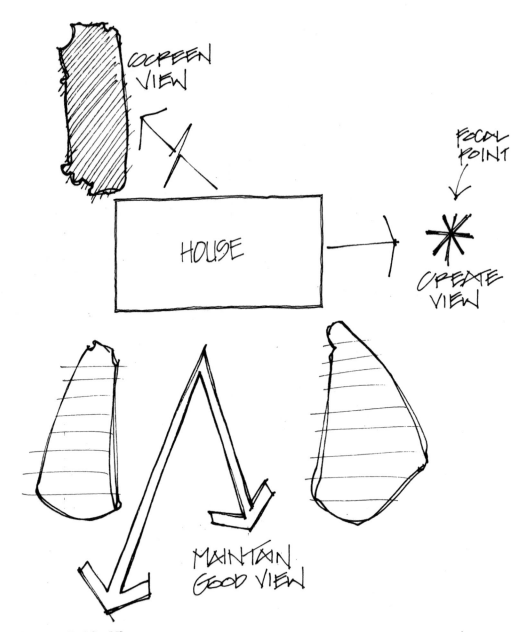

**Figure 5-12  Views**
The concept plan should address the views in analysis. The broken arrow indicates screening view, the star refers to a proposed focal point, and the large arrows indicate major views.

## Poor Views

Plantings or fences screen poor views such as unsightly trash areas, storage, or traffic. These areas are noted on the concept plan to be blocked from common views, such as from an entertainment area or public area.

## Potential Views

Some areas of viewing (entertainment or inside views) have very few interesting views. To increase the interest of these areas of viewing something can be created. This may be a focal point, such as a water feature or sculpture, or other themes, such as butterfly gardens.

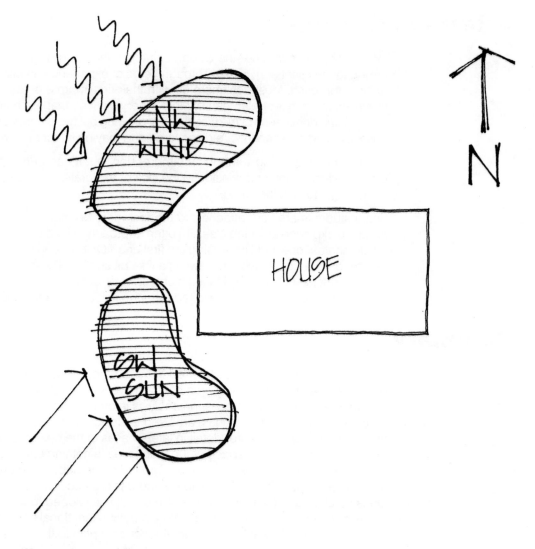

*Figure 5-13* **Exposure**
The concept plan should screen the sun and wind according to analysis for energy efficiency.

# Exposure

There will be areas on the site that need to be protected from the elements (Fig. 5-13).

## Shade

Create shade for an entertainment area or to cool the southwest side of the house.

## Wind

Provide a wind block to protect entertainment areas or the northwest side of the house when prevailing wind is a problem.

## Enclosure

Create a sense of enclosure at entertainment areas or other gathering areas such as the front door, which makes them more comfortable.

# Alternate Concepts

Most designers can "see" the design solution after being on site for a short while and talking to the client (Fig. 5–14). Through years of experience an intuition develops for a design approach. Most designers go with their first impression as the design solution. However, the concept plan can explore other solutions that are hardly considered because of the dominance of the first idea. By drawing out two or three concept plans, other fresh, exciting approaches are discovered and may be integrated with the original idea.

There is nothing wrong with the first impression, but it can become a blinder to other creative ideas. Another downside to the lack of exploration is hitting a rut, where all designs begin to look the same.

Some students are very attached to the first idea. So much so that they are very resistant to exploring anything else. I'm often approached by a student with the response, "I'll do another one, but I'll be using the first one." Or, between two concept plans, there are few differences. Maybe the lawn is a little bit smaller. Those students who finally relent and decide to go off and take an entirely different approach are often pleased with the results. They find they are excited with original, unique solutions never considered.

# Summary

The concept plan, sometimes referred to as a bubble diagram or functional diagram, organizes the ground plane to create a framework on which the design will be built. It is fundamental that it addresses the analysis in order to be fully functional. Bubbles, which are somewhat amorphous, are used to designate areas of activity or material that will be refined in greater detail in later phases of the design process. These bubbles will fill the entire space of the plan to leave nothing undefined. The size and placement of the bubbles organize the ground plane depending on the intended function of the area, as well as visibility and desired access. A number of concept plans, each addressing the analysis, are quickly developed to work through new and different ideas in order to come up with a creative, functional solution to the analysis. Occasionally a designer may present the concept plan to the client to support the master plan.

# Key Terms

**Bubbles:** outlines that define an area or activity

**Bubble diagram:** see concept plan

**Concept plan:** organization of ground plane to create a functional design

**Functional diagram:** see concept plan

**CONCEPT A**

(labels within drawing: TURF, BED, BED, ENTRY, BED, WORK, BED, WALK, BED, DRIVE, TURF, BED, DITCH, SCREEN)

**Figure 5–14  Grant Concept Drawings**
Three different concept plans that address the analysis of the Grant residence.

*(continues)*

**Figure 5–14   Grant Concept Drawings—continued**

144

**Figure 5-14 Grant Concept Drawings—continued**

# 6 Design Principles

## Objectives

- Become familiar with attributes of form, color, and texture and their use in design
- Understand approaches to balance in the landscape
- Be able to establish connection or unity in the design
- Know various means of creating visual interest in the design
- Be able to create a sense of flow or transition in the landscape
- Understand the application of mass planting

As the concept plan creates the useful or functional component of the landscape design, design principles create the aesthetic, or visual appeal. Design principles are useful not only to develop visual interest but also to create a sense of unity and order in the design concept. The goal should be to create a landscape that appears as a big picture where every component of the landscape belongs to the overall design. Compare it to a framed work of art (Fig. 6–1). There are interesting components within the work itself, with each individual part having a unique aspect. These differences within the frame make it interesting, keeping our attention moving throughout the work. But when you step back and look at it in its entirety, all the individual unique components belong to a theme.

The following design principles are proposed to help bring unity, order, and interest to your design.

(a)                                                            (b)

***Figure 6–1*  Cohesive Design**
Like a framed work of art, the landscape design should be composed of individual components yet be connected as if part of one composition (a) rather than random individual parts (b).

# Design Attributes

Before discussing design principles, let us take a look at design **attributes,** in particular those that pertain to plants. Becoming familiar with these attributes will make it easier to understand design principles.

## Form

**Form** is the outline of an object or plant, often thought of as the silhouette (Fig. 6–2). It is easiest to see it in an individual plant. Form can also be the total mass of plants when they are grouped together.

Form is manipulated when shrubs are tightly **sheared,** creating geometric forms out of the plants (Fig. 6–3). This may be the intention in formal gardens or in the practice of

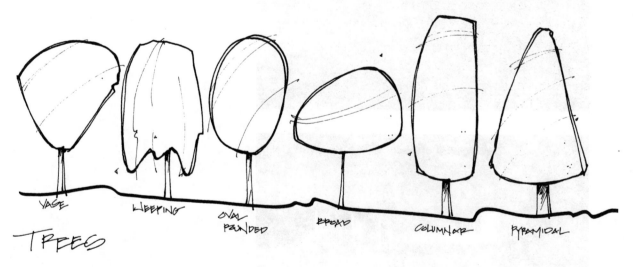

(a)

***Figure 6–2*** **Form**

(a) There are various forms in which plants can be categorized, from upright and columnar to broad and spreading.

*(continues)*

(b)

***Figure 6–2*  Form—continued**
(b) Plant forms can be very unique and, in this case, should be used carefully. Too much of a "loud" form that demands attention can be disruptive. (c) The vine growing up a white wall creates an interesting pattern or form. (d) This weeping form creates the effect of water falling into a dry creek. (e) The planting beds create a curving form of turf on the ground plane.

(c)

(d)

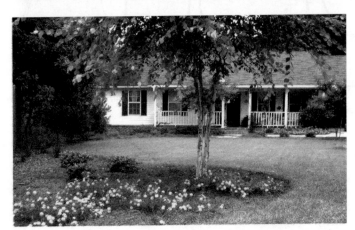

(e)

**topiary,** when a plant form is pruned into shapes of spirals or animals (Fig. 6–4). **Espalier** manipulates form by training a tree or shrub to grow flat against a wall or fence (Fig. 6–5). However, shearing is often abused and the natural form is lost.

There are a variety of natural plant forms to be aware of. It's important to be familiar with the various forms, so as not to have too much variety in the design.

*Figure 6–3*  **Shearing Form**
Pruning, in particular shearing, can dramatically change a plant form. Oftentimes it destroys the natural form.

*Figure 6–4*  **Topiary**
The technique of pruning plants into specific shapes, such as pom-poms, spirals, or animals. *(Photo Courtesy of Visual Impact software.)* www.visualimpactimaging.com

*Figure 6–5*  **Espalier**
The technique of pruning plants to grow flat against a wall or fence.

**Shrubs**

- Creeping
- Prostrate
- Mounded
- Rounded
- Upright
- Irregular

**Trees**

- Vase-shaped/fastigate
- Weeping
- Round
- Broad
- Oval
- Columnar
- Pyramidal

# Color

**Color** in the landscape can be introduced from several parts of the plant. Most commonly color comes by way of flowers, but color is also useful from foliage, fruit, and branching. Color has an impact on human emotion. **Warm** colors (red, orange, yellow) create excitement while **cool** colors (blue, green, purple) have a calming effect.

## Foliage

There are many shades of green that foliage can display: light green, silver green, blue green, and dark green (Fig. 6–6). Together a nice variety of green colors can create visual interest and contrast. Although foliage is commonly green there are selections that maintain foliage of other colors such as shades of red, purple, and yellow (Fig. 6–7). Burgundy, most popular with Japanese maples, is a common alternative and can be a nice change of pace among green foliage.

***Figure 6–6***   **Shades of Green**
Variety of green colors can create interest, from light green and blue green to dark green, as well as variegation.

***Figure 6–7***   **Foliage Color**
Colors other than green, such as the burgundy foliage of a Japanese Maple, can add a nice change of pace. *(Photo courtesy of William A. Hoch. http://www.midwestlandscapeplants.org)*

*Figure 6–8* **Variegation**
Variegated foliage is a popular selection because it is unique in color and pattern. It is often a good selection to create a focal accent because it attracts attention.

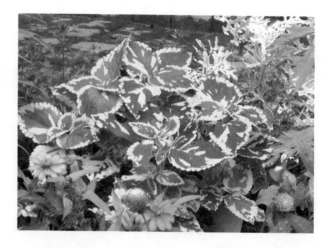

*Figure 6–9* **Fall Color**
Not all plants have an appealing fall color like the brilliant red of these Firepower Nandina.

**Variegation**   Another consideration is **variegation,** which is the mottling or striping of foliage (and sometimes flowers) (Fig. 6–8). Variegation offers a unique display of foliage and can be used to create accent points among green foliage.

**Fall Color**   Some plants are well known for brilliant displays of fall color (Fig. 6–9). This may be bright colors of orange, yellow, red, or purple. These plants offer a great burst of color toward the end of the growing season when flowering colors are rare. Be aware that some plants have very little color in the fall, simply turning brown and falling to the ground.

## Flowers

Flowers are often the most revered of many plants, whether it's for their color, shape, or fragrance. Some plants are highly prized for their flowering and as a result have numerous cultivars with a wide variety of flower characteristics. This is evident with roses, camellias, and azaleas. In contrast, other plants have flowers of insignificance, such as sycamores, maples, and conifers. Many people think the value of flowers lies mostly in the color (Fig. 6–10).

**Length of Bloom**   In many cases, color is provided by annual flowers that bloom all season long (Fig. 6–11). Perennial flowers, trees, and shrubs only flower for a portion of the season. However, the length of time varies greatly. Some may be a short bloom of a few days while other plants go on for several weeks.

***Figure 6–10*** **Flower Color**
Flower color is a very common means of introducing color into the landscape.

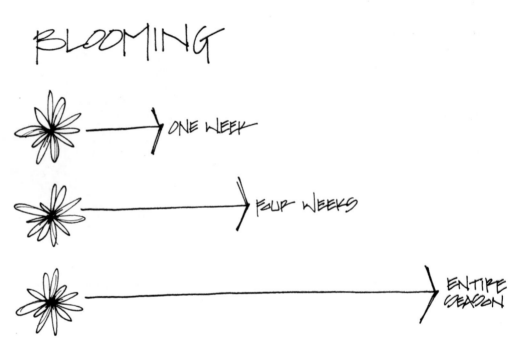

***Figure 6–11*** **Length of Bloom**
Be aware of how long a plant will bloom. Annuals bloom all season, while perennials range from a short week to several weeks of color.

**Sequence**    Another consideration when selecting flower color is timing (Fig. 6–12). Select plants so there is a **sequence** of flowering throughout the growing season. This creates a movement of change and interest throughout the entire season. Contrast this to a scenario where all plants in the design flower at the same time, creating an overwhelming blast of color and then after a few weeks appear green for the remainder of the season.

**Spring flowering:** Most plants flower during the spring. However, there is a lot of variation in spring flowering. Flowering can occur in early, mid, or late spring.

**Summer flowering:** There are fewer plants that flower during the summer and even fewer in the fall. However, in southern parts of the country some plants will flower in the winter.

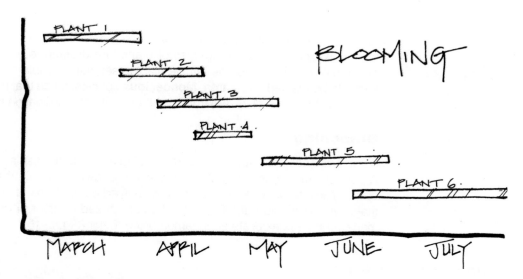

**Figure 6–12  Timing of Bloom**
Note when plants bloom, in particular perennials. Ideally, plants should provide a succession of blooms that provide a variety of color from early spring to late summer.

(a)

(b)

(c)

**Figure 6–13  Fruit**
Another way to introduce color into the landscape is fruit. It is often a great way to get color late in the growing season when few things are blooming. (a) Hollies are a popular shrub that gets bright red clusters of fruit, commonly used during the Christmas holiday. (b) Some fruit is valuable as a food source to attract birds, although beware of fruit sources that attract birds that make an enormous mess. (c) Pyracantha is valued for large clusters of bright red fruit.

## Fruit

Some plants offer a great display of fruit that may even outdo the flowering. This may be in the form of color, shape, and edibility. Fruit can be used in conjunction with flowering as a sequence of color (Fig. 6–13). This is especially valuable when fewer plants are flowering late in the summer, but fruit is often starting to set and display.

Be aware of plants that offer very little fruit display. Hollies are a great example. Known for a heavy set of bright red fruit in the winter, some species of holly, valued for their glossy foliage, will not fruit. Some species of plants are **dioecious,** meaning that a plant is either male or female. For the female plant to set fruit, it requires a male plant, or **pollinator,** to be planted in the area. **Monoecious** species, those that have male and female flowers on the same plant, will fruit by self-pollination or pollination from nearby plants.

## Branching

Some branches are brightly colored, creating a wonderful display in winter (Fig. 6–14). A perfect example is some of the multi-stem dogwood shrubs that have bright red or bright yellow twigs. Color can also be displayed on the trunk of trees, especially those that have exfoliating bark. Paper birches are prized for their bright white trunks, while many other trees exfoliate a cinnamon brown color (Fig. 6–15).

**Figure 6–14   Twig Color**
Colorful branches can introduce color in the winter.
*(Photo courtesy of William A. Hoch. http://www. midwestlandscapeplants.org)*

(a)

(b)

**Figure 6–15   Trunk Color**
Colorful trunks add color, especially exfoliating varieties. (a) Paper birch. (b) River birch.
*(Photo (a) courtesy of William A. Hoch. http://www.midwestlandscapeplants.org)*

# Texture

The **texture** of a plant may refer to the foliage or branching and be classified as fine, medium, or coarse.

## Foliage

Foliage often refers to the size of the leaves (Fig. 6–16). Large leaves are coarse and small leaves are fine in texture, although this may be relative to the surrounding plants. Oakleaf hydrangea is considered a coarse-textured plant when growing next to yaupon holly, but next to a fatsia, which has enormous leaves, it appears less coarse.

## Branching

Large, blocky branching appears coarse in texture compared with thin, wispy branching (Fig. 6–17). Thus, a plant with fine-textured foliage may appear coarse once the leaves have dropped. A great example is the honeylocust, which has small leaves but knobby, coarse branches compared with the thin, flexible whips of the willow tree. The bark of the trunk can also have a coarse or fine texture.

(a)

*Figure 6–16*  **Foliage Texture**
The size of the leaf is often the measure of a plant's texture. (a) The largest leaf (left) is coarse while the smallest leaf (right) is the finest texture. (b) The plant at the top is considered the coarsest. *(Photo (b) courtesy of Visual Impact software. www.visualimpactimaging.com)*

(b)

*Figure 6-17*  **Branch Texture**
Texture can also be a measure of the branching.
Large, gnarly branches (left) are coarse while the
thin, wispy branches (right) are fine textured.

*Figure 6-18*  **Texture Accents**
Coarse texture is more dominant than fine texture.
The large leaf herbaceous plant has a welcoming,
unique texture in the patio setting. It also has a warm
reddish color and contrasts nicely with the fine textured vine and bamboo behind it.

**Coarse Texture**   Coarse texture has a more dominant quality than fine texture and
can be used to accent an area (Fig. 6–18). It also tends to make a space feel smaller
and can be used to make wide-open spaces feel more enclosed (Fig. 6–19).

**Fine Texture**   Fine texture is often used in formal designs, such as tightly sheared
hedges. It is less dominant than coarse texture and often used as a unifying effect. Fine
texture also has a distant quality that creates a larger, more open feeling. This can be
used to open up, or "expand," small spaces such as a courtyard (Fig. 6–19).

***Figure 6–19  Texture and Space***
Coarse texture can make large spaces feel smaller and more intimate. Fine textures can make smaller spaces feel larger.

# Balance

**Balance** is a sense of equality. When an area has many items gathered on one side and only a few on the other an imbalance exists (Fig. 6–20). The same goes for a residence—when a house has several large trees on one side but only low-growing shrubs on the other side, it can appear unbalanced (Fig. 6–21).

Without balance, the design loses a sense of order. Approaching the house in the previous example, regardless of the plant selection and placement, something feels out of place, unbalanced . . . out of order.

There are two general forms of balance that are utilized in landscape design.

*Figure 6–20* **Imbalance**
Like a balancing scale, a design must feel proportionately balanced to be cohesive.

(a)

(b)

*Figure 6–21* **Landscape Balance**
(a) Too much of the landscape is located to the right along with the tallest part of the house, while (b) this landscape appears balanced. *(Photos courtesy of Visual Impact software. www.visualimpactimaging.com)*

# Symmetrical Balance

**Symmetrical balance** is a mirror image of both sides (Fig. 6–22). If a line were drawn down the middle, a symmetrical design would have the exact same placement and selection of plants and material on both sides (Fig. 6–23).

Think of a balancing scale and spherical weights (Fig. 6–24). If you placed a large weight in the right side, you would need to place a large weight of the same size and weight in the left to achieve symmetrical balance. If smaller weights were then placed in the right side, the same number of weights of the same size and weight would then be placed in the left side to achieve balance again.

## Formal Character

Symmetrical balance is rather structured in how it is attained because of the exact repetition on both sides (Fig. 6–25). Because of this structured appearance, it has a formal nature. Symmetrical balance is normally seen in formal gardens where the hedges are tightly sheared.

HOUSE

**_Figure 6–23_ Symmetrical Placement**
The same objects are placed on each side in the same location (top) to achieve symmetrical balance, while the bottom example uses a variety of objects to achieve asymmetrical balance.

## Figure 6–24 Symmetrical Scale

As an example, symmetrical balance is achieved on a scale using the same exact object on both sides.

(a)

(b)

## Figure 6–25 Formal and Informal Balance

(a) Symmetrical balance (top) lends itself to formal design, while asymmetrical (bottom) is often used for a loose, natural balance. (b) Some botanical gardens utilize symmetrical balance to create formal design.

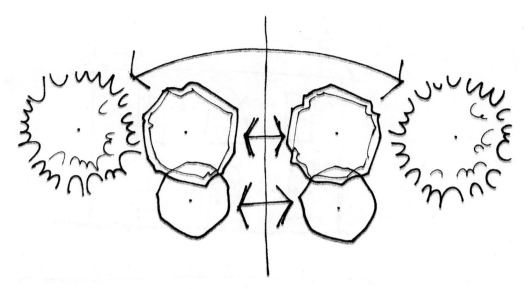

***Figure 6–26*** **Formulaic Balance**
Symmetrical balance is formulaic in the sense that objects are repeated on each side
of an axis.

## Formulaic Balance

This is considered the easiest form of balance to achieve because it only has to be repeated on both sides (Fig. 6–26). Students new to design often find this to be a simple
approach to achieving balance, although they should be aware that the overuse of symmetrical balance can begin to lack interest because it is too predictable.

## Symmetrical Houses

Some houses have symmetrical balance, front door in the middle of the house with the
exact number and placement of windows on both sides (Fig. 6–27). If the house has this
character, then it would be natural to repeat this style with a symmetrically balanced
landscape as well.

# Asymmetrical Balance

**Asymmetrical balance** is unstructured, relying more on a "gut feeling" of balance
rather than the calculated placement of material on both sides of an axis as in symmetrical balance (Fig. 6–28).

With asymmetrical balance, if a large spherical weight were placed in the right side of
a balancing scale, the left side would be balanced by adding something other than the
exact same size and weight, such as several smaller weights that would equal the
weight on the right side. Balance would be achieved without using the exact same material (Fig. 6–29).

## Natural and Informal

Because of the unstructured nature of asymmetrical balance, it is more of an informal
balance. It appeals to a loose, natural sense of balance.

(a)

(b)

(c)

***Figure 6–27*** **Balanced Houses**
The house can impact the type of balance used in the landscape. (a) The top house is symmetrical while the bottom is asymmetrical. (b) Symmetrical house. (c) Asymmetrical house.

# Connection

A common element creates **connection** among the entire design, also referred to as **unity.** Without something that creates a visual recall of similar elements throughout the design, it can appear chaotic and lack a sense of unity. A couple of ways to create connection is by repetition and physically linking space.

**Figure 6–28  Asymmetrical Balance**
Asymmetrical balance uses a variety of material that appears balanced more by feel.

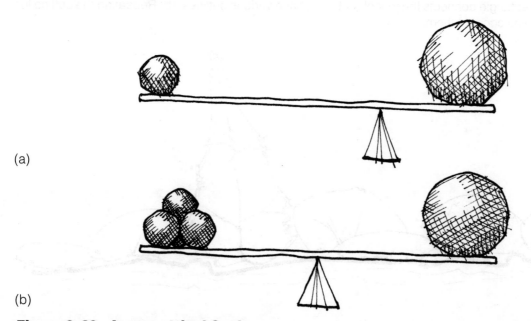

(a)

(b)

**Figure 6–29  Asymmetrical Scale**
(a) Asymmetrical balance is achieved by balancing a larger object with a smaller object and space, or (b) a collection of smaller objects to equal the weight of the larger object.

# Repetition

Repeating elements such as hardscapes or plants throughout a design is critical to creating unity (Fig. 6–30). Visual recall of seeing the same plants or a similar plant quality helps create connection.

Pay attention to qualities that you are using and repeat them throughout an area to connect space (Fig. 6–31). Beware of overzealously pursuing the unique qualities of too many different plants and hardscapes and losing the big picture (Fig. 6–32). Too many differences are disruptive.

(a)

(b)

**Figure 6–30   Repetition**
(a) Repeating the rectangle connects the four objects that have various outlines. (b) Repeating the outline for different objects helps connect them.

**Figure 6–31   Repeating Objects**
The left to right connection in this example comes from repeated plant material and only one different (taller) shrub for variety.

(a)

(b)

*(continues)*

*Figure 6–32* **Repeating in the Plan—continued**
(c) Too much repetition is boring.

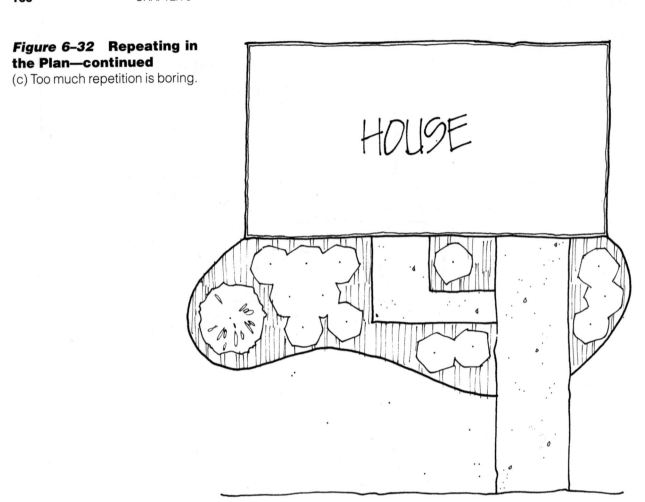

(c)

However, a word of caution to not be too repetitive or the design will become boring. There is nothing interesting about the same one or two plants used for the entire design.

## Plant Repetition

Repeating the same plant throughout the design is the easiest approach to creating visual recall (Fig. 6–33). This is most effectively done with **foundation plants** (Fig. 6–34). Foundation plants are plants that have a nice, simple form but little outstanding qualities. They are valuable in the landscape because they balance the attention demanded from specimen plants. Foundation plants bring unity to the design, or lay the foundation (not necessarily plants used to cover the foundation of the house).

Foundation plants can be used in several different areas of the design because they have a subtle appearance. Therefore, they provide a good visual recall throughout the design by being seen in several places and helping connect the space between these areas.

## Material Repetition

The same principle of repetition can be applied to hardscapes (Fig. 6–35). Using the same pavers or flagstone for walks and patio can create visual recall in different parts of the residence.

*Figure 6–33*  **Plant Repetition**
Plants are sufficiently repeated in the plan to help connect or unify space.

*Figure 6–34*  **Foundation Plants**
The plants on the right are low-profile without stand-alone qualities; typically repeated to help unify design. The plant on the left would be more suitable as a specimen or an accent. *(Photo courtesy of Visual Impact software. www.visualimpactimaging.com)*

**Figure 6–35  Material Repetition**
Hardscape material is repeated in the plan to help connect the front and back portions of the design.

## Characteristic Repetition

Instead of repeating the same plant, plant characteristics can be repeated for a sense of connection.

**Texture:** Similar textures of various plants can create a visual relationship (Fig. 6–36).

**Color:** Use color in various forms. For instance, red may appear in foliage, fall color, fruit, and flowers of several plants in the landscape.

**Form:** Repeat similar forms, such as low mounding shrubs (Fig. 6–37).

# Linking Space

Another means of connecting space throughout the design is by physically linking plants with a common material or continuing ground lines.

***Figure 6–36*  Characteristic Repetition**
Repeating plant characteristics, such as similar leaf shape of the pittosporum shrub (left) and the akebia vine (right), can help connect the design.

***Figure 6–37*  Form Repetition**
Repeating plant forms can help unify design.

## Common Material

Seemingly random plants can be connected with a common material, such as a mulched planting bed, fence, or wall (Fig. 6–38). Enclosing plants in a bed of mulch or groundcover is one of the easiest ways to create connection in the landscape (Fig. 6–39). Even in existing random plantings, connection can be improved and appear to fit within the same design by pulling a bed around them.

(a)                                                                    (b)

***Figure 6–38*  Linking Space**
Connect space with a common material, (b) such as a fence, to link the two plantings. *(Photos courtesy of Visual Impact software. www.visualimpacting.com)*

(a)

***Figure 6–39*  Linking Space with Common Material**
(a) Without a mulched bed plantings feel less connected.

*(continues)*

(b)

(c)

(d)

**Figure 6-39  Linking Space with Common Material—continued**
(b) A mulched bed can connect plantings. (c) These plants appear randomly planted in the corners and lack unity. (d) Simply placing a bed helps draw them together.

## Ground Lines

Another means of linking space is continuing lines from beds, house, or other structures. One technique that some designers do with beds for a good sense of connection is to continue a bed line on the other side of a sidewalk or driveway (Fig. 6–40). This is a good way to connect across the broad expanse of concrete (Fig. 6–41). The same principle applies to continuing the ground lines from driveways, sidewalks, patios, and beds to improve flow and unity (Fig. 6–42).

Establish a bedline that continues from corners, doors, or windows of the house. This could also include the corners of other structures such as decks or patios. By continuing the lines from these structures the design integrates the residence, with the landscape creating a more effective and smoother connection with indoor and outdoor living.

***Figure 6–40*  Ground Lines**
By continuing a bed line across pavement, a sense of connection can be created.

(a)                                                    (b)

**Figure 6–41   Continuing Bed Line**

(a) The nearest planting appears disconnected with the bed on the other side of the driveway, unless (b) the bed is changed to continue where the far bed left off to appear cohesive.

**Figure 6–42   Connect Ground Lines and Corners**

Continuing beds from corners of the house or other structures helps connect indoor and outdoor living. Unity is further improved by connecting ground lines from the driveway, sidewalks, patio, and beds.

# Interest

The design has to have visual interest. For many residents, curb appeal (visual interest) is the most important aspect. The design needs to have qualities that make people admire the residence and even spark a desire to experience walking through the landscape. To be successful it has to stir an element of curiosity.

## Accent

Interest can be stirred by elements of **accent.** This can be achieved with a focalized accent or interesting effects such as contrasting textures.

### Focalized Accents

**Focalized accents** are objects or plants that would directly attract an observer's attention. An example would be a sculpture, water feature, or specimen plant (Fig. 6–43).

(a)

(b)

(c)

**Figure 6–43  Focalized Accents**
(a) An object or space that draws attention, such as a water feature, sculpture, or unique plant, is a focalized accent. (b) The infamous "gazing ball," not looked upon kindly by many designers, is an attempt at creating a focalized accent. (c) The waterfall, in addition to the sound, is a great focal point of motion for the entertainment area. *(Photo (a) courtesy of Chris Briand, http://www.salisbury.edu/arboretum; Photo (c) courtesy of Big Sky Landscaping, Inc., Clackamas, OR. www.bigskylandscaping.com)*

**Specimen plants** refer to plants with some unique characteristics which can be planted alone as a focal accent (Fig. 6–44). Some of these characteristics may be continual, such as a unique form, or short-lived, such as when the plant flowers.

Characteristics of Specimen Plants

**Form:** Unusual forms such as weeping or contorted

**Texture:** Striking foliage, whether extremely fine or extremely coarse

**Bark:** Exfoliating bark that reveals interesting colors and texture

**Flowering:** Unique shapes or vivid color

**Foliage:** Interesting color or unique variegation

The attention and appeal of specimen plants is balanced, and enhanced, by surrounding foundation plants. Due to simple qualities, foundation plants, help accentuate the unique qualities of specimen plants. The outstanding quality of the specimen stands out amid the foundation plants as opposed to an entire collection of specimen plants that can make the unique qualities less special.

(a)

(b)

***Figure 6–44*  Specimen Characteristics Form**
(a) This contorted tree creates an interesting form. (b) The broad, coarse texture of the foliage can be used as a bold specimen plant. *(Photo (b) courtesy of Josh G. Silliman.)*

*(continues)*

(c)

(d)

(e)

*Figure 6–44* **Specimen Characteristics Form—continued**
(c) Bark: This mottled brown and gray trunk is very appealing in the winter. (d) Flower: The unique shape and/or color of the flowers can attract attention. (e) Foliage: This lacy burgundy foliage of the weeping tree has a specimen quality.

***Tip Box***

## Avoid "Overaccenting"

Be careful and don't become overzealous with accents (Fig. 6–45). Too many accents and the design becomes chaotic. It loses a sense of unity. Every aspect of the design should not demand the same attention.

(a)

(b)

***Figure 6–45*** **Overaccenting**
(a) Too many specimens become too busy and void out the uniqueness of each plant. (b) The use of foundation plants helps to enhance the outstanding quality of a specimen plant.
*(Photos courtesy of Visual Impact software. www.visualimpactimaging.com)*

## Contrast

**Contrast** is the juxtaposition of two opposing qualities (Fig. 6–46). Contrast sparks a drastic change in the flow of surroundings and attracts attention. It can be created by one of the following:

**Texture:** Planting a fine-textured plant next to one of coarse texture. Texture can be measured as the size of the foliage or stems.

**Form:** A vertical form, such as yucca or ornamental grass, can be used to contrast with rounded or horizontal forms.

**Color:** Using plants with bright variegation near plants with green foliage.

# Curiosity

**Curiosity** can be used to pique the interest of an observer. When people are interested, they are stirred to investigate. Hiding, or screening, portions of the landscape or accenting narrow walks and corners can heighten curiosity.

## Screening and Sound

Breaking up a large space with screens keeps one from experiencing the entire area and can lead one to investigate each space of the residence (Fig. 6–47). Take for instance a backyard. Using fences or shrubs keeps one experiencing a smaller outdoor room. By utilizing various forms or accents, one can be led from one outdoor room to the next by curiosity. A good example is the use of water (Fig. 6–48). The low trickling sound of a small fountain can draw one down a path to investigate what is around the corner.

(a)

(b)                                                    (c)

***Figure 6–46*** **Contrasting Texture**
(a) Contrasting the fine texture of the vine with the coarse texture of groundcover draws attention. (b) Contrasting the vertical, sharp form of the grass with the rounded broadleaves is appealing. (c) Contrasting the bright colored foliage with the surrounding green shrubs is attention-getting. *(Photos courtesy of Visual Impact software. www.visualimpactimaging.com)*

***Figure 6–47*** **Curiosity of Space**
Breaking up a large space with screens creates outdoor rooms that heighten curiosity about what is in the next space.

(a)

(b)

(c)

**Figure 6–48 Curiosity of Sound**
(a) The sound of trickling water can draw one's interest into other areas. (b) This fountain creates an echoing sound of water splashing at the end of a path. (c) This large water feature is a great addition to the entertainment area. *(Photo (c) only courtesy of Blue Ribbon LLC, Maryland. www.blueribbonllc.com)*

**Tip Box**

Fish are a great addition to ponds to add interest: living movement and brilliant color (Fig. 6–49).

**Figure 6–49 Goldfish and Koi**
Fish are a great addition to add interest: living movement and brilliant color.

## Narrow Walks and Corners

Traffic naturally flows through space that is long and narrow (Fig. 6–50). Corridors and sidewalks naturally pull people in that direction. To heighten this intuitiveness, curiosity can be stirred by placing a focalized accent at the end of the path, such as a water feature or sculpture. Something that grabs attention stirs one to wonder what else may be at the end of the path and around the corner.

The same can be applied at the corners to attract attention. Placing a focalized accent, such as a striking specimen, at a corner can stir curiosity about what's around it (Fig. 6–51).

# Flow

**Flow** is the quality that carries the eye smoothly through the landscape. It is also referred to as **transition** or sequence. The flowing character may be formal or informal, but with both, one moves visually through the landscape with comfortable fluidity.

***Figure 6–50   Curiosity of Narrow Paths***
Placement of an accent, such as this water feature, at the end of a narrow space can entice observers down the path to see what's at the end.

**Figure 6-51  Curiosity of Corners**
Placement of an accent on a corner can draw one's attention around to the next outdoor room.

## Line

A **line** can be seen where two materials meet or along the outline of a form. It can most
easily be seen and created with the outline of planting beds. Bed lines stand out in the
landscape because of the contrast created by green grass next to brown mulch. Good
edging surrounding a bed should not be noticed, only the line created by the junction
of materials.

> ### Tip Box
>
> Although this is more related to maintenance, a sharp bed line is the most
> appealing. Steel edging has great value to beds not because it looks good,
> but because it creates a sharp, bending arc that holds this line with minimal
> maintenance.

Lines can be used to develop the character of the landscape in three ways:

**Curving:** Lines of the bed can create a nice flow through the landscape with broad sweeping arcs that gracefully move throughout the landscape (Fig. 6–52). Bed lines should flow in broad arcs and move easily from one arc to the next (Fig. 6–53). Curving lines are typically used to create an informal, loose character, often in conjunction with asymmetrical balance.

**Straight:** Lines of the bed are straight and typically meet in 90-degree corners (Fig. 6–54). They are typically used to create a formal character, oftentimes in conjunction with symmetrical balance.

**Arc and tangent:** A unique approach that combines straight and curving lines, creating a structured layout with the flow of curves (Fig. 6–55).

---

### Tip Box

The overzealous use of line movement, in an attempt to create interest, can lead to a busy, chaotic feeling and disrupt the quality of flow (figs. 6–52 and 6–54). The eye of the observer no longer moves smoothly through the landscape.

---

(a)

**Figure 6–52  Curving Lines**
(a) Wide sweeping bed lines create a natural moving flow.

*(continues)*

(b)

**Figure 6–52 Curving Lines—continued**
(b) Overzealous curves get chaotic and breakup the flow.

(a)

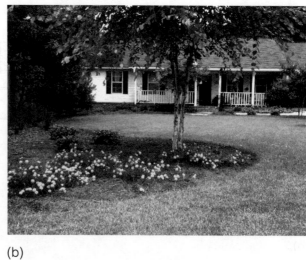

(b)

**Figure 6–53 Curving Beds**
(a) Example of a curving ground plane. (b) A wide sweeping bed line has a nice motion. *(Photo (a) courtesy of Visual Impact software. www.visualimpactimaging.com)*

(a)

(b)

(c)

**_Figure 6–54_ Straight Lines** (a) Straight lines and square corners create a formal, structured flow. (b) Too many corners disturb the structure of the ground plane. (c) Example of straight-line beds. *(Photo (c) courtesy of Visual Impact software. www.visualimpactimaging.com)*

(a)                                         (b)

***Figure 6–55   Arc and Tangent Lines***
A unique combination of straight lines and curving arcs. *(Photo courtesy of Visual Impact software.*
*www.visualimpactimaging.com)*

## *Tip Box*

**Berms** are a good way to create a sense of flowing form. A berm is a change
in the topography by mounding soil, often to create a planting bed. The
changes in elevation add another dimension to the flowing interest of the
ground lines (Fig. 6–56).

***Figure 6–56   Berms***
A change in the topography creates a flowing element in elevation.

**Figure 6–57 Flowing Form**
Flow can be present in the form, such as the sweeping arcs on a fence.

(a)

(b)

**Figure 6–58 Transition**
Transition smoothly (a) between plants and (b) up from the ground plane for gradual flow.

# Form

Lines that can lead the eye can also be created with the edges of walls, hedges, fences, and other construction (Fig. 6–57). Form is often used to develop a smooth transition from the ground plane to the house and surroundings (Fig. 6–58).

# Mass Planting

Trees, shrubs, and groundcover are often planted in groups referred to as **mass planting.** For one reason, large collections of a common material add a sense of balance. When allowed to grow together, several small shrubs can form one unique mass that can balance another large plant. Second, the small size of many shrubs and groundcover would have minimal impact if planted alone. Plants tend to lose connection throughout the design and the design begins to appear segmented with all the various plants growing as individuals. Third, with improved connection, mass planting can improve the flow of the design. As plants merge together, the eye travels through the landscape easier.

## Spacing

Generally speaking, plants should be spaced so they begin to merge into each other at about 70 percent of their mature spread (Fig. 6–59). This creates a good mass without the negative effects of overcrowding (Fig. 6–60). If plants are spaced extremely close to mass together, they will begin to compete for water and nutrients and weaken the general health of each other. If they are overcrowded, they are less able to overcome drought and pests.

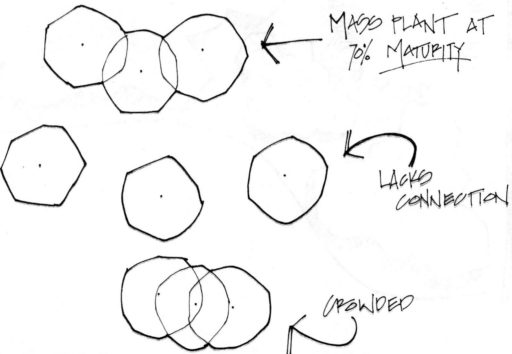

**Figure 6–59  Mass Spacing**
Mass plant with proper spacing to create a group of merging trees or shrubs. Too close and the plants will compete with each other.

(a)

(b)

**Figure 6–60   Mass Spacing**

(a) The plants are evenly spaced and lack mass appeal. (b) Massing plants together creates better connection within the bed.

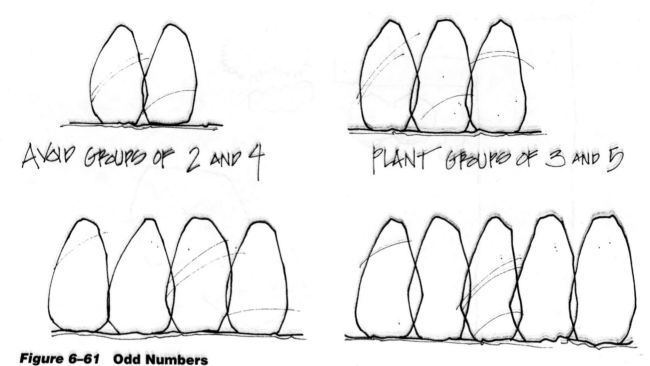

**Figure 6–61   Odd Numbers**
Mass plant with groups of odd numbers for better balance, in particular groups of three and five.

## Odd Numbers

To improve the balance of massing and create a solid planting, groups of shrubs and trees should be planted in odd numbers (Fig. 6–61). In particular, groups of three and five. As the masses get larger the number of plants isn't easily discerned (Fig. 6–62). When two trees or shrubs are planted as a mass, the even number tends to be visually divided by the eye. A third plant establishes a solid grouping (Fig. 6–63).

## Staggered Placement

When grouping plants together, consider staggering the placements rather than a straight line (Fig. 6–64). Staggering can be more appealing because the placement has a flow rather than a rigid row of plants, although there will be times to mass in a straight line, such as formal hedges. Staggering can also improve the massing appeal, making it more solid, because the plants will be growing closer together more so than in a straight line.

(a)

(b)

**Figure 6-62 Odd Numbers**

(a) Groups of two tend to visually divide in half. (b) Groups of three appear grounded and better balanced.

**Figure 6-63 Mass Planting**

(a) Lacks proper spacing and numbers. (b) Good spacing that merges plants together in numbers that appear better balanced.

(a)

STAGGERED PLACEMENT

**Figure 6–64 Staggered Placement**
(a) Lay out plants in a staggered placement for interest and balance. (b) An even number of plants can be improved with a staggered placement.

(b)

# Summary

As the concept plan creates the useful or functional component of the landscape design, design principles create the aesthetic or visual appeal. Form, texture, and color are attributes to plants and objects that are used to create an appealing landscape. Balance is important to create a sense of equality or order. Symmetrical balance is the formulaic approach of mirroring each side to achieve balance and is often associated with a formal characteristic. Asymmetrical is an informal balance that utilizes plants or objects of various sizes and types and is not a mirrored image of each side. Unity or connection helps to pull all the elements of the design into a big picture. Repeating plants or elements creates visual recall for a sense of connection. It can also be achieved by linking space with common materials, such as mulch or a fence, and continuing ground lines, such as the continuation of a planting bed on the other side of a driveway. Interest helps to create visual appeal. Focalized accents or interesting effects have striking qualities that grab attention. These are often enhanced with the balance of foundation plants, those that have few outstanding qualities, rather than a chaotic mass of specimens plants. Effective placement of accents, such as in corners or at the end of narrow paths, stirs curiosity and enhances the visual appeal. Flow is the smooth transition throughout the landscape, influenced by the line of the ground plane or outline of the form. Mass is the technique of plants placed close enough to merge together to create a large grouping of several smaller plants. It helps to unify and balance the design. Planting masses in odd numbers provides additional balance to the mass.

# Key Words

**Accent:** striking effect of quality that gets attention

**Arc and tangent:** unique approach that combines straight and curving lines, creating a structured layout with the flow of curves

**Asymmetrical balance:** unstructured balance relying more on a "gut feeling" rather than the calculated placement of material on both sides of an axis as in a symmetrical balance

**Attributes:** inherent characteristics or qualities

**Balance:** sense of equality

**Berm:** change in the topography by mounding soil; often used to create a planting bed

**Color:** elements in the design to attract attention or impact mood; flowers, foliage, branches, trunk, fruit

**Connection:** sense that all components of design are part of the big picture

**Contrast:** juxtaposition of two opposing qualities

**Cool colors:** have a calming effect; blue, green, purple

**Curiosity:** a quality or effect that piques the interest of an observer

**Curved lines:** sweeping bed lines in landscape; loose, informal quality

**Dioecious:** plant is either male or female; requires a male plant, or pollinator, to be planted in the area for a female plant to set fruit

**Espalier:** manipulates form by training a tree or shrub to grow flat against a wall or fence

**Flow:** quality that carries the eye smoothly through the landscape; transition or sequence

**Focalized accents:** objects or plants that would directly attract an observer's attention

**Form:** the outline of an object or plant, often thought of as the silhouette

**Foundation plants:** low-profile plants that are not particularly striking

**Line:** can be seen where two materials meet or along the outline of a form

**Massing:** shrubs and groundcover are often planted in groups; also referred to as mass planting

**Monoecious:** plant has both male and female flowers; will fruit by self-pollination or from nearby plants

**Pollinator:** male plant of a dioecious species

**Sequence:** see flow

**Shear:** tightly prune shrubs into geometric shapes

**Specimen plants:** have some unique plant characteristics that are visually appealing; form, texture, bark, flowering, or foliage

**Straight lines:** straight bed lines at 90° corners; more formal

**Symmetrical balance:** each side is a mirror image of the other

**Texture:** may refer to the foliage or branching and be classified as fine, medium, or coarse

**Topiary:** plant form pruned into shapes of spirals or animals

**Transition:** see flow

**Unity:** see connection

**Variegation:** the mottling or striping of foliage

**Warm colors:** create excitement; red, orange, yellow

# 7 Preliminary Design

### Objectives

- Understand the role of preliminary design
- Learn how to construct a preliminary design
- Know how to draw a preliminary design

The preliminary design will take shape using the design principles outlined in the previous chapter. The design process, as mentioned earlier in this book, continues to proceed from general to specific with each phase. This is when the plan begins to resemble the landscape design. In this case, the preliminary design takes the bubble diagram of the concept plan and develops a plan with a defined ground plane and plant symbols. It is very important to follow the concept plan because it addresses the analysis and is fundamental to the functional aspect of the design.

*Analysis → Concept Plan → Preliminary Design*

# Client Presentation

Some designers present the preliminary design to the client, whereas others will present the master plan. For the client, the preliminary will be the first look at the proposed design. Presenting the preliminary design has the advantage of getting feedback from the client and allows the designer to make any changes before establishing the specifics in the master plan.

## Feedback

Feedback allows the clients to give their input on the design (Fig. 7–1). Having the opportunity to have an impact on the design makes the clients feel more involved in the project, which will increase their satisfaction with the final product. In many cases, the designer will create more than one preliminary design based on one or more concept plans from which the clients will choose or give feedback.

Having the feedback from the client during the preliminary design reduces the amount of time the designer would spend making changes after drawing the master plan.

## Design Theft

Some designers may be concerned with design theft. This may happen when a client gets a master plan and decides not to accept. Afterward, a very similar design is installed. To reduce the chance of theft, some designers may leave an unlabeled copy of the preliminary design with the clients to look over on their own and to make changes. Don't hand over a completed master plan until the contract is completed in full.

***Figure 7-1*** **Preliminary Feedback**
Some designers present the preliminary design to get feedback before proceeding with the master plan.

## Graphics

Since the preliminary is presented to the client, it should be illustrated with presentation graphics (covered later in this chapter). This allows the client to read the plan easier when symbols are representative of the plant characteristics and the ground plane texture represents the material.

# The Preliminary Design Process

The following are steps to developing the preliminary design. Not all designers employ all of the following steps, but they usually use some form of them during the design process.

## Utilizing the Concept Plan

The preliminary design builds on the concept plan (Fig. 7-2). Some designers like to place the concept plan directly underneath a piece of tracing paper so that they can draw the preliminary over the top of it. The concept plan can also be next to the preliminary for reference. Either way, the idea is the same—the preliminary design is refining the bubbles of the concept plan into definitive lines and symbols.

## Sketching the Preliminary Design

Start by drawing more than one preliminary design freehand with a soft lead on tracing paper (Fig. 7-3). Be very loose and quick and do not worry about the detail. This allows the designer to approach the organization of the ground plane and the balance of the design efficiently, as well as try a couple of ideas for comparison before committing to a definitive preliminary design.

***Figure 7–2* Building a Preliminary Design from the Concept Plan**
The preliminary design should work from the concept plan. Some designers will place the concept plan under the preliminary to address the conceptual layout, while others will refer to it lying off to the side.

***Figure 7–3* Sketching the Preliminary**
Start by loosely sketching preliminary ideas with soft lead on tracing paper.

## Starting with the Ground Plane

This doesn't have to be the next step, but many beginning students find that organizing the ground plane first makes it easier to start (Fig. 7–4). Once bed lines, lawn, and hardscapes are established, then symbols can be placed.

Sketching preliminary designs allows you to experiment with various bed lines such as curving or straight. Be consistent with the theme of the bed lines in the various areas of the residence. However, the bed line character doesn't necessarily have to be used over the entire property. The front yard may be straight, having more of a formal feeling, while the backyard can be free flowing and have a more relaxed and informal feeling.

***Figure 7–4*** **Sketching the Ground Plane**
Start by roughly sketching the ground plane: bed
lines, walks, driveway, and so forth, according to
the concept plan.

***Figure 7–5*** **Points of Extension**
Corners of the house, deck, or patio are major points of extension; windows and doors
are minor points.

**Connecting the Ground Plane**    Work on integrating the ground plane by continuing lines from the house and the surroundings (as discussed in the "Connection" section of the previous chapter). Corners of the house, porch, deck, and patio are major points to extend into the landscape. Minor points of extension are things such as windows, doors, or change of materials (Fig.7–5). When sketching the ground plane, experiment with lines that begin or end at these points (Fig. 7–6).

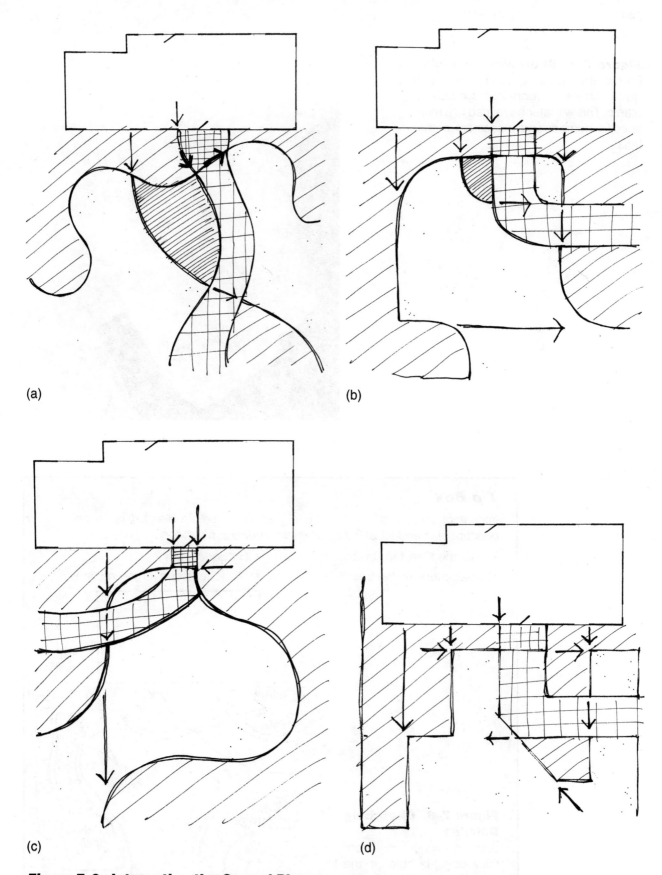

**Figure 7–6  Integrating the Ground Plane**
Various examples of integrating the ground plane with points of extension on the house: (a) curved theme, (b) arc and tangent theme, (c) curved theme, and (d) straight-line theme.

***Figure 7–7*  Sketching Symbols**
Follow the rough ground plane with quick circles to represent symbols of plants. This will later be refined to a more specific number and placement of material.

## Tip Box

Instead of using symbols, some designers may use bubbles similar to the concept plan and label the bubbles with general plant descriptions (Fig. 7–8).

- Low, medium, tall shrubs
- Small, medium, tall trees
- Groundcover
- Deciduous or evergreen plants

***Figure 7–8*  Sketching Bubbles**
Some designers will continue using bubbles in the preliminary instead of symbols to define areas of plant types and sizes.

## Placing the Plant Symbols

Once the ground plane is sketched, do quick symbol placements to get an idea of balance and flow (Fig. 7–7). These can just be quick and loose circles, both large and small. Do not be concerned with specific plants since plant names will not be addressed until the master plan. And do not spend too much time on the details of size, proportion, and exact placement since this is an exercise. These details will be developed in the next step.

# Drafting the Preliminary Design

Now that you have some idea of direction for the preliminary design, it is time to draft an illustrative preliminary for the presentation. This draft should be accurate with size and placement of plant symbols, and the proportion and location of ground plane areas. It will be a much different approach than sketching, utilizing quality drawing techniques for a clear, legible plan drawing.

### Drafting Versus Computer-Aided Drawing (CAD)

**Computer-aided drafting systems** (or computer-aided drawing) are referred to as CAD. AutoCAD, originally released in 1982, is a software program that allows the user to draw lines, arcs, and circles. The advantage for designers using computer design is the ease of application and change. Symbols can be dropped onto the design with a click of a button, filling an area in a matter of minutes, and can be moved around just as easy. Labeling, coloring, and line drawing are just as quick and easy. Many pro-CAD users feel like computer design appears much more professional, while designers that draft by hand appeal to the artistry of line drawing. The disadvantage is the investment. Computer design can cost thousands of dollars in hardware and software, while drafting equipment can cost less than a hundred dollars. For this reason, many small freelance designers and especially beginning design students start by drafting. This chapter will look at drafting techniques (hand drawn) and computer drawing to compare the end results. However, for more in depth information of computer drafting, refer to Appendix D for application techniques.

### Drafting

The preliminary design should be drafted on vellum paper for quality lines and reproduction. Using lead pencils of various degrees of hardness is the easiest and most forgiving approach for beginning students. Ink creates excellent line quality but is much less forgiving. If ink is to be used, consider drafting on Mylar, which is a drafting film from which ink can be erased (Fig. 7–9).

*Figure 7–9* **Drafting Tools**
Tools used to draw a plan.

## Figure 7–10  Border and Title Block

Border helps define the working area while the title block provides vital project information. (a) Drafted.  (b) Pre-drawn.

(a)

A Landscape  Design For:

p.o. box 817 bluffton, south carolina  29910
phone no.   1 (803) 681-2334

The
Evergreen
Co.  Inc.

(b)

A **border** around the perimeter of the paper may be used to define the drawing area, although some designers prefer not to use one. There should be a **title block** included that contains the following information: client name and address, scale, north arrow, designer name, and date (Fig. 7–10).

# The Ground Plane

Choose one, or a combination of a few, sketches to further develop into the preliminary design. The areas and symbols will be refined so that they are precisely drawn with sharp lines.

## Ground Angles

Students tend to draw lines that meet at very acute angles, especially with curving lines. The idea is to allow for a smooth transition and to provide an easier approach to mowing the turf. However, acute angles can be difficult to maintain and often fail over time. It is often where concrete cracks or mulch and groundcover don't remain. As a general rule, the lines of the ground plane should meet close to square, or a 90-degree angle (Fig. 7–11).

(a)

(b)

***Figure 7–11  Square Corners***
(a) Corners on the ground plane should not meet at an acute angle because it can be difficult to maintain and hardscapes can crack. (b) Instead, have the ground meet at angles closer to 90 degrees.

*(continues)*

***Figure 7–11* Square Corners—continued**
(c) Where the turf meets the patio is a strong connection. *(Photo (c) courtesy of Big Sky Landscaping, Inc., Clackamas, OR. www.bigskylandscaping.com)*

(c)

## Ground Labels and Textures

Use general labels in areas such as lawn, driveway, deck, patio, etc. (Fig. 7–12). This will help clarify the layout for the client. Textures help develop and aid the visual component (Fig. 7–13).

**Turf**   Areas of turf are typically designated by stipples. **Stippling** creates tonal value by placing dots close together. As dots are placed closer together, the value becomes darker.

**Concrete and Exposed Aggregate**   To symbolize concrete and exposed aggregate, use stipples of a coarser texture, using a combination of dots, circles, and triangles.

**Groundcover**   Groundcovers generally cover a large area. There are several textures that represent a loose foliage and can be drawn quickly.

**Mulch**   Mulches are used throughout beds to reduce weeds and moisture loss. Textures used for mulch are fairly nondescript, representing the coarse dark qualities.

**Stone and Bricks**   Don't be concerned with patterns during the preliminary design. Specific patterns and construction will be established later in the master plan.

***Figure 7–12  Label the Ground Plane***
Place labels on the ground plane to avoid confusion.

There are many types and sizes of bricks and stones. **Stone** is often used in the form of flagstone, which is a sheet-like stone that comes in various colors and sizes. **Bricks** are smaller units when compared with stone. These also come in similar forms of **pavers.**

**Wood**   Decking is the most common feature utilizing wood.

**Water**   Water features are used as focal points because of their fluid movement, soothing sound, and naturalizing effects. They can easily be drawn with a rippling texture that reflects water movement.

**Figure 7-13 Ground Plane Textures**
Turf, concrete, groundcover, mulch, hardscape, water, and boulders.

**Boulders**   **Boulders** and stones are often used with water features and as a naturalizing effect. These are drawn with a variety of hatching and cross-hatching textures.

# Plant Material

Once the ground plane has been established, begin placing the plant material. Again, in the preliminary plan the designer does not work with specific plants, rather general plant characteristics: size, placement, and type. Plants should be thought of in terms of trees, shrubs, groundcover, flowers, and specimen or foundation plants.

Beginning students often get hung up in the design process because they look at the empty base map and begin to place specific plants. What may result from this approach is losing sight of the overall design concept by being too focused on plants, or a creative block when becoming overwhelmed with all the options. It is all right to have plants in mind and rather difficult to not think of any plants, especially if the client has favorite plants to use. But the idea is not to get caught up in naming plants as they are placed. If there is an area to be screened, then place a large shrub and move on. The master plan may completely rearrange this area, so do not waste time on it at this point. Some designers may jot down a few plant names as they go, but, again, they are not trying to identify the symbols.

## Symbols

The information that the symbols should convey include

- Size
- Placement of material
- Character (broadleaf, needle)

**Size**   The symbols should be drawn relative to scale to represent the diameter of a suitable plant. Use a circle template to place symbol outlines in the appropriate placement and at the correct diameter. Since specific plants are not being considered, the following is a general guideline for symbol diameters that can later be changed when specific plants are used (Fig. 7–14).

### Trees

Large trees: 25'

Medium trees: 20'

Small trees: 15'

### Shrubs

In the preliminary, shrubs may be represented by a mass outline and not necessarily show the individual shrubs.

Large shrubs: 10'

Medium shrubs: 5'

Small shrubs: 3'

**Placement**   The symbol helps locate the plant material. A center dot in the middle of the symbol represents the placement of the plant (Fig. 7–15). In the preliminary design, center dots may not be used since it is a generic design. However, the master plan will utilize center dots for all plant placements.

TREES

25'
LARGE

20'
MEDIUM

15'
SMALL

SHRUBS

6'
LARGE

5'
MEDIUM

3'
SMALL

GROUNDCOVER

ANNUALS/PERENNIAL

**Figure 7-14  Symbol Diameter**
The diameter of symbols should be generally related to large, medium, and small trees and shrubs. Other massing areas include groundcover and flowers, which can be represented by an outline.

***Figure 7–15*  Symbol Placement**
Center dots locate the proposed plant.

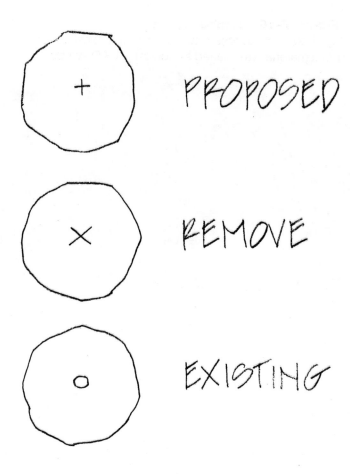

**Character**   Symbols are developed to help the client understand the plan as well as appear more presentable. Figure 7–16 presents examples of drawing symbols to more accurately depict general characteristics of plants.

**Generic: Generic symbols** are used to represent any type of plant. They are typically foundation plants.

**Broadleaf:** Any plant that has a flat, wide leaf is a **broadleaf.** These are typically deciduous plants, such as maples and oaks, but some evergreen plants also have a broadleaf as well, for example, hollies and magnolias.

**Needle:** The **needle symbol** refers to any plant that has needle-like foliage, which are typically evergreens such as pines and spruce. There are some deciduous plants that have needle-like foliage, such as redwoods and cypress. It can also include barrier plants that have a prominent spiny nature.

**Branched:** The **branched symbol** is typically used to represent deciduous plants since they lose their leaves, but can also be used for any plant with strong or unique branching habits. Branching symbols are often used for specimen plants that attract attention. These branching symbols tend to attract the most attention.

# Grant Preliminary Design

Examples of completed preliminary design, both drafted and CAD, are illustrated in Figure 7–17.

## Figure 7-16 Symbol Types

Symbols can represent types, or characteristics, of plant material. (a) Drafted symbols; (b) CAD symbols.

 GENERIC

  BROADLEAF

  NEEDLE

 BRANCHED

(a)

(b)

### *Figure 7–17* **Preliminary Sketches and Designs**

Two preliminary plans, including a preliminary sketch for each one, based on concept plans presented in the previous chapter. Each preliminary set (A and B) includes sketch, drafted and a CAD drawing.

*(continues)*

Figure labels within the drawing:

TURF

SHED

MULCH

DECK    FUTURE SUNROOM

DRIVEWAY

TURF

CURB

NORTH

PRELIMINARY PLAN A

GRANT RESIDENCE
724 WEST MARKET ST
ANYTOWN, USA

PELICAN DESIGNS

**Figure 7–17** **Preliminary Sketches and Designs—continued**

SCALE: 1/8"=1'-0"

TURF

MULCH

SHED

DECK

FUTURE SUNROOM

RESIDENCE

Driveway

TURF

PRELIMINARY PLAN A

GRANT RESIDENCE
721 WEST MARKET ST.
ANYTOWN, USA

PELICAN DESIGNS

REVISIONS BY

*Figure 7–17*  **Preliminary Sketches and Designs—continued**

*Figure 7-17* **Preliminary Sketches and Designs—continued**

PRELIMINARY PLAN B

GRANT RESIDENCE
724 WEST MARKET ST
ANYTOWN, USA

PELICAN DESIGNS

*Figure 7–17* **Preliminary Sketches and Designs—continued**

SCALE: 1/8"=1'-0"

TURF

SHED
MULCH

DECK | FUTURE SUNROOM

RESIDENCE

Driveway

TURF

PRELIMINARY PLAN B

GRANT RESIDENCE
721 WEST MARKET ST.
ANYTOWN, USA

PELICAN DESIGNS

REVISIONS BY

**Figure 7-17 Preliminary Sketches and Designs—continued**

# Summary

The preliminary design refines the concept plan into distinct ground lines and symbols. It can be developed to present to the clients as a working design to get feedback before drawing the final master plan. Some designers will draw more than one preliminary design to allow the clients a choice. The preliminary plan will have ground lines and areas clearly labeled. Plant symbols will not be labeled with names; instead they will represent general plants to indicate plant size, placement, and characteristics.

# Key Words

**Border:** perimeter of the paper that may be used to define the drawing area

**Boulders:** used with water features and as a naturalizing effect

**Branching symbol:** represents deciduous plants since they lose their leaves, but can also be used for any plant with strong or unique, branching habits

**Brick:** rectangular blocks typically 8″ × 4″ and a couple of inches thick, made of clay or concrete; used to pave

**Broadleaf symbol:** represents any plant that has a flat, wide leaf

**Computer-aided drafting systems:** software programs that allow the user to draw lines, arcs, and circles to create a landscape design

**Generic symbols:** used to represent any type of plant, typically foundation plants

**Mulch:** used throughout beds to reduce weeds and moisture loss

**Needle symbol:** represents any plant that has needle-like foliage, which are typically evergreens such as pines and spruce

**Paver:** see brick

**Stippling:** creates tonal value by placing dots close together; as dots are placed closer together, the value becomes darker

**Stone:** often used in the form of flagstone, which is a sheet-like stone that comes in various colors and sizes

**Title block:** contains client name and address, scale, north arrow, designer name, and date

# 8 Plants and Hardscapes

## Objectives

- Learn the criteria affecting plant selection
- Understand general plant characteristics
- Become familiar with helpful resources in plant selection
- Be familiar with hardscape material uses and construction

The preliminary design has given shape to a balanced, functional plan. Now plants and hardscapes need to be considered because up to this point in the design process, specific materials have not been considered.

## Plant Material and Selection

Many clients are interested in a landscape design to beautify their home with plants. Up to this point, the preliminary design has integrated the analysis of the residence with the client's wishes to come up with a functional plan that is interesting, balanced, and useful. There is great variety of plant material available for the designer to use, many interesting forms, colors, sizes, scents, and so on. There are several factors that limit this selection if the design is going to be not only visually pleasing but also hardy and durable as well. The entire design process has led to an organized, visually appealing design, but if the plant selection is poor, the design will ultimately be a failure. Plants growing in the wrong location will not develop, and often eventually die. For instance, the placement of a shade plant in full sun will result in poor growth and eventually death, bringing in to question the designer's reputation (Fig. 8–1).

> ### Tip Box
>
> The importance of proper plant selection cannot be overemphasized. Plants not adapted to growing conditions will fail, as will the design.

**Figure 8–1  Plant Selection**
This shade plant, Acuba, is sunburned (black margins) because of too much sun.

# Plant Selection Books and Software

This section will cover much of the criteria that influence the decisions of plant selection. It does not cover specific plants. Refer to the Appendix B for books and software for selection resources. There are many good books that list plants and categorize them in their best uses, such as flower color, sun exposure, fall color, and more. Color photos are helpful to make selections as well as discuss unfamiliar plants with clients.

In addition to books, there are several software programs that have selection capabilities based on given criteria (Fig. 8–2). This makes plant selection much easier for beginning students with limited plant experience. A user can select the hardiness zone of their area along with other conditions such as moisture, exposure, flower color and timing, form, size, fruit, thorns, and so on. The criteria can be set to filter out plants that

(a)

(b)

***Figure 8–2*** **Plant Software and Websites**
Plant selection can be aided by the use of books or, as shown, database software. (a) This is an example of *Horticopia* software. (b) Example of Web site *(http://www.Salisbury. edu/arboretum).* Some books will categorize uses of plants while software can suggest plants that fit selected criteria such as size, moisture, shade, hardiness, etc.

don't fit. For instance, set criteria to look for a shrub that is 3 feet tall and adapts to wet, shady conditions. The software database can then show a list of plants that meet these conditions in your selected hardiness zone.

Also make note of free Web sites that offer great databases of plant images and selection options that operate in a similar fashion to the software programs.

---

### Tip Box

A good way to keep up to date with the latest and most popular books and software is through the American Nurseryman Publishing Company (http://www.amerinursery.com).

---

# Availability

Obviously plant selection will vary depending on location. There are a few guidelines that will simplify selection and improve the likelihood of success.

## Regional Plants

Start by limiting the plants to those that can be easily purchased in the area. Beginning students often overburden themselves by looking at an extensive plant materials book or lists from class of over 300 plants. Although there may be hundreds of excellent plants that can grow in the area, many of them will be difficult to find locally. There is nothing wrong with using unique plants, it is just difficult to attain them and can cause a problem for installation due to the time and cost of special ordering.

## Local, Reputable Nurseries

Become familiar with regional plants and their availability and cost by compiling lists and catalogs from local reputable plant nurseries (Fig. 8–3). These plants will best adapt to the regional climate. The nursery should sell quality plant material that will be important to the development of the landscape design. Poor quality may be diseased, damaged, or stressed, which will reduce the chances of its establishment and survival.

## Developing a Plant Palette

Consider creating a **plant palette** of the most adapted plants in your area. This can help limit the number of plants and simplify the selection process. It can also serve as a reference page whenever you are selecting plants for future projects. This list can be divided into various categories based on characteristics or cultural requirements as listed in this textbook. The list will continue to grow with experience.

# Hardiness

The design will not be successful unless the plants thrive. Plants not adapted to the climate grow slowly, are susceptible to insects and disease, and simply look bad. Eventually they will not survive the cold winter or hot summer.

**Hardiness zones** are areas of average annual minimum temperature assigned throughout the United States that were established by the USDA (Fig. 8–4). The hardiness zone map was first published in 1960 and then updated in 1990. Plants are as-

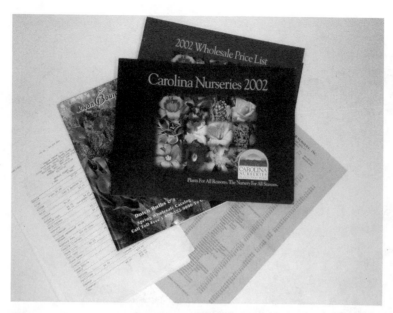

***Figure 8-3*** **Local Reputable Plant Nurseries**
Collect and become familiar with local reputable plant nurseries and their inventory. It's a good indication of plants adapted to the region and makes availability easy.

signed a range of zones in which they will grow based on their cold hardiness, which is often the factor limiting where plants can grow year after year. Palms, for instance, can grow in the summer but cannot over winter in northern climates. The United States is assigned zones 2 through 10. Each zone contains a range of 10 degrees, for instance areas within zone 2 have an average annual minimum temperature between −50 and −40, zone 3 is between −40 and −30, and so on. Plants are assigned a range of zones in which they are adapted to grow based on these minimums.

Be aware that heat hardiness has not been considered to the degree as cold hardiness, and that many factors affect plant adaptation such as moisture, soil conditions, and microclimates. Heat damage is much less apparent than cold damage because plants can survive for several years in a stunted, chlorotic condition before they fail. The American Horticultural Society (http://www.ahs.org) has produced a heat adaptability map that serves as a reference much like the cold hardiness map (Fig. 8–5). **Heat zones** are based on the average number of days over 86 degrees Fahrenheit, considered the threshold beyond which plants begin to suffer physiologically. For example, zone 1 is less than one day and zone 12 is over 210 days. It also assumes there are no other stresses, such as water deficiency, which can make plants more susceptible to heat damage.

Beginning students often find it difficult to select plants because they are new to the horticulture field. Researching what zones plants are assigned is important, but be aware that the extremes of adaptation can result in marginally healthy plants that do not look like the picture in the book. Beyond plant research, consult local nurseries or seasoned designers about the best plants to use in the area.

Also, be aware of the supplier. Just because a vendor is selling the plant doesn't mean it is adapted to the area. Some are guilty of selling plants marginally adapted at best (you might be surprised how little plant knowledge the manager possesses). It is advisable to buy from local reputable nurseries, especially those that buy from regional wholesale growers.

## USDA PLANT HARDINESS ZONE MAP
Courtesy of Agricultural Research Service

AVERAGE ANNUAL MINIMUM TEMPERATURE

| Temperature (°C) | ZONE | Temperature (°F) |
|---|---|---|
| −45.6 and below | 1 | Below −50 |
| −42.8 to −45.5 | 2a | −45 to −50 |
| −40.0 to −42.7 | 2b | −40 to −45 |
| −37.3 to −40.0 | 3a | −35 to −40 |
| −34.5 to −37.2 | 3b | −30 to −35 |
| −31.7 to −34.4 | 4a | −25 to −30 |
| −28.9 to −31.6 | 4b | −20 to −25 |
| −26.2 to −28.8 | 5a | −15 to −20 |
| −23.4 to −26.1 | 5b | −10 to −15 |
| −20.6 to −23.3 | 6a | −5 to −10 |
| −17.8 to −20.5 | 6b | 0 to −5 |
| −15.0 to −17.7 | 7a | 5 to 0 |
| −12.3 to −15.0 | 7b | 10 to 5 |
| −9.5 to −12.2 | 8a | 15 to 10 |
| −6.7 to −9.4 | 8b | 20 to 15 |
| −3.9 to −6.6 | 9a | 25 to 20 |
| −1.2 to −3.8 | 9b | 30 to 25 |
| 1.6 to −1.1 | 10a | 35 to 30 |
| 4.4 to 1.7 | 10b | 40 to 35 |
| 4.5 and above | 11 | 40 and above |

### *Figure 8-4* Hardiness
Plant temperature adaptation is based on cold hardiness, the annual average minimum temperature. Zones are assigned a hardiness zone number that is shown on the above map established by the USDA.

**American Horticultural Society**
**Plant Heat-Zone Map**

Zone

Average Number
of Days per Year
Above 86°F (30°C)

< 1
1 to 7
> 7 to 14
> 14 to 30
> 30 to 45
> 45 to 60
> 60 to 90
> 90 to 120
> 120 to 150
> 150 to 180
> 180 to 210
> 210

Scale for the mainland U.S.

Scale for Alaska

Scale for Hawaii

AMERICAN HORTICULTURAL SOCIETY
7931 East Boulevard Drive
Alexandria, VA 22308 U.S.A.
(703) 768-5700 Fax (703) 768-8700

Coordinated by:
Dr. H. Marc Cathey, President Emeritus

Compiled by:
Meteorological Evaluation Services Co., Inc.

Underwriting by:
American Horticultural Society
Goldsmith Seed Company
Horticultural Research Institute of the
American Nursery and Landscape Association
Monrovia
Time Life Inc.

Copyright © 1997 by the American Horticultural Society

*Figure 8-5* **Heat Zone Map**
Plant temperature adaptation based on heat tolerance established by the American Horticultural Society. Zones are assigned similar to the cold hardiness map. *(Photo Courtesy of the American Horticultural Society; www.ahs.org)*

## Tip Box

## Microclimate

**Microclimates** are areas or pockets that are warmer or cooler than predominate growing conditions in the area (Fig. 8–6). This may be due to urbanization, changes in topography, or surrounding trees. This is most noticeable in areas that are partially enclosed by walls. These areas are protected from cold, hard wind that can dry out plants and increase the chances of winter damage. Plants marginally adapted to the climate can survive these conditions much better in protected areas.

(a)

### Figure 8–6  Microclimate
An area within a hardiness zone that is warmer or cooler due to protection or urbanization. (a) Often buildings protect a planting area from harsh winter wind and exposure to temperature extremes. (b) The dogwood tree is protected in the corner of the building and has grown about 20 feet, while dogwoods around the corner in full sun grew little and eventually failed.

(b)

# Cultural Requirements

**Cultural requirements** refer to growing conditions required for optimal growth. Two of the most important requirements are exposure and moisture.

## Exposure

**Exposure** refers to the location of the plant with respect to light, wind, salt, city conditions, and durability (Fig. 8–7).

**Light**    There are sun-tolerant plants and shade-tolerant plants, as well as those adapted to a degree of both sun and shade. Shade plants in full sun will burn and sun plants in shade will grow poorly, if at all. Some plants have a broad range of sunlight adaptation that can grow in either full sun or full shade. Make note of plants that are adapted to both sun and shade because they are very versatile.

---

### *Tip Box*

### Southwest Exposure Is the Hottest

What time of the day does the plant receive sun exposure? Late afternoon sun is the warmest. Some shade-tolerant plants can tolerate full sun in early morning because temperatures are relatively low.

---

**Planting for Future Shade?**    Be careful when planting for future shade. A newly planted large tree will not provide significant shade for several years. If shade-requiring plants are planted under the future large tree, they will be scorched in the full sun and fail before shade is there. One good way to address these areas is to select plants that tolerate full sun and shade.

*Figure 8–7*   **Cultural Requirements**
There are several factors to consider when selecting a plant best adapted to the area.

***Figure 8–8*** **Urban Impact**
Paving raises the temperature around plants. These plants are growing in tight wells in a hot area with a high level of pedestrian traffic.

**Wind**   Windy areas can mechanically ruin some plants by physically damaging foliage and branches or rapidly drying the plant. Examples include coastal regions and the Midwest prairie.

**City Conditions**   Some plants are not very tolerant of city conditions. Ozone and smog have a negative impact. This can greatly limit plant selection. Another impact of urban environments is paving and walls that can significantly raise the temperature (Fig. 8–8).

**Durability**   Know which plants don't handle rough exposure, such as to pets and children. Delicate plants that have stems and leaves that break easily will not survive a big outdoor dog unless some protection is provided (Fig. 8–9).

**Salt**   Coastal regions have the limitation of exposure to salt water, either to the roots or blown onto foliage. As a result, plants have to be salt-tolerant to survive (Fig. 8–10).

## Moisture

Be familiar with predominately wet or dry conditions. Wet soil can cause root rot and lack of soil oxygen, while dry conditions can stunt growth and weaken tolerance and health. Choose plants adapted to either extreme.

### Typically Wet Conditions

- Heavy soils
- High water table
- Areas near downspouts

### Typically Dry Conditions

- Sandy soils
- Nonirrigated
- Arid climates

***Figure 8–9* Durability**
Plants may have to handle the rough conditions of pets or children. In this example, ornamental grass handles the surrounding playground well.

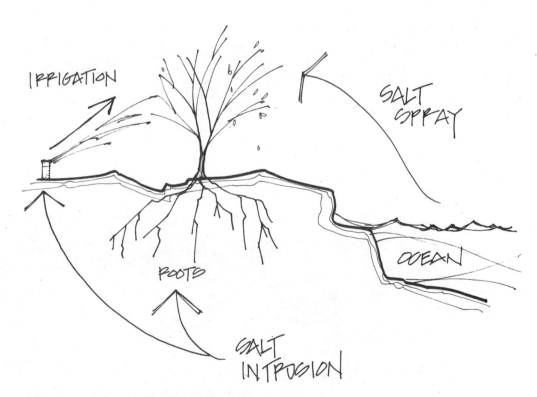

***Figure 8–10* Saline Conditions**
Plants must be salt-tolerant if the foliage is sprayed or the roots are exposed to saline water.

# Soil

There are several facets of soil, which can be studied in Chapter 3, "Inventory and Analysis." The main components considered are: pH, structure, texture, and fertility (Fig. 8–11). Be sure if any soil conditions that are not correctable are noted before plant selection so that the plants selected are tolerant of such conditions. For instance, as mentioned in an earlier chapter, plants such as azaleas and rhododendrons are adaptable to acidic soils.

# Wildlife

Plants can be used to attract or repel wildlife. Birds, butterflies, and even sometimes squirrels are appreciated by some people. (See Appendix E for suggestions on attracting birds and butterflies.)

## Birds

Hummingbirds are valued because of their unique flying habit. They are attracted to flowers to feed on nectar, in particular flowers that are red such as the orange-red flowers on the trumpet creeper vine, or red flowers on a bottlebrush shrub (Fig. 8–12). Other birds are attracted to fruit and seeds as a food source. Be aware that attracting birds to consume fruit can also create problems! Certain fruit, in particular Mulberry, will cause birds to defecate in unwanted areas such as the driveway, automobiles, and entertainment areas.

***Figure 8–11*** **Soil Conditions**
Consider soil factors when selecting plants, or whether the soil will need to be or can be altered to plants.

**Figure 8–12  Birds**
Birds are attracted to fruit of some plants, while hummingbirds are attracted to flowers of others, such as this trumpet creeper vine. *(Photo courtesy of Chris Briand. http://www. salisbury.edu/arboretum/.)*

**Figure 8–13  Butterflies**
Attract immature butterflies with larval food sources or adult butterflies with nectar sources. *(Photo courtesy of Chris Briand. http://www.salisbury.edu/ arboretum/.)*

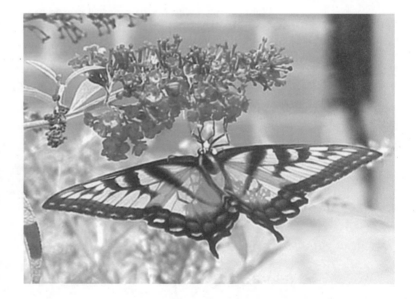

## Butterflies

Butterflies are a great addition to any landscape, especially along a pathway where they flutter up when people approach (Fig. 8–13). To attract butterflies, there are food sources to attract the larval (caterpillar) stage and food sources to attract the adult butterfly. The caterpillar will consume the foliage of food source plants so they should be planted to allow insect damage. Herbs are often a great source of food for caterpillars. Nectar is provided to the adult butterfly from flowers. There are numerous resources for creating a successful butterfly garden that will attract a great variety during the growing season.

### Deer

Deer are the most notable wildlife that wreak havoc on a landscape by devouring flowers and foliage overnight, leaving behind nothing but bare ground or stems. The intensity of deer problems will depend on the deer population, drought conditions, and time of year. During dry summers, deer search harder for food that is limited in nonirrigated regions. Spring is the height of intense feeding because foliage is flush, succulent, and nutritious. Winter, when food is most difficult to find, may bring deer into the landscape to feed on woody stems.

Be aware if deer problems exist in the region of the design. If so, take precautions to select plants (or other methods) to resist deer. There are several good resources online for plants and methods, such as http://www.mydeergarden.com.

## Plant Characteristics

Many plant characteristics were discussed in Chapter 6, "Design Principles," in reference to color and texture. This section will take a look at some other characteristics that will impact selection.

### Thorns and Spines

Plants armed with sharp pointed stems or leaves, such as a cactus, are sometimes referred to as barrier plants (Fig. 8–14). These are often used to repel people or animals, to direct traffic, or keep traffic out of sensitive areas.

**Thorns** are sharp, woody extensions that technically are a modified branch. **Spines** are sharp points that can grow on the margins or at the tips of foliage and are technically modified leaves.

(a)

(b)

***Figure 8–14*** **Thorns and Spines**
Barrier plants have (a) thorns or (b) spines to repel people or animals.

## Branching

Although branching is covered in Chapter 6, there are other considerations worth mentioning.

**Exfoliating** trunks and branches are valued assets to some plants (Fig. 8–15). These are especially noticeable when leaves have fallen from deciduous plants exposing a rich texture. Exfoliating trunks are noticeable anytime of the year, while the exfoliating branches are more valued after leaf drop.

One of the most unique plant characteristics is the **contorted,** or **corkscrew,** effect of branches that are twisted and curled (Fig. 8–16). These are highly coveted branches used in flower arrangements. This branching habit can make a great accent plant.

The **weeping** form has branches that are flimsy enough that there is little structural support (Fig. 8–17). As a result, these branches, which are typically newer growth, hang from the older limbs in a pendulous fashion. They move easily in the wind and lend a graceful form to the landscape.

(a)

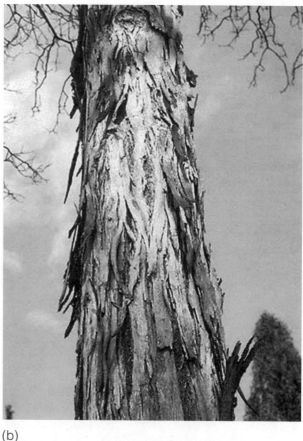

(b)

### *Figure 8–15* **Exfoliation**

Exfoliating trunks and branches adds rich texture to trees and shrubs. (a) Paperbark Maple; (b) Shagbark Hickory. *(Photo (a) courtesy of Chris Briand, http://www.salisbury.edu/arboretum/; photo (b) courtesy of William A. Hoch, http://www.midwestlandscapeplants.org)*

*(continues)*

(c)

(d)

(e)

(f)

***Figure 8-15*** **Exfoliation—continued**
(c) Stewartia; (d) Chinese Elm; (e) Musclewood (no exfoliation but interesting texture); (f) Oakleaf hydrangea, exfoliating branches. *(Photo (f) courtesy of Chris Briand. http://www.salisbury.edu/arboretum/; photos (c), (d), and (e) courtesy of William A. Hoch. http://www.midwestlandscapeplants.org)*

(a)

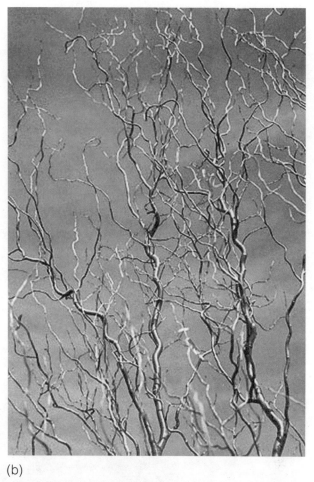

(b)

*Figure 8–16* **Contorted Branches**
The contorted branches of (a) Hardy Orange Flying
Dragon, (b) Corkscrew Willow, and (c) Harry Lauders
Walking Stick are unique specimens, especially in
the winter. *(Photo (b) courtesy of William A. Hoch.*
*http://www.midwestlandscapeplants.org)*

(c)

## Fragrance

The effect of fragrance adds another dimension to the landscape in addition to visual.
Fragrance typically emanates from flowers and some, like gardenia, honeysuckle, and
jasmine, can fill an entire yard (Fig. 8–18). Be aware that some plants have a good
fragrance only when you stick your nose into the flower but have minimal effect on the
surrounding area.

(a)                                                    (b)

### *Figure 8-17*  **Weeping Branches**

(a) Branches have less structural support than nonweeping varieties and hang gracefully from main limbs of the tree, such as these weeping pines and (b) weeping willow. (*Photo (b) courtesy of William A. Hoch. http:// www.midwestlandscapeplants.org.*)

### *Figure 8-18*  **Fragrance**

The flowers of Tea Olive are visually insignificant but are highly valued for their potent fragrance.

This is a wonderful dimension to add to an entertainment area or entrance where they would be most noticeable. Even planting these flowers near open windows can fill the house with fragrance.

Be aware that some plants may be malodorous. The Bradford Pear, for example, is valued for its white showy flowers in early spring but smells something like vomit, which can be overpowering at the entrance.

***Figure 8–19*** **Nuisance Fruit**
Some plants drop fruit that can be messy or malodorous. This ginkgo fruit is pulpy and when dropped on the ground can break open and reveal a rank odor. (*Photo courtesy of Chris Briand. http://www.salisbury.edu/ arboretum/.*)

## Nuisance Fruit

Be aware of plants that drop messy fruit (Fig. 8–19). This is a major concern in areas of traffic where the fruit would drop on sidewalks or parked cars. One example is ginkgo. The female tree produces a fleshy fruit that when broken open, smells awful!

# Plant Size and Quality

The landscape designer will specify the size of plants to be installed and should be familiar with plant quality.

## Size

The designer should understand the impact that plant size has on the cost of the design as well as how plants are sold (Fig. 8–20). This will have a great impact on the rate at which the design develops.

### Larger Plants

- More expensive

- Fill in the intended design quicker

### Smaller Plants

- Less expensive

- More time to fill the design

Inform the client that the design needs time to develop and grow into the plan that has been proposed. Some clients may expect the landscape to look like the plan drawing at the time of installation. Ideally, clients would like to install plants that fill the area immediately. But large plants are more expensive, take longer to establish, and are often not economically feasible. However, installing very small, inexpensive plants will look undersized and take too much time to fill.

*Figure 8–20* **Plant Size**
The designer will specify plant size and the client should be aware that the proposed design will take time to mature. Larger plants will fill the intended design quickly but will cost more to purchase.

## Plant Production

Plants are grown at wholesale nurseries and sold to contractors or retail nurseries. Retail nurseries sell to contractors and the general public. Plants are produced and sold in plastic containers or balled-in-burlap.

**Container Grown**   **Container grown** plants are grown in a plastic pot. They have the relative convenience of easy handling and planting anytime of the year (Fig. 8–21). The approximate volume of the plastic container is measured in gallons. For smaller containers, such as those used to sell annuals and perennial flowers or groundcover, inches may be used to describe the diameter of the container. Four-inch containers are a common size for annual flowers and some perennials.

> **One gallon:** Some perennials are sold in 1-gallon containers. One-gallon shrubs are also available but often considered too small for many applications because of the size and time required to fill the design.
>
> **Three and five gallon:** Three-gallon containers are commonly used for small to medium shrubs because they are economical and reasonable in size.
>
> **Ten, fifteen, thirty gallons and larger:** These sizes are used for shrubs and trees. Of course, the larger sizes are the most expensive.

**Balled-in-Burlap**   **Balled-in-burlap** are field-grown plants that are dug and wrapped in burlap to contain the rootball (Fig. 8–22). This type of production is often referred to as B and B. It is often specified for large trees and shrubs.

(a)

(b)

(c)

***Figure 8–21*  Container Grown Plants**
(a) Trees and shrubs are conveniently grown in black plastic containers. Sizes are measured in gallons: 1, 3, and 5 gallons are common examples, but larger sizes are used as well. (b) At a nursery, 1-gallon shrubs are grown on the right and 15-gallon trees on the left. (c) Annual and perennial flowers are typically sold in 4-inch containers.

The size of B and B plants can be specified by either

- Height from the ground to the top of the plant

  Example: Ten-foot *Acer rubrum,* Red Maple

- **Caliper,** which is the diameter of the tree trunk measured at 6 inches from the ground for trunks up to 4 inches in diameter and 12 inches from the ground for larger trees.

  Example: 1.5-inch caliper *Acer rubrum,* Red Maple

**Bare root**   **Bare root** plants are generally small plants sold without soil around the roots. They are limited to planting during dormancy and are not often used by designers.

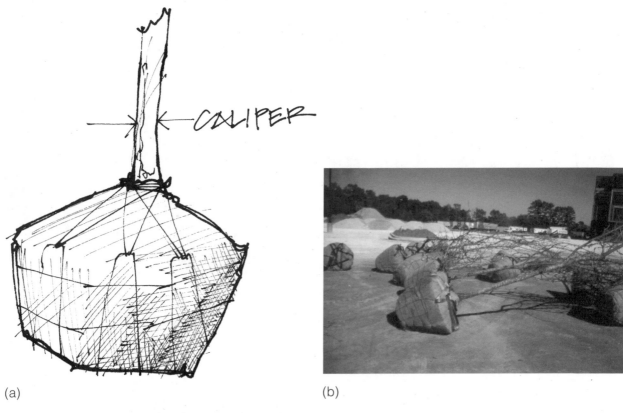

(a)  (b)

***Figure 8–22*** **Balled-in-Burlap**
A common method of plant production is the rootball wrapped in burlap. (a) The size is often dictated by caliper, the diameter of the trunk 6 inches from the rootball, although it can also be measured as the height of the plant. (b) Balled-in-burlap trees are ready to plant.

---

*Tip Box*

**What Is the American Standard for Nursery Stock?**

**American Standard for Nursery Stock,** sometimes referred to as the **ANSI Standards** or just the **Standard** for short, is from the American Association of Nurserymen (http://www.anla.org). The nursery industry recognizes this as the primary reference for the standardization of plant terminology. Many designers simply write in their specifications, "All plant material must conform to the American Standard for Nursery Stock."

---

# Hardscapes and Other Materials

This section covers hardscapes, those components of the landscape other than plants, which are used to build walks, driveways, walls, decks, and so on. Other materials discussed include drainage, mulch, and lighting.

Although many times landscape designers are hired to design with plants after the general contractor has done much of the hardscaping, this chapter addresses hardscaping components so that the designer has some understanding of their uses and construction. In many cases, the designer will have little impact on designing the driveway, sidewalks, and patio. Landscape architects are more often hired rather than landscape designers at the initial planning phases and will have much more control of the hardscape portion of the landscape design.

## Concrete

**Concrete** is one of the most inexpensive forms of paving. When installed properly it is very effective at supporting traffic safely without wear. Typically a minimum of 4-inch-thick concrete is used for the sidewalk, patio, and driveway. The driveway may be thicker and reinforced with steel rods to support the weight of automobiles.

Because the driveway is large, the expanse of concrete can be visually overwhelming (Fig. 8–23). The uninterrupted gray slab of concrete can also be a dull, uninteresting feature. To break up the monotonous expanse of concrete, there are different finishes to make an interesting surface (Fig. 8–24).

**Figure 8–23   Driveways**
Driveways are often very large, visually dominant features of the landscape.

(a)

**Figure 8–24   Unique Driveways**
(a) Ways to break up the large expanse of concrete are dividing it with rows of pavers or stone, or the use of alternate materials. (b) Paving a driveway is a good alternative to concrete and is more appealing in color and texture, but more expensive. *(Photo (a) courtesy of Visual Impact Software; photo (b) courtesy of Blue Ribbon LLC, Maryland. www.blueribbonllc.com)*

(b)

(a)

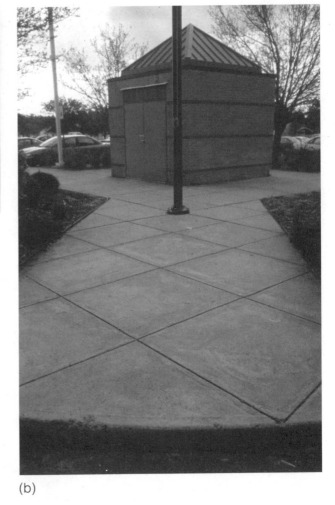

(b)

***Figure 8–25* Contraction Lines**
(a) Grooves in the concrete visually help break up the large driveway. (b) On this large concrete sidewalk at an elementary school, contraction lines are used to add visual interest by breaking up space and repeating the angle of the brick structure.

## Surface Finishing

There are several finishes to the surface of concrete that can add interest. Consult a concrete contractor for specialty finishes.

**Contraction Jointing**   Concrete often cracks as it dries. **Contraction joints** are 3/8″ deep grooves that help control cracking. Jointing creates a weak line in the concrete where the cracking will occur, rather than running randomly across the slab.

Jointing lines are often seen as grooves running perpendicular across sidewalks, but they can also be used to create patterns over large slabs of concrete to be more visually interesting (Fig. 8–25).

**Exposed Aggregate**   **Exposed aggregate** is one of the more attractive surfaces and has a natural appeal. It has pea gravel embedded in the surface of the concrete (Fig. 8–26). The pea gravel adds a textural element that is visual and physical.

**Colored Concrete**   **Colored concrete** has a color additive that can be added to concrete before it is poured (Fig. 8–26). Warming the concrete with a slight tan color adds an attractive earth-tone appeal that complements the natural colors of the surrounding mulch and soil. This can also be used in conjunction with the exposed aggregate technique.

(a)

(b)

**Figure 8–26  Exposed Aggregate and Colored Concrete**
Exposed aggregate concrete has pea gravel embedded into the surface. (a) This concrete is warmed with an addition of tan coloring. Deep contraction lines that help control cracking also help break up the large slab. (b) Close-up of exposed aggregate.

(a)

(b)

(c)

**Figure 8–27  Stamped Concrete**
(a) Concrete can be colored and stamped into patterns, such as this herringbone paver pattern.
(b) Driveway stamped into basketweave pattern;
(c) Entrance stamped into flagstone pattern. *(Photos (b) and (c) courtesy of King's Materials, Cedar Rapids, IA. http://www.kingsmaterial.com.)*

**Stamped Concrete  Stamped concrete** uses numerous approaches to create specialty effects on the concrete surface (Fig. 8–27). It can be used in conjunction with colored concrete to create a brick paving effect, cobblestone, or any number of patterned effects.

# Stone and Pavers

Paved areas are more expensive to install than concrete but are more decorative and just as functional (Fig. 8–28). There are many types and sizes of bricks and stones.

## Stone

**Stone** is often used in the form of flagstone, which is a sheet-like stone that comes in various colors, shapes, and sizes (Fig. 8–29). It's often used as an informal walkway because the stones are of the irregular variety. **Cut stone** is shaped, or cut, into various rectangular shapes that are more consistent in shape and size. Cut stone has a more formal appeal than flagstone.

(a)                                                              (b)

***Figure 8–28*** **Stone and Pavers**
(a) Pavers, or bricks, used in conjunction with concrete in this example are an effective way to create a visually interesting walk. (b) Stone is large and flat and can be irregular or square shaped. *(Photos courtesy of Visual Impact Software. www.visualimpactimaging.com)*

(b)

***Figure 8–29*** **Stone**
(a) Irregular-shaped stone, often referred to as flagstone. (b) Square stone is often referred to as cut stone, or bluestone (a common type of stone that is cut). *(Photos courtesy of Visual Impact Software. www.visualimpactimaging.com)*

(a)

**Stone Tiles**   Stone tiles are concrete paving modules that are colored and textured to simulate a natural appearance. Much like cut stone, seams fit tightly and there are numerous textures, colors, and patterns to choose from (Fig. 8–30a).

## Pavers

**Pavers** are like bricks made from concrete or clay and come in various shapes and colors (Fig. 8–30b). They can be used in patios, sidewalks, and driveways (Fig. 8–30c). Shapes can be rectangular, square, or interlocking. There are numerous patterns that can be created with pavers. A few of the commonly used patterns are

- Running bond
- Herringbone
- Basket weave
- Interlocking
- Fan

## Stone and Paver construction

Stone and pavers are commonly constructed free-laid with sand or wet-laid with mortar (Fig. 8–31).

**Dry-Laid**   **Dry-laid** construction utilizes a foundation of crushed granite or limestone (or similar material) and a setting bed of sand on which the pavers are laid (Fig. 8–32). Once all the pavers are laid, sand is swept into the cracks between the pavers. Some techniques mix dry mortar with sand to sweep in the cracks to set up a weak cement bond. Dry-laid installation is a quick means of installation, but very reliable when done properly. Since it uses porous materials such as sand, water will infiltrate through the hardscape and reduce runoff. **Flagstone** is more susceptible to weeds since the cracks are often wider than pavers or cut stone.

**Wet-Laid**   **Wet-laid** construction sets pavers or stone in **mortar,** a concrete mixture that bonds units together (Fig. 8–33). This uses a concrete foundation with a setting bed of mortar which the pavers or stone are laid. Space between the pavers and stone are then filled and leveled with mortar for a smooth, durable surface. This is much more stable for stone and there is no potential for weeds to grow in cracks.

*Figure 8–30a*   **Stone Tiles**
Paving modules that come in a variety of shapes, colors, and textures. *(Photo courtesy of King's Materials, Cedar Rapids, IA. http://www. kingsmaterial.com.)*

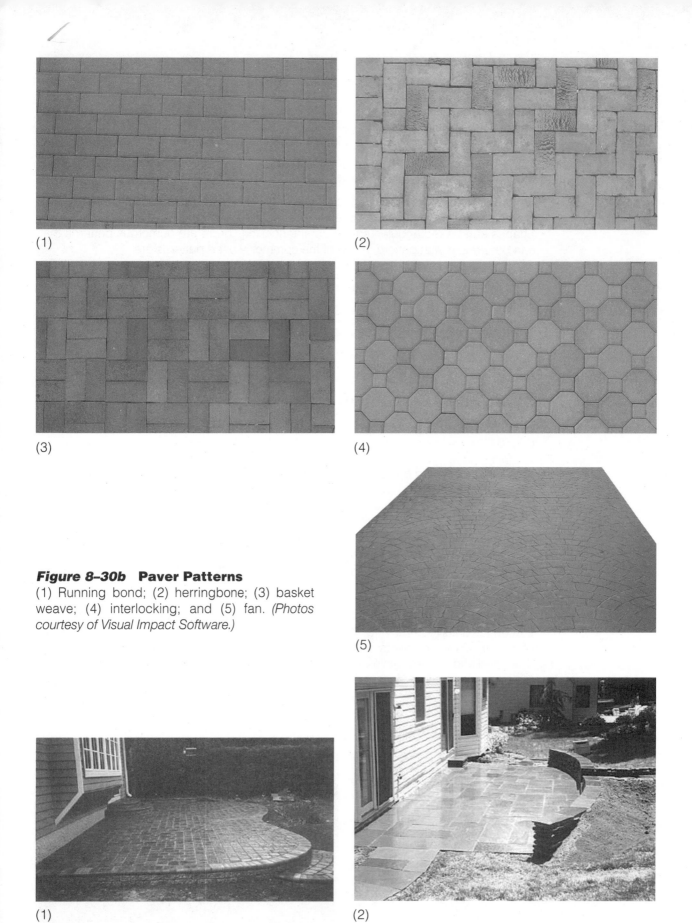

**Figure 8–30b** **Paver Patterns**
(1) Running bond; (2) herringbone; (3) basket weave; (4) interlocking; and (5) fan. *(Photos courtesy of Visual Impact Software.)*

(1)

(2)

(3)

(4)

(5)

(1)

(2)

**Figure 8–30c** **Patio**
Patio constructed with (1) pavers and (2) stone. *(Photos courtesy of Robert J. Kleinman Landscaping, East Lansdowne, PA. www.kleinberg.com)*

***Figure 8–31* Stone and Paver Construction**
(a) Dry-laid construction lays pavers or stone in a thin layer of sand over a compacted layer of crushed limestone. Sand is swept into the into cracks. (b) Mortar construction lays pavers or stone in a layer of wet mortar over a base of concrete. Mortar is pressed into the cracks of pavers or stone.

# Wood

Wood has numerous uses in the landscape, in outdoor furniture, edging, and storage sheds, as well as decks and fences, which will be covered in this section.

## Decks

Some designers will be asked to design the layout of the deck that will be integral to the landscape. Designers often will provide a contractor with the layout who will then determine the substructure required to build it.

(a)

(b)

(c)

### *Figure 8–32* **Dry-Laid Construction**

(a) Pavers are laid on a compacted layer of sand. (b) Stone set in crushed aggregate. (c) Stone set in soil for informal path that allows groundcover and moss to grow between stones. *(Photo (c) only courtesy of Big Sky Landscaping, Inc., Clackamas, OR. http://www.bigskylandscaping.com)*

***Figure 8–33* Wet-Laid Construction**
Stone is set in wet mortar.

***Figure 8–34* Single Level Deck**
This single level provides a dry, level area for a small gathering and to cook out.

**Single Level Versus Multilevel**   **Single level** is the simplest construction that works fine for small gatherings and outdoor cooking (Fig. 8–34). **Multilevel** decks are effective in creating different rooms on the deck (Fig. 8–35). Smaller areas can be developed for cooking, eating, a hot tub, or intimate relaxation, while main areas can be developed for entertaining larger groups.

**Circulation**   Be aware of the flow of traffic as it goes into the house and out into the yard (Fig. 8–36). Access points should allow for convenient access to the deck and house. Try to direct traffic around gathering areas and not through them.

**Seating**   Make considerations for seating space, whether it's going to be built-in seating along the perimeter of the deck or deck furniture (Fig. 8–37).

(a)

(b)

(c)

## Figure 8–35  Multilevel Decks

(a) Deck has multiple levels for entertaining large parties. (b) This single deck (upper deck) had a lower deck added to create another outdoor room for entertainment. (c) The vine on the railing provides some separation between the upper and lower deck, while the vine growing up the arbor will provide overhead enclosure. *(Photo (a) courtesy of JRW Decks in Seattle. www.jrwdecks.com)*

## Figure 8–36  Entertainment Circulation

Lay out the entertainment area to account for circulation through the area.

**Figure 8–37 Deck Seating**
These benches are built into the deck to provide seating as well as a railing. (*Photo courtesy of JRW Decks in Seattle. www.jrwdecks.com*)

(a)

(b)

**Figure 8–38 Steps**
(a) Steps should be placed at convenient access points to circulate into the surrounding landscape. (b) Combining deck and patio materials for interest. (*Photos courtesy of JRW Decks in Seattle. www.jrwdecks.com*)

**Steps**  Steps will be the access points connecting the deck to the yard. They should make access convenient from the house to deck to yard (Fig. 8–38a).

**Combining Materials**  Wood decking and paver/stone patios can be combined for visual interest and to develop outdoor rooms (Fig. 8–38b).

## Fences

Fences are typically used to enclose the backyard for children and pets as well as provide entertainment privacy (Fig. 8–39). Many regional codes prevent privacy fences in the front yard. Fencing in the front yard is often limited to 3 feet high picket fences (Fig. 8–40).

There are many different patterns of fences. Some of the more common ones are mentioned here (Fig. 8–41).

**Figure 8–39  Fencing Dimensions**
Privacy fences are typically limited to 6 feet tall in the backyard. Construction with fence panels that are 6 feet high and 8 feet wide is a common approach where posts are set on 8 foot centers to attach the panel.

**Figure 8–40  Front Yard Fence**
Regional codes restrict fences in the front yard to 3 feet high or none at all.

***Figure 8–41*  Fence Styles**
(a) Solid board; (b) board-on-
board; (c) basket weave;
(d) lattice-top; and (e) picket.

(a)

(b)

(c)

(d)

(e)

**Solid Board Privacy (Dog-Ear)**  One of the most common patterns is the **solid board privacy fence,** sometimes referred to as **dog-ear** (Fig. 8–42). This pattern has all the fence boards on one side. This offers complete privacy, but the downside is that the fence has a "bad side" showing the **stringers** where the fence boards attach. The fence board side is considered the "good side." Most codes require that the good side must face out toward the public.

**Board-on-Board (Shadowbox or Alternate Board)**  Another common fence pattern is **board-on-board,** sometimes referred to as **shadowbox** or **alternate board.** This pattern alternates the fence boards on each side of the stringer. This creates a semi-private barrier since you can see through the fence at an angle (Fig. 8–43). The advantage is there is no bad side.

**Basket weave**  Basket weave has a strong horizontal effect since the fence boards are installed horizontally to the posts. The horizontal pattern is considered to have a calming effect on the area. Like board-on-board, it has no bad side since there are no stringers.

**Lattice-Top**  With **lattice-top fencing,** the bottom portion of the fence is solid board or board-on-board. There is a decorative effect with a panel of lattice across the top of the fence.

*Figure 8–42* **Bad Side of Fence**
Solid board fence has a good side (boards) and bad side showing where the stringers are to support the fence boards. Some
codes stipulate that the bad side needs to be constructed facing
the property and the good side facing outward to the public.

(a)

(b)

*Figure 8–43* **Semiprivate Board-on-Board**
(a) A view through the board-on-board fence; (b) at an angle.

**Picket**   Decorative picket fencing is often used in the front yard to contain and define the property, but offers no privacy.

# Retaining Walls

**Retaining walls** have numerous functional properties as well as design value (Fig. 8–44).

**Reduce the slope of the ground:** Retaining walls create a level surface on a sloped area. For large slopes, terracing the area with more than one wall will level it out in sections.

**Lower maintenance:** Steep slopes can be difficult to maintain. Turfgrass is hard to mow and trees and shrubs are difficult to water. Groundcovers work well, but getting them established can be difficult. Any bare ground on a slope is prone to erosion.

**Raised planting bed:** Raised beds can utilize trailing vines and groundcover to grow over the edge.

**Elevations:** Retaining walls create a stepping effect. The change in elevation adds another dimension to the landscape.

(a)

*Figure 8–44*  **Retaining Walls**
(a) Retaining walls can be used to reduce the slope of the ground, lower maintenance, and create visual interest; (b) multilevel retaining wall. *(Photo courtesy of King's Materials, Cedar Rapids, IA, http://www.kingsmaterial.com.)*

(b)

Most residential retaining walls are generally kept less than 3 feet high. Higher walls will require more expertise to offset the higher degree of failure.

## Retaining Wall Materials

Retaining walls can be constructed with landscape timbers, railroad ties, concrete blocks, or free stone. Regardless of the material, retaining walls have to be built on a solid foundation and have sufficient drainage to avoid wall failure.

**Landscape Timbers and Railroad Ties**   **Landscape timbers** are wooden timbers that are often 6″ × 6″ in dimension or greater (Fig. 8–45). Use timbers that are treated for ground contact to avoid decay. **Railroad ties** are similar to timbers but are treated with creosote, a preservative to reduce wood decay. Railroad ties should be weathered with age to reduce detrimental effects of the creosote on plants.

*Horizontal construction* stacks timbers and can either stagger the seams or stack the seams in a line (Fig. 8–46). Wall support is achieved by deadman installation and/or vertical posts. Deadman support is a timber installed perpendicular in the backfill that acts like an anchor. Walls that don't utilize support posts or a deadman are built with **batter,** which is the leaning back or stepping back of the wall toward the hill.

*Vertical construction* installs the timbers and ties on end into the ground. To achieve stability, the timbers/ties are installed as deep as the wall is high above the ground in addition to attaching a 2″ × 6″ along the back side.

(a)

(b)

*Figure 8–45*   **Timber Walls**
(a) Timbers used to reduce slope by terracing.
(b) Landscape timbers, such as 6″ × 6″ or
8″ × 8″ lumber, is commonly used. (c) Vertical
construction is a unique approach.

(c)

**Figure 8–46 Timber Wall Construction**
(a) Horizontal construction (top) installs a course below grade for stability. Vertical construction (below) installs each timber at a depth below grade equal to how high it is above grade. (b) Batter, the leaning of the wall, or vertical posts are used to stabilize the wall.

(a)

BATTER

VERTICAL POST

(b)

(c)

FRONT VIEW

STAGGERED          DEADMAN

STACKED

VERTICAL
POST

(d)

TOP VIEW

DEADMAN

SIDE VIEW

DEADMAN

(e)

*Figure 8–46* **Timber Wall Construction—continued**
(c) example of batter; (d) stacked vs. staggered horizontal construction; (e) deadman installed like an anchor for stability.

**Concrete Blocks**   **Concrete blocks** for the retaining wall construction come in a variety of sizes and colors (Fig. 8–47). Choosing an appropriate color may depend on the color of surrounding material, such as the house. There are variations of block types, but two commonly used blocks are lipped and pinned.

**Lipped Blocks**   **Lipped blocks** have an extended edge, or lip, on the bottom rear portion (Fig. 8–48). This lip hangs over the top of the block below it creating a built-in stepping-back effect with additional support to prevent slippage.

(a)

(b)

***Figure 8–47*   Block Retaining Walls**
(a) Retaining walls built with segmental, concrete blocks providing a raised foundation bed with variations in height. (b) This wall provides visual interest where the groundcover will grow and trail over the wall.
*(Photo (a) courtesy of King's Materials, Cedar Rapids, IA, http://www.kingsmaterial.com.)*

***Figure 8–48*   Lipped Blocks**
One of the easier to come by blocks has a lip on the bottom back portion for wall stability and creates a step-back effect of the wall to offset backfill pressure.

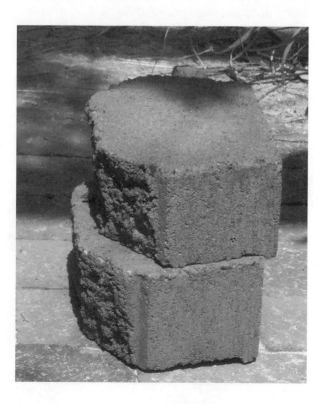

**Pinned Blocks**   **Pinned blocks** utilize fiberglass rods, or pins, that slide through internal holes that attach them to the block above (Fig. 8–49). **Geogrid** is laid between courses for additional support. These are typically used for larger wall construction.

**Stone**   Stone is an effective material with a natural appeal that can be either free-laid or mortared (Fig. 8–50).

***Figure 8–49*  Pinned Blocks**
These types of blocks utilize pins that interlock the top course (row) to the bottom one.
*(Photo courtesy of King's Materials, Cedar Rapids, IA. http://www.kingsmaterial.com.)*

***Figure 8–50*  Stone Walls**
Stone used to create retaining walls.
*(Photo (b) courtesy of Big Sky Landscaping, Inc., Clackamas, OR. www.bigskylandscaping.com)*

(a)

(b)

(c)

***Figure 8–51*** **Edging**
Edging is valuable to keep mulch and beds separate and to maintain a sharp bed line. Without edging, the turf will encroach into the mulched bed and create a weak bed line that is higher maintenance.

# Edging

The edge that separates the planting bed from the turf needs to be defined and reinforced (Fig. 8–51). It's important that the edge be sharply maintained. A sharp edge dramatically improves the definition of the beds and the flow of the line throughout the design. It also helps to keep turf from encroaching into the bed.

Edging material can be decorative or relatively unseen. Regardless, it should perform two functions:

**Easy to maintain:** Avoid edging materials that require a lot of trimming.

**Reduce Turf Encroachment:** It should be set deep enough (3″ to 4″) to keep turf from growing under.

## Strip Edging

**Strip edging** is a solid, thin strip of material made of steel, aluminum, or plastic (Fig. 8–52). This type of edging is best installed so it is unseen and only draws attention to the sharp edge of the bed and not the edging itself. Therefore, the edging is best installed with the top as high as the turf grows and no higher. Strip edging works best to establish curving bed lines because it is very flexible. Anchoring with spikes will reduce edging from frost heaving in northern climates.

**Steel and Aluminum**   Steel and aluminum are the most durable and create one of the sharpest lines, but are more expensive than plastic.

**Plastic**   There are some favorable plastic edgings that are rigid enough to create a crisp bed line, however, most brands of inexpensive plastic edging are not durable and often create a weak line (Fig. 8–53).

## Wood

Straight bed lines are created with 2″ × 4″, 2″ × 6″, or 4″ × 4″ wood (Fig. 8–54). Curved bed lines can be created with 1″ × 6″ wood because 1″ dimension is much more flexible. Anchor wood edging with spikes to prevent frost heaving.

## Concrete, Brick, and Stone

Unlike strip edging, concrete, brick, and stone define the bed with a decorative appeal (Fig. 8–55). In these cases, the edging is meant to be seen as the defining edge. This type of edging is effective in keeping out turfgrass encroachment because of the width and is also very easy to maintain.

(a)

(b)

(c)

**Figure 8–52** **Strip Edging**
(a) The edging maintains a sharp bed line and the integrity of the design with minimal maintenance. (b) Strip edging and weed barriers shortly after installation. (c) After 3 years, this bed line has maintained its integrity with minimal maintenance.

**Figure 8–53** **Plastic Edging**
A popular strip edging used by homeowners is black, plastic edging. Often it creates a weak line and has poor longevity. Another common shortcoming is that the edging is installed too high, increasing maintenance and susceptibility to damage from equipment.

***Figure 8–54*  Wood Edging**
Wood that is 1 inch thick and can
be bent to create curves. Two inch
or 4 inch thick wood is most likely
used for straight lines.

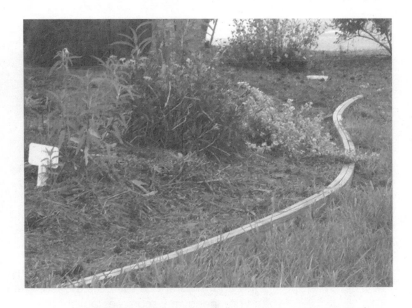

***Figure 8–55*  Brick Edging**
Bricks and pavers used as an edging material.

# Mulch

**Mulch** is used to cover planting beds and around the base of trees (Fig. 8–56). The
advantages are numerous:

- Reduces weed competition
- Reduces mowing
- Adds organic matter to the soil
- Conserves moisture
- Reduces temperature fluctuation and extremes

***Figure 8–56*  Mulch**
Mulching material is used to cover beds, conserve moisture, moderate temperature, and control weeds.

The demands for mulch will be high at the installation of the design, since plants will be small and more space will be exposed. The demand for mulch will reduce as shrubs and groundcover become established.

## Mulching Materials

**Organic**   **Organic mulch** is decomposable (Fig. 8–57). The advantage is it helps condition the soil. However, the disadvantage is it has to be replenished annually.

There's a great selection of organic mulches, most of which are wood products.

**Bark**   These are chunks of **bark,** often from pine (Fig.8–57a). This type of organic mulch is often described as **nuggets.** They can be small to very large. Nuggets break down slowly because of lesser surface area and have to be replenished less often.

**Wood**   This material is usually shredded (Fig. 8–57b). The degree of shred varies from very fine to coarse. Shredded mulch works well on slopes and will resist washing down. Wood mulch can also be chipped more like mini-nuggets.

>   **Cedar:** Has a reddish color and is aromatic, but these effects will fade. It is relatively expensive.

>   **Cypress:** A blonde color that is relatively expensive.

>   **Pine** and **hardwood:** These are inexpensive mulches.

(a)                                                      (b)

***Figure 8–57*  Organic Mulch**
Organic mulch decomposes and can be used to amend the soil. It needs to be occasionally replenished. (a) Bark nuggets; (b) shredded mulch.

> ### *Tip Box*
>
> Shredded mulch works well in annual flower beds because it can be tilled at the end of the season to condition the soil. **Double-hammered mulch** is shred extremely fine for this reason.

**Recycled Wood**   **Recycled wood mulch** comes from wood products such as disposed pallets and is shredded and often dyed. Colors range from bright red to tan to black. Beware that recycled wood can serve as a food source to termites and should be used with caution around the foundation of the house.

**Non-Wood**   **Pine straw** is one of the most popular mulches in the South (Fig. 8–58). It's relatively inexpensive, and effectively holds to slopes. The disadvantage is that it breaks down rapidly and has to be replenished more than once a year. Other non-wood materials include **shells of cocoa bean, pecan,** and **peanuts.** Some of these materials will release as much as 3 percent nitrogen as they decompose. Cocoa shells can be poisonous to dogs because they are derived from the bean to make chocolate.

**Figure 8–58   Non-Wood Mulch**
A non-wood organic mulch popular in the Southeast is pine straw.

> ### *Tip Box*
>
> On slopes or berms, use shredded mulch or pine straw that will knit together and resist washing out during heavy rain. Do not use nuggets because they are prone to washing out (Fig. 8–59).
>
>
>
> **Figure 8–59   Mulching Slope**
> Use shredded mulch on slopes instead of nuggets to avoid washing out.

***Figure 8–60*** **Inorganic Mulch**
Inorganic mulch, such as stone, does not need to be replenished, although it can elevate temperatures in planting beds.

***Figure 8–61*** **Rubber Mulch**
Another inorganic mulch is recycled rubber that can appear like bark or shredded mulch.

**Inorganic**   **Inorganic mulch** will not decompose, and thus does not have to be replenished like organic mulch. The disadvantages can be higher temperatures around plants and the fact that it does not condition the soil.

**Gravel and Stone**   The most common form of inorganic mulch is **gravel,** or stone (Fig. 8–60). There are numerous sizes, shapes and colors available. It is commonly used in dry regions to reduce turf areas.

**Recycled Rubber**   Another inorganic mulch that is popular in some regions is **recycled rubber** (Fig. 8–61). Old tires are shredded or ground up and look very much like organic mulch.

## Weed Barrier

One big concern with mulched beds is weed competition (Fig. 8–62). Weedy beds can weaken a design because it looks poorly done. In addition, weeds will compete with the plantings and slow their establishment.

***Figure 8–62* Weed Barrier**
Weed barrier under mulch creates a physical barrier to prevent weeds from growing.

One good approach to controlling weeds is using a high-quality grade weed barrier underneath the mulch. **Weed barrier** is a mat of material, often a woven fabric or similar material, which creates a physical barrier preventing weeds from emerging in planting beds. If done correctly, beds can appear virtually weed free for years. The cost up front will reduce the need to spray herbicides and pull weeds.

---

### Tip Box

Avoid using plastic as a weed barrier. It can create a moisture lock and have a suffocating effect on the roots.

---

## Drainage

The degree of drainage required depends on the region. In some areas, the design will have to implement drainage, either subsurface tile or surface grading (Fig. 8–63). The designer should have some knowledge of common approaches to drainage.

***Figure 8–63* Drainage**
Water needs to drain in the correct direction on the surface. Drain tile can be used to collect subsurface water and direct it to an acceptable outlet.

## Surface Drainage

**Surface drainage** is directing water flow over the surface of the ground. Any changes to the surface should allow water to drain toward a catch basin or storm sewer in the road. At the very least, do not create drainage problems by grading surface water toward traffic areas, house, or creating water problems in the neighbor's yard.

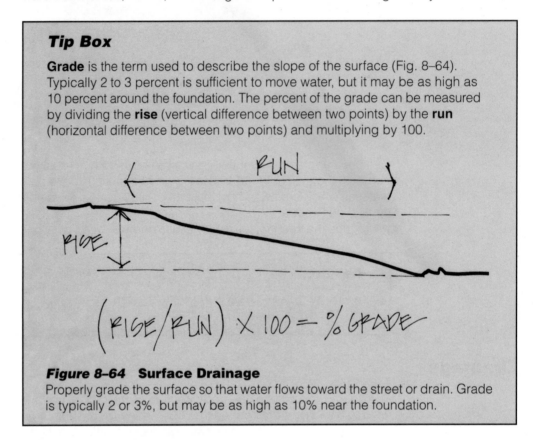

**Tip Box**

**Grade** is the term used to describe the slope of the surface (Fig. 8–64). Typically 2 to 3 percent is sufficient to move water, but it may be as high as 10 percent around the foundation. The percent of the grade can be measured by dividing the **rise** (vertical difference between two points) by the **run** (horizontal difference between two points) and multiplying by 100.

**Figure 8–64   Surface Drainage**
Properly grade the surface so that water flows toward the street or drain. Grade is typically 2 or 3%, but may be as high as 10% near the foundation.

## Subsurface Drainage

Where soil moisture is a problem, the construction of **subsurface drainage** will facilitate the removal of excess soil moisture (Fig. 8–65).

**French drains** are trenches that are filled with drainage gravel to increase pore space to the ground. The main purpose of the French drain is to allow water to drain off the soil surface and into the ground. The French drain does not have an outlet since it acts mostly like a holding tank that facilitates water percolation off the surface. They are relatively short-lived, being effective for 5 to 10 years.

**Tile drainage** utilizes a 4-inch perforated drain pipe installed in a trench and surrounded by drainage gravel (Fig. 8–66). Its main purpose is to take subsurface water and direct it to an outlet. It is much more efficient at removing water from an area than a French drain.

## House

One of the most important areas of drainage is to get water away from the house (Fig. 8–67). This is especially true for houses built over a basement or crawl space. When water drains back toward the house, moisture causes mildew problems, promotes wood decay, and can create termite problems.

**Figure 8–65  French and Tile Drains**
A French drain is a ditch filled with pea gravel that allows a high degree of pore space to get water below the surface. Tile drain utilizes a perforated pipe that will collect water and carry it to an outlet.

(a)

**Figure 8–66  Black Plastic Drain Tile**
(a) Drain tile is sold in rolls (100') or lengths (10'). (b) Perforated tile has slots around the entire perimeter to allow water to seep in. Drain tile can also be nonperforated to simply carry water to an outlet.

(b)

***Figure 8–67* Drain Away from the Foundation**
Be sure that water drains away from the foundation to reduce moisture problems.
Shrubs should keep enough space from the foundation to allow ventilation.

(a)

(b)

***Figure 8–68* Planting at the Foundation**
(a) Shrubs should be far enough away from the foundation to allow adequate ventilation. (b) These shrubs
are planted right against the foundation, limiting their growing space and possibly causing moisture problems
around the house.

Homebuilders should grade the soil so that surface drainage runs away from the house.
Do not disturb this surface drainage by building up beds or berms around the house.

**Foundation Planting**   Avoid planting up against the house (Fig. 8–68). This will create a high humidity microclimate that can cause wood decay. This is often evident by
the molding around windows rotting because the wood is not treated.

Plant shrubs so that their mature diameter leaves a couple feet of space from the house to allow enough air movement to keep things dry. Some recommendations suggest keeping as much as 5 feet of space.

**Gutters**   If the house has gutters, subsurface tile systems can take water from the downspouts and direct it to an outlet away from the house (Fig. 8–69). This can be done with nonperforated drain tile that will dump all water at an outlet. Oftentimes, a pop-up outlet can be installed at the curb and disperse water when it rains. The advantage to this setup is that water is directed away from the house without any downspout extensions lying on the ground that often get damaged or create wet areas around plantings.

# Lighting

The aspect of low-voltage lighting adds an entirely new dimension to the design at night in addition to improved security and safely lit paths (Fig. 8–70).

## Basic Lighting Effects (Fig. 8–71)

**Uplighting:** The light source shines up into the canopy of a tree or shrub from below.

**Downlighting:** A light is secured within a tree or to an outside structure and shines down through the canopy of a tree, shrub, or object. It can also serve to put light on the path nearby and serve as an indirect path light.

**Pathlighting** and **Spreadlighting:** Pathlights are short lights that illuminate a walking area. Spreadlighting diffuses the light out over a larger area that may light up a bed or path.

## Lighting Techniques

- Ideally the light source is not visible. The illuminated effect is softer and more appealing without the bright spot of the fixture.

- Avoid overlighting area. A common mistake is placing too many fixtures that overloads the area with light, washing out the effect created by light and dark.

# Summary

Plant selection is vital to the success of the landscape design. Incorrect selection will result in plants with poor health that may eventually die. Many factors need to be considered when selecting plants besides the design attributes such as plant size, thorns, attractive bark, fragrant flowers, and appealing fruit. This includes things like hardiness, availability, and cultural factors (exposure, moisture, and soil). Many resources are available that aid the beginning designer with plant selection, including books, software, and Web sites.

In addition to plants, hardscapes are an important component of the landscape. This includes concrete, pavers, and stone used to establish surfaces for sidewalks, patios, and driveways. Fences are important to establish boundaries and decks create a

(a)

(b)

(c)

(d)

**Figure 8–69  Downspouts**
(a) Downspouts from gutters should drain away from the foundation or into a nonperforated drain tile that carries water (b) to a pop-up outlet. (c) This is a pop-up outlet installed. (d) This downspout gets water away from the house but interferes with the sidewalk.

***Figure 8–70*** **Lighting**
Consider the impact of low-voltage lighting on the landscape at night (digitally enhanced).

***Figure 8–71*** **Basic Lighting Effects**
Uplighting; downlighting; and spreadlighting.

comfortable entertainment area. Retaining walls can be functional by reducing slopes while creating planting areas. Edging is important to maintain a sharp boundary between planting bed and turf. Mulch will cover the planting beds for visual appeal as well as reduce weeds, while a weed barrier can be used in addition to mulch to reduce weed growth. Drainage is important to manage excess water and runoff for healthy plants and sound house maintenance. Lighting can be added to create another dimension to the landscape at night.

# Key Words

**Alternate board fence:** see board-on-board fence

**American Standard for Nursery Stock:** standardization of plant terminology established by the American Association of Nurserymen

**ANSI Standards:** see American Standard for Nursery Stock

**Balled-in-burlap:** field-grown plants dug and wrapped in burlap to contain the rootball

**Bare root:** small plants sold without soil around the roots

**Bark:** chunks of organic mulch; referred to as nuggets

**Basket weave fence:** fence boards installed horizontally to the posts; strong horizontal effect; no bad side

**Batter:** the leaning back or stepping back of the wall toward the hill

**Board-on-board fence:** alternates the fence boards on each side of the stringer; semiprivate barrier since you can see through the fence at an angle; no bad side

**Caliper:** the diameter of the tree trunk measured at 6 inches from the ground for trunks up to 4 inches in diameter and 12 inches from the ground for larger trees

**Cedar:** organic mulch; reddish color and aromatic; relatively expensive

**Cocoa bean shells:** organic mulch

**Colored concrete:** a color additive added to concrete

**Concrete blocks:** used for retaining wall construction; come in a variety of sizes and colors

**Concrete:** one of the most inexpensive forms of paving

**Container grown:** plants for sale grown in a plastic pot

**Contorted branches:** branches that are twisted and curled

**Contraction joints:** 3/8″ deep grooves that help control cracking in concrete

**Corkscrew:** see contorted branches

**Cultural requirements:** the growing conditions for optimal growth

**Cut stone:** shaped, or cut, into various rectangular shapes that are more consistent in shape and size

**Cypress:** organic mulch; blonde color; relatively expensive

**Dog-ear:** see solid board privacy fence

**Double-hammered mulch:** organic mulch shred extremely fine

**Downlighting:** light is secured within a tree or to an outside structure and shines down through the canopy of a tree, shrub, or object

**Dry-laid:** construction that utilizes a foundation of crushed granite (or similar material) and a setting bed of sand

**Exfoliating:** peeling characteristics of trunks and branches

**Exposed aggregate:** attractive concrete surface that has pea gravel embedded in the surface

**Exposure:** location of the plant with respect to light, wind, salt, city conditions, and durability

**Flagstone:** see stone

**French drains:** trenches filled with drainage gravel to increase pore space to the ground

**Geogrid:** laid between courses of pinned blocks for additional support of retaining walls

**Grade:** the term used to describe the slope of the surface

**Gravel:** common inorganic mulch

**Hardiness zones:** areas of average annual minimum temperature assigned throughout the United States

**Hardwood:** organic mulch; inexpensive

**Heat zones:** areas based on the average number of days over 86 degrees Fahrenheit, considered the threshold beyond which plants begin to suffer physiologically

**Inorganic mulch:** stone or gravel that will not decompose; creates higher temperatures around plants; does not condition the soil

**Landscape timbers:** wooden timbers that are often 6″ × 6″ in dimension or greater

**Lattice-top fence:** bottom portion of the fence is solid board or board-on-board; decorative effect with a panel of lattice across the top of the fence

**Lipped blocks:** used for retaining wall construction; have an extended edge, or lip, on the bottom rear portion

**Microclimates:** areas warmer or cooler than predominate growing conditions in the area

**Mortar:** concrete mixture that bonds units together

**Mulch:** covers planting beds and around the base of trees

**Multilevel decks:** effective in creating different rooms on the deck

**Nuggets:** see bark

**Organic mulch:** mulch that is decomposable and helps condition the soil

**Pathlighting:** short lights that illuminate a walking area

**Pavers:** bricks made from concrete or clay and come in various shapes and colors

**Peanut shells:** organic mulch

**Pecan shells:** organic mulch

**Pine straw:** popular organic mulch in the South

**Pine:** organic mulch; inexpensive

**Pinned block:** used for retaining wall construction; utilizes fiberglass rods, or pins, that slide through internal holes that attach them to the block above

**Plant palette:** compilation of plants and their uses and cultural requirements

**Railroad ties:** similar to timbers but treated with creosote

**Recycled rubber:** inorganic mulch; old tires are shredded or ground up and look very much like organic mulch

**Recycled wood mulch:** wood products such as disposed pallets are shredded and often dyed

**Retaining walls:** create a level surface on a sloped area

**Rise:** vertical difference between two points

**Run:** horizontal difference between two points

**Shadowbox fence:** see board-on-board fence

**Single-level deck:** simplest construction that works fine for small gatherings and outdoor cooking

**Solid board privacy fence:** the fence boards are on one side; offers complete privacy; has a "bad side" showing the stringers

**Spines:** sharp points that can grow on the margins or at the tips of foliage, technically are modified leaves

**Spreadlighting:** diffuses the light out over a larger area that may light up a bed or path

**Stamped concrete:** specialty effects on the concrete surface; creates a brick paving effect, cobblestone, or any number of patterned effects

**Standard:** see American Standard for Nursery Stock

**Stone:** sheet-like stone that comes in various colors, shapes, and sizes

**Stringers:** boards that support fence boards

**Strip edging:** solid thin strip of material made of steel, aluminum, or plastic

**Subsurface drainage:** the removal of excess soil moisture with an underground drainage system

**Surface drainage:** directing water flow over the surface of the ground

**Thorns:** sharp, woody extensions that are a modified branch

**Tile drainage:** Four-inch perforated drain pipe installed in a trench and surrounded by drainage gravel

**Uplighting:** light source that shines up into the canopy of a tree or shrub from below

**Weed barrier:** a mat of material, often a woven fabric or similar material, which creates a physical barrier preventing weeds from emerging in planting beds

**Weeping branches:** flimsy branches with little structural support

**Wet-laid:** construction that sets pavers or stone in mortar

# The Master Plan

**9**

## Objectives

- Understand the components and role of the master plan
- Know how to label symbols
- Be familiar with a plant list and its application

In the final step of designing, the master plan refines the preliminary plan with detail.

*Analysis → Concept Plan → Preliminary Design → Master Plan*

The **master plan** is the final document that based on changes at the preliminary phase, will illustrate all materials, amounts, and specifications (Fig. 9–1). Materials include all plants and hardscapes as well as their location, and may also include construction details. Plant and hardscape materials covered in the previous chapter will be used to fully detail the master plan. The master plan may be drawn with presenta-

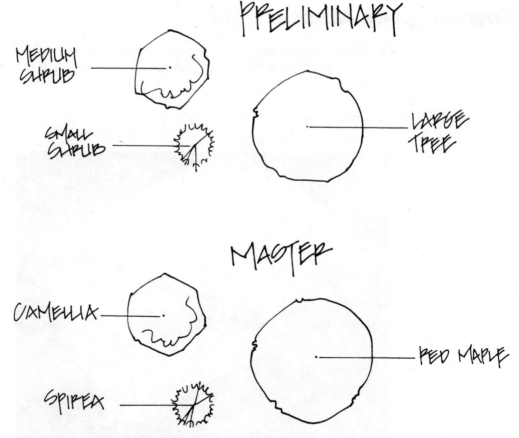

***Figure 9–1   Preliminary versus Master Plan***
While the preliminary plan uses general plant material to convey the overall design concept, the master plan specifies plant name and number.

tion graphics, especially when presented to the client. It will maintain all the preliminary design criteria, such as client information, scale, north arrow, and so on.

## Implementation Plans

The master plan may be the final document presenting all the information including installation. Many small landscape design companies use the master plan for presentation and implementation, while many large landscape design firms use the master plan primarily for presentation while other plans are drawn and bundled together for installation and construction (Fig. 9–2).

A project may include all or some of the following (Fig. 9–3):

- **Planting plan** is used to specify planting specifications: name, number, and size.
- **Layout plan** shows the location of all plants and dimensions of ground plane areas.
- **Construction drawings** show three-dimensional drawings of planting methods, paver construction, edging installation, or other construction.
- **Grading plan** illustrates the proposed changes in slope.
- **Irrigation plan** shows the irrigation system.

## Drawing the Master Plan

As with the preliminary plan, the order of these steps is not necessarily the only approach to completing the master plan but seems logical and easy for many beginning students.

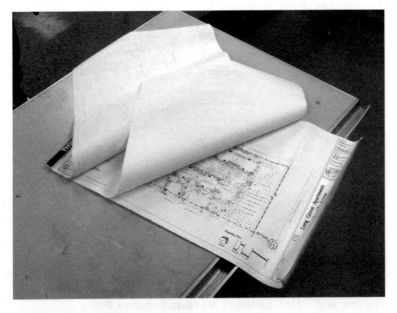

***Figure 9–2   Bundled Plans***
Large design projects may have several plans that are bundled together.

(a)

## *Figure 9–3*  **Implementation Plans**

Other plans may be drawn and included with the master plan, especially from larger projects. (a) Construction details. *(Plans courtesy of Sandy Plance.)*

*(continues)*

**Figure 9–3 Implementation Plans—continued**

(b) Irrigation plan.

# Rough Sketching the Master Plan

Doing a rough sketch from the preliminary (or directly on the preliminary plan) allows students to place symbols to accurately scale and label without concern for detail. This will often combine preliminary plans and include feedback from the client. This can also be a quick way to work out final, specific details such as plant selection, before the final drawing. Sketch on tracing paper and once complete, draw the master on vellum (or mylar). As mentioned in a previous chapter, vellum is higher quality paper that reproduces good line drawings and avoids tearing easily.

# Lay out Ground Plane and Label

When drawing the final plan on vellum, start by drawing the ground plane with any changes worked out in the sketch. Once the ground plane is completed, clearly label areas of turf, driveway, mulch, and so on. Some designers may choose to label the ground plane after all the symbols are completed so that a label doesn't appear misplaced.

# Symbols and Textures

Symbols are drawn as they were in the preliminary plan. They should be accurately placed in the plan with a center dot illustrating the exact spot where the trunk is to be located. Each symbol will be labeled with the name and amount of plants in the grouping. Textures will be applied to the ground plane to identify the illustrated materials. Each of these areas should be clearly labeled as well.

## Labeling symbols

All symbols, objects, and areas need to be accurately labeled (Fig. 9–4). While objects other than plants and ground plane areas need to be simply labeled, plants should be labeled to provide the following:

• Number of plants in each grouping

• Botanical name of the plant or key

There are several ways that designers label information. The botanical name of the plant may be written out in its entirety on each label or a key may be used referring to a plant list where all information is organized. In some cases, a legend may be created to identify the symbols.

# Plant List

The **plant list** contains pertinent information pertaining to plants and hardscapes (Fig. 9–5). This is sometimes referred to as a **planting schedule.**

Plant lists should contain columns of the following information:

**Key:** includes all the keys from the plan drawing

**Botanical name:** Genus, species, and cultivar (if necessary)

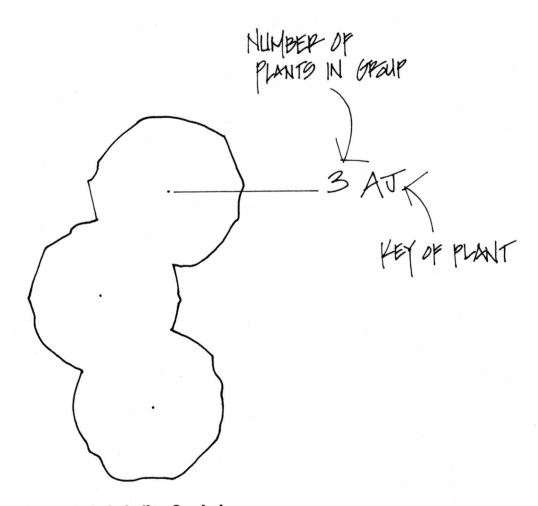

NUMBER OF PLANTS IN GROUP

3 AJ

KEY OF PLANT

***Figure 9–4*** **Labeling Symbols**
Plant symbols need to be clearly labeled. Each label includes the plant name or plant key that refers back to a plant list and the number of plants in the group.

**Common name:** common name of plant (some designers omit this column)

**Quantity:** total number of each plant in the design

**Size:** specifies the planting container, caliper, or height and width of plant

**Spacing:** refers to distance on center of plants in mass. Some designers omit this column and include spacing notations in the "Notes" column. **"On center"** may be abbreviated as O.C.

**Notes:** additional comments, if necessary. This might include flower color, growth habit (such as multi-trunk), or plant spacing (if "Spacing" column is not used).

The plant list may be drawn directly on the plan or created on a separate document. If created on a separate document, the plant list can be copied and attached to the plan drawing for reproduction. If changes to the plant list are required at a later time, the document can be reprinted to replace the preceding plant list. This is much easier to edit than redrawing the plant list on the plan.

| KEY | BOTANICAL NAME | COMMON NAME | QTY | SIZE | NOTES |
|---|---|---|---|---|---|
| AEG | Abelia x 'Edward Goucher' | Edward Goucher Abelia | 21 | 3 gal | |
| AP | Acer palmatum 'Dissectum' | Cutleaf Japanese Maple | 1 | 10 gal | |
| BC | Bignonia capreolata | Crossvine | 7 | 1 gal | |
| BT | Berberis thunbergii var. Atropurpurea 'Crimson Pygmy' | Japanese Barberry | 1 | 3 gal | |
| CA | Clethra alnifolia 'Compacta' | Summersweet | 7 | 3 gal | |
| CC | Callistemon citrinus 'Compacta' | Dwarf Bottlebrush | 3 | 3 gal | |
| CR | Cycas revoluta | Sago Palm | 2 | 30 gal | |
| CS | Cortaderia selloana | Pampas Grass | 1 | 3 gal | |
| CAR | Cupressus arizonica | Arizona Cypress | 1 | 30 gal | |
| EP | Elaeagnus pungens | Elaeagnus | 5 | 5 gal | |
| FJ | Fatsia japonica | Fatsia | 3 | 3 gal | |
| FS | Feijoa sellowiana | Pineapple Guava | 5 | 3 gal | |
| GA | Gardenia agusta | Gardenia | 1 | 3 gal | |
| IG | Ilex glabra 'Densa' | Inkberry | 15 | 1 gal | |
| KP | Koelreuteria paniculata | Goldenraintree | 1 | 1.5" cal | |
| LC | Lantana camara | Lantana | 17 | 1 gal | |
| LCH | Loropetalum chinese | Fringetree | 9 | 5 gal | |
| LN | Lagerstroemia x 'Natchez' | Natchez Crape Myrtle | 3 | 30 gal | |
| LS | Liriope spicata | Liriope | 300 | 4" | 12" O.C. |
| MB | Mahonia bealei | Mahonia | 3 | 3 gal | |
| MC | Muhlenbergia capillaris | Sweetgrass | 54 | 1 gal | |
| OF | Osmanthus fragrans | Tea Olive | 3 | 5 gal | |
| OP | Ophiopogon planiscapus 'Nigrescens' | Black Mondograss | 50 | 4" | 6" O.C. |
| QV | Quercus virginiana | Live Oak | 1 | 1.5 cal | |
| WF | Weigela florida | Weigela | 1 | 3 gal | |

(a)

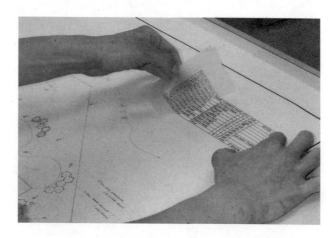

(b)

***Figure 9–5*** **Plant List**
(a) The plant list includes information of plant material, and occasionally other material, in the master plan. Columns include key (if symbols are labeled with key instead of entire plant name), botanical and common name, total quantity of each item, size of each plant to be installed, and a column for miscellaneous notes such as substitutions or plant spacing. (b) Placing a plant list on the master plan.

# Print

Once the master plan is completed, a copy should be obtained to give to the client and/or contractor (Fig. 9–6). The original drawing should remain with the designer. If implementation plans are included in the project, they will be bound together at the top.

# Storage

The originals should be stored in a safe, dry area. Ideal storage is lying flat in shelf storage, but they can be rolled for storage as well. If it is rolled, have the design facing out so that it lies flat when it is unrolled.

(a)

***Figure 9–6*** **Master Plan**

The master plan, based on the preliminary plans, has been labeled and drawn to completion. (a) Sketch.

*(continues)*

(b)

**Figure 9–6  Master Plan—continued**

(b) Hand-drafted master plan.

## PLANT LIST

| QTY. | BOTANICAL NAME | COMMON NAME | SIZE | NOTES |
|---|---|---|---|---|
| 21 | Abelia x 'Edward Goucher' | Edward Goucher Abelia | 3 gal. | |
| 1 | Acer palmatum 'Dissectum' | Cutleaf Japanese Maple | 10 gal. | |
| 7 | Bignonia capreolata | Crossvine | 1 gal. | |
| 1 | Berberis thunbergii var. atropurpurea 'Crimson Pygmy' | Japanese Barberry | 3 gal. | |
| 7 | Clethra alnifolia 'Compacta' | Summersweet | 3 gal. | |
| 3 | Callistemon citrinus 'Compacta' | Dwarf Bottlebrush | 3 gal. | |
| 2 | Cycas revoluta | Sago Palm | 30 gal. | |
| 1 | Cortaderia selloana | Pampas Grass | 3 gal. | |
| 1 | Cupressus arizonica | Arizona Cypress | 30 gal. | |
| 5 | Elaeagnus pungens | Elaeagnus | 5 gal. | |
| 3 | Fatsia japonica | Fatsia | 3 gal. | |
| 5 | Feijoa selloviana | Pineapple Guava | 3 gal. | |
| 1 | Gardenia augusta | Gardenia | 3 gal. | |
| 15 | Ilex glabra 'Densa' | Inkberry | 1 gal. | |
| 1 | Koelreuteria paniculata | Goldenraintree | 1.5" cal. | |
| 17 | Lantana camara | Lantana | 1 gal. | |
| 9 | Loropetalum chinense | Fringetree | 5 gal. | |
| 3 | Lagerstroemia x 'Natchez' | Natchez Crape Myrtle | 30 gal. | |
| 300 | Liriope spicata | Liriope | 4" | 12" o.c. |
| 54 | Muhlenbergia capillaris | Sweetgrass | 1 gal. | |
| 3 | Osmanthus fragrans | Tea Olive | 5 gal. | |
| 50 | Ophiopogon planiscapus 'Nigrescens' | Black Mondo Grass | 4" | 6" o.c. |
| 1 | Quercus virginiana | Live Oak | 1.5" cal. | |
| 1 | Weigela florida | Weigela | 3 gal. | |

**SCALE: 1/8"=1'-0"**

5 'Edward Goucher' Abelia

1 Pampas Grass

mulch

31 Sweetgrass

10 Lantana

7 'Edward Goucher' Abelia

St. Augustine Turf

mulch

1 Southern Live Oak

7 Lantana

5 Elaeagnus

5 Pineapple Guava

mulch

Herb Garden

Herbs

Herb Garden

mulch

1 Goldenraintree

3 Crossvine

FLAGSTONE PATIO

1 Crape Myrtle

5 'E.G.' Abelia

SHED

1 Tea Olive

3 Dwarf Bottlebrush

4 'Edward Goucher' Abelia

1 Gardenia

DECK

FUTURE SUNROOM

1 Crape Myrtle

1 Japanese Barberry

mulch

1 Tea Olive

1 Weigela
3 Mahonia

WORK BENCH

DRY LAID FLAGSTONE

4 Crossvine

RESIDENCE

3 Loropetalum

St. Augustine Turf

3 Fatsia
6 Inkberry

COMPOST BIN

1 Crape Myrtle

1 Japanese Maple

Tea Olive

7 Summersweet

50 Mondo Grass @ 6" O.C.

1 Sago Palm
9 Inkberry

3 Loropetalum

1 Sago Palm

FLAGSTONE SIDEWALK

3 Loropetalum

23 Sweetgrass

St. Augustine Turf

1 Arizona Cypress

mulch

CONC. DRIVE

mulch

300 Liriope @ 12" O.C.

Existing edge of pavement

## MASTER PLAN

EXISTING LIVE OAK

**GRANT RESIDENCE**
721 WEST MARKET ST.
ANYTOWN, USA

PELICAN DESIGNS

REVISIONS BY

(c)

***Figure 9–6*** **Master Plan—continued**
(c) CAD master plan. *(Photo (c) courtesy of Sandy Plance.)*

# Summary

The master plan is the final plan in the landscape design process. It includes all specifications and details in the design illustrated on the plan with plant symbols and ground plane textures that are all clearly labeled. A plant list concisely organizes all the names, quantities, and sizes of material included in the design. A copy of the design (print) is presented and given to the client and/or contractor, the original is kept by the designer and stored in a cool, dry place, either rolled or flat, to preserve the longevity of the design. Sketching the master plan to combine preliminary plans and make changes from feedback allows the designer to work out the final plan before drawing it on vellum.

# Key Terms

**Botanical name:** scientific name of plant

**Common name:** name plant is commonly referred to

**Construction plan:** shows three-dimensional drawings of planting methods, paver construction, edging installation, or other construction

**Grading plan:** illustrates the proposed changes in slope

**Irrigation plan:** shows the design of the irrigation system

**Key:** an abbreviated code used to label symbols; appears in the plant list with plant information

**Layout plan:** shows the location of all plants and dimensions of ground plane areas

**Master plan:** final document that based on changes at the preliminary phase, will illustrate all materials, amounts, and specifications

**On center:** space between plantings; abbreviated O.C.

**Plant list:** includes plant material names, quantities, sizes, and other information; located on the master plan

**Plant list schedule:** see plant list

**Planting plan:** specifies planting specifications: name, number, and size

# 10 The Presentation

### Objectives

- Understand how to present the design
- Learn how to assist in the client's understanding of the design
- Learn an orderly approach to selling the design

The presentation of the design is as important as the drawing itself. It is essentially *selling the design.* This is a product that needs explanation and guidance for most clients to fully understand and appreciate. Without the explanation of the layout, design concepts, and plants, the client may not understand or recognize the potential of the design. Instead it may appear only as a pretty picture.

---

### Tip Box

There are instances where an average drawing can appear as a brilliant design purely on the enthusiasm and clarity of the presentation.

---

# What to Bring to the Presentation

## A Copy of the Design

Present the design rolled out on a table or attach the design to **foam** or **posterboard** to prop up or even to walk around the property and discuss each part of the design, giving the client better ability to visualize it (Fig. 10–1).

(a)

(b)

**Figure 10–1   Copy of Design**
(a) A copy of the design will be used to present; (b) attaching it to foam or posterboard makes it easier to prop up on a wall or carry around the yard.

## Pictures

If not walking around the residence, bring along pictures and refer to them with each point of the design. Help the client visualize the design by flipping through the pictures while discussing each area.

# What the Presentation is NOT

So how does a designer present a design? Every designer has his or her own style and procedure, but let's take a look at what makes it less effective.

## NOT Reading the Plant List

The presentation is NOT just reading the plant list to the client. This can take the form of pointing to each symbol and telling the client the name of the plant without describing anything about it. This may continue until every single symbol has been identified and named before the presentation ends abruptly.

In the classroom, students are often dealing with the stress of public speaking as well as presenting their ideas. In addition to having the clients' attention (or the entire classroom!), offering their own ideas is stressful for fear of being criticized, especially in the beginning of the design process when they may not have a lot of confidence in the first few attempts.

## NOT Speaking to the Design

Speaking to the design refers to the designer looking at the plan drawing, sometimes with his or her back to the client, for the entire presentation. This, again, is often due to nervousness about making eye contact, but results in a cold, less engaging approach with the client.

## NOT Overly Critical of Design

There will be many times that right in the middle of a class presentation a student will suddenly realize an oversight or mistake. Avoid criticizing or apologizing for your design. Some beginning students lack confidence in their ideas and feel more comfortable talking about their indecision or lack of talent. (Some students even introduce their design as "this is not a good design.") And, in some cases, this may be a subconscious effort to lower expectations and avoid criticism from others. In other words, "I know my design stinks, so you don't have to tell me."

## NOT Unprepared

Avoid giving presentations without preparation. This may be more applicable to a classroom or formal presentations to a group of clients (such as a board of directors) rather than the informal presentation with a couple at their residence. Even though the designer has spent many hours with the design, without prior thought and preparation, the presentation will often lack confidence and clarity.

# What the Presentation IS

The presentation needs to consist of more than what appears on the drawing. As with the interview, be warm and personable with the client while presenting the design. It is important to continue to be engaging and enthusiastic. Guide the client through the design with excitement and explain the site potentials, the types of plants and materials in the plan, and how the design will improve the quality of living and value of the property.

## Answer the Question "Why?"

Give a brief explanation with each plant symbol and ground plane texture. As mentioned earlier, the client can look at the symbols and read the plant list without the aid of the designer. What the clients need is the designer to explain to them WHY those plants are there.

What ideas and knowledge is the client buying?

What is it about the plants and the layout that makes them a good selection?

In general, what makes it a good design?

It does *not* have to be a major explanation of every plant and material; just a simple reason may sometimes be enough.

For instance, "In this shady area under the tree there is a group of Fatsia, which has a striking leaf shape and is very shade tolerant." This is a simple explanation of why the Fatsia is used, as opposed to pointing to the symbol and saying, "That's Fatsia."

---

**Tip Box**

In a nutshell, *every point mentioned should answer the question "Why?"*

---

The following is another way of how it may, but should not be, presented:

*"This is a Gardenia, that is a Pyracantha, and that is a Bloodtwig Dogwood."*

Instead present it this way:

*"This Gardenia provides a* nice scent in the spring, *this Pyracantha has* brilliant orange fruit during the late summer and early winter when few things are flowering, and the *Bloodtwig Dogwood has* bright red twigs in the winter that add color to a gray landscape."

## Speak to the Client

*Make eye contact* and engage the client with a discussion of the design (Fig. 10–2). Be excited about the project the clients are receiving—enthusiasm is contagious! *Smile,* be open and animated during the presentation so the clients feel the same energy. Flat, monotonic presentations are boring, they lack the luster and shine that a warm personality can add to the design. The clients will believe the design is good if the designer tells them it is, verbally and nonverbally.

(a)

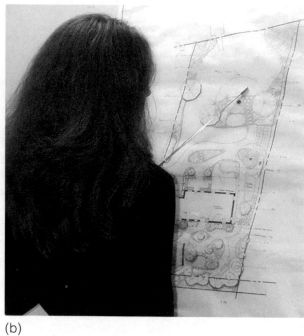

(b)

***Figure 10–2*  Make Eye Contact**
A presentation to a group or committee (or classroom). (a) Speak to the client about the design. (b) Do not speak to the design with your back to the client.

## Be Confident

Resist any temptation to bring undue attention to oversights or mistakes, particularly minor ones. Most people don't notice small mistakes unless they are pointed out. This is not to suggest lying about an inaccuracy. If needed, discuss it honestly and straight-forwardly while asking for feedback.

A poor approach to this example may be

> *"There is a barberry over there that has thorns and would scratch you when walk-ing by . . . that probably was not a good idea. I should have put something else there."*

Instead put a positive spin on the decision and, if needed, recommend a possible alternative.

> *"That's a barberry that will add color with deep red foliage throughout the summer. However, it does have thorns and if that looks like it would be problem, there are other plants that would work."*

## Be Prepared

Practice, practice, practice. This is especially true for a formal presentation to a group of people, such as a classroom or board of directors (Fig. 10–3). This is the key to good public speaking. The more it is practiced, the more familiar it becomes. For many people it is hard to think clearly when addressing a group, which makes it easy to for-get topics and details, often resulting in a person "freezing" because the train of thought is too disrupted. Being familiar with the information makes it much easier to know the

***Figure 10–3*  Practice the Presentation**
Going over note cards to remind the student about the order and key points of the presentation is helpful to keep it smooth and organized.

order of presentation. Make **note cards** of all the points that you want to cover and go through the presentation alone a few times. This helps you become familiar with the flow of the presentation and what direction it may go.

# Starting the Presentation

Some designers like to begin by briefly discussing the analysis before pulling out the design. This explains how the design addresses the landscape potentials and solves problems. This may be a discussion with pictures or even include some rough sketches of the analysis.

## Start with the Positives

Clients may feel good about their property if they hear about the upside first. This may just be references to the potential of particular areas and how they can be developed.

## Don't Be Overly Critical of the Site

The existing landscape may be unimaginative and poorly installed. But some people may take criticism of their property personally, especially if they have been working on it. Opening a presentation by blatantly criticizing the residence may be offensive and cause the clients to be less receptive to new ideas.

## Display a Copy of the Design

Once initial discussions have concluded, roll out a copy of the design. This will be the copy the clients will keep.

### Orient the Client to the Plan Drawing

To many people, a plan drawing can be confusing. They may not recognize the house on the plan. In this case, quickly orient them to what they are looking at. Briefly mention, "This is the front door of the house, the front yard is here, and of course this would be the backyard." It can be as quick as that and would avoid the look of confusion on their faces and prevent them from feeling embarrassed to ask a simple question like "Where's the garage?"

### Explain the Plan Details

It's a good idea to briefly explain a few other concepts that you may take for granted, such as scale. Briefly state, "This plan is drawn so that every 1/8 inch is equal to 1 foot." Then refer to the graphical scale to show them what a 5- or 10-foot line looks like.

Other things might include which way is north, property lines, right-of-way, and easements.

# Present in an Orderly Fashion

Have some order in the way the design is presented. For example, start in the front yard and cover all the points before moving to the side yard then to the backyard. The one thing to avoid is jumping all over the design, from front to back to front to side . . . in no apparent order. It's easier to follow along when presented in an organized, sequential manner.

# Introduce the Design Goals

Ease into the presentation with an overview of the goals that the design achieves. Give the "big picture" of the design first, what they can expect to see in the design. This may repeat some of the requests from the interview organized into a checklist. Some examples are

"Approached your residence with low maintenance in mind . . . "

"Since you don't care for mowing, this design reduces the amount of turf . . . "

"Created comfortable areas for entertaining and relaxation . . . "

"Developed some interesting views from the back of the house . . . "

"This design will improve the curb appeal of your residence . . . "

# Know the Plant Material

The designer is the expert; therefore he or she should know the contents of the design with minimal referencing. Know what every symbol represents. Many beginning students, as a result of being unprepared or extremely nervous, rely on looking up all the symbols in the plant list. This can give the impression of unfamiliarity with the design.

The designer should be intimately familiar with the plant material to answer any additional questions a client may have about it. This will include discussing outstanding qualities or the reasons it was selected, such as

When does it bloom?

What color does it bloom?

Does it handle dry conditions?

How fast does it grow?

## Repeat the Clients' Requests

Instill competence in the design by repeating the clients' requests (from the interview) and show them how it has been incorporated in the design. This helps the client recognize how the design addresses their wants and needs. Statements may include

"You mentioned you liked palms . . . "

"During the interview, you said you liked scented plants . . . "

"You were interested in creating an entertainment area and deck . . . "

"Because you don't like the neighbor's view into your backyard . . . "

"You spend a lot of time looking out the office window . . . "

"Since you don't like backing out of the driveway . . . "

## Explain the Design Concepts

You may need to explain the design concepts because many people will not understand the significance of repeating plant material to create a sense of connection, or how placing certain plants of unique character creates interesting views, or the effect of sweeping lines in the beds. For instance, briefly explain how, "I've used Indian Hawthorne in these three areas to create a sense of connection, by means of visual recall, between the front and side yard." Another example is, "This is a sharply variegated plant that will draw your attention to this part of the yard as you enter the back and will help provide a sense of direction."

## Address the Analysis

The analysis was discussed briefly in the beginning of the presentation, but be sure to repeat these points during the presentation. This helps explain how the design will improve the functional aspect of the property.

Widen the sidewalk for better access?

Accommodate two people?

Interesting approach?

Screen the air-conditioning unit?

Accent an interesting view or plant?

# Visually Support Your Design

Verbal descriptions may be very good, but nothing works like actually seeing the product (Fig. 10–4).

## Books and Catalogs

Use books or catalogs to give the client a visual idea of certain aspects of the design (Fig. 10–5). This is helpful when discussing outstanding characteristics of specimen plants or the look of hardscape materials. It can be useful to show someone what bluestone looks like, or a particular paving pattern like herringbone. Other examples can be water features, fountains, flowers, fruit, retaining walls, arbors, and fence construction.

***Figure 10–4*  Visual Support**
This student, presenting to a church group, has ample visual support—pictures, digital imagery, and samples.

***Figure 10–5*  Books and Catalogs**
Pictures from books and catalogs can help clients visualize plants and materials used in the design.

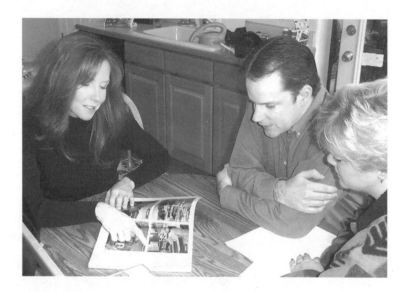

Some designers include pictures of plants and material in their portfolio to always have a reference available.

## Personalize the Visual Support

One way to personalize the visual aids is to use plant software (see Appendix B) to print pictures of each plant and material in the design. These images can be loosely bound together and given along with the design for reference, or can be recorded on a compact disc.

In addition to photos, a brief explanation of each plant's characteristics and its management provides the client with comprehensive information about the design they can refer back to at a later time. These little blurbs can be saved in a document and each time the plant is used in different projects it can be simply cut and pasted to the client's plant list.

# Elevation Illustrations

Many people will have difficulty imagining three-dimensional aspects from the bird's-eye view of the plan drawing (Fig. 10–6). To help them visualize the idea, it is helpful to provide an **elevated drawing,** even if it is a rough sketch.

**Figure 10–6   Section Elevations**
Elevated drawings can help the client visualize the design concept and spatial
relationships.

# Digital Imaging

With the aid of computer design, a client can see what the proposed design looks like
on their house (Fig. 10–7). This sidesteps the artistic interpretation of the planting and
uses an actual picture of the house while images of plants and other materials are
blended into the photo. Car dealers rely on buyers seeing, touching, driving, and even
smelling (new car smell!) the car to get them to visualize themselves owning it. The
automobile is a very tangible product that can hook the buyer. The landscape design
is a product that relies on descriptions, sketches, and imagination that is ultimately
*intangible*. **Digital imaging** makes the design more real because it appears as an actual photo of the project.

(a)

(b)

(c)

***Figure 10-7*** **Digital Imaging Software**
(a) The designer is presenting computer-generated renditions of the design. Computer graphics can be used to build a picture of the design. (b) Before and (c) after.

# Plant and Hardscape Samples

When appropriate, have samples of some of the material in the landscape design. This would be limited to materials that are a highlight of the design, such as stone tile on the patio or exceptional foliage or flower. In these cases, bring in a sample of the stone tile or a cutting of the foliage or flower (if available). Clients are more excited with the design when they can see the and feel elements of it.

Word of caution, don't overdue samples. Limit them to the special elements, such as accents and specimens. Too many samples can be overwhelming.

# Concluding the Presentation

Quite often the client will have questions that come up that you will answer during the course of the presentation. Once you have covered all the points of the design, ask if there are any final questions or input that the clients would like to add.

## Set a Date for the Next Meeting or Conclude the Contract

If presenting a preliminary design, be sure to agree on the next meeting to give the clients the **master plan** and collect the rest of your fees. If this is the presentation of the master plan, then collect the remainder of the contract due and conclude the transaction.

# Summary

The presentation is as important as the design itself. It should be informative so that the client better understands the functional and design aspects as well as the plant material. It should not be simply reading the plant list to the client without explanation. The presentation should explain why plants were selected and their value to the design. It should address the analysis to explain the functionality of the design. And the presentation should visually support the design with pictures from catalogs and software or digital imaging.

# Key Words

**Digital imaging:** software used to create the design from a picture of the site

**Elevated drawing:** sketch that illustrates width and height of design

**Foam board:** used to mount design for presentation

**Master plan:** the final design that includes all detail, specifications, and names

**Note cards:** used to prepare key points for presentation

**Posterboard:** see foam board

**Print:** a copy of original drawing presented to client

# A The Design Process

This appendix is an in-depth look at the landscape design project (Ann and Jeff Grant) illustrated in this text. It contains a lengthy interview with the clients and an inventory and analysis of the site. The third section is an example of presenting the design to the Grants. The fourth section contains all the drawings illustrated throughout the text sequentially arranged, ending with the final master plan.

# Grant Interview

## Family

**How many family members?**

- Ann, 52, works as a full-time nurse
- Jeff, 55, teaches English at a local college
- Children are grown up
- Grandchildren, ages 2 to 11, frequently come to visit

**Are there any allergies to consider, such as bees or to specific plants?**

None.

**Are there any pets to consider?**

Ann has a toy poodle that is mostly an indoor pet.

## Design Goals

Ann and Jeff had several items they wanted to address:

- Widen the driveway to develop a turnabout.
- Develop perennial and herb beds, as well as her gardening nook.
- Reduce the maintenance of the front drainage ditch.
- Screen some of the views coming into their yard.
- Develop a wildlife habitat to attract birds and butterflies to the backyard.
- Create an informal, low-maintenance landscape in their front yard.

## Lifestyle

**What kind of things do you do in the** . . .

**Front yard?**

They spend little time in the front, other than going from the driveway to the front door or from the front door to around the corner of the house.

**Side yard?**

The left side of the house has the driveway so it's mainly just to get from the front to the back. The right side of the house is where Ann would like to develop a gardening work area.

### Backyard?

They spend most of their time here, either relaxing on the patio, gardening, or playing with the grandchildren.

## Hobby

### Do you have any outdoor hobbies?

Ann loves to work in the garden and would like to develop areas for herbs, perennials, and vegetables. Jeff is mainly an indoor person.

They're interested in developing a playground for the grandchildren.

## Entertaining

### Do you spend time entertaining guests?

Besides family, they usually only have a few friends over on occasion. For the most part it's just the two of them relaxing with a great view to the marsh.

They would like to improve their sitting area but not really expand it.

### Do you need to develop an area for outdoor cooking and eating?

No. They rarely cook outside.

## Views

### Are there views you would like to keep?

They purchased the house because of the exceptional view over the marsh.

### Are there views you would like to block?

They spend a lot of time in the office, which has a large bay window looking over the front and another looking out to the backyard. They want to keep the view open to the backyard but would like to create a screening from the road into the front window.

### Are there any unpleasant items to be screened?

They don't care for the view of the neighbor's privacy fence, which appears barren, or the telephone pole and fire hydrant in the front yard.

### What about from inside the house?

Ann also spends a lot of time looking out a small kitchen window and would like to develop something pleasant to look at.

They also have a grand view from the living room to the marsh, which they want to keep.

### Is there any need for more privacy from neighbors' views?

They'd like to have a bit more privacy in the backyard from the neighbors on each side, not anything enclosing, just something partial.

# Taste

### Do you prefer informal, natural areas, or formal, well-defined areas?

They insist on something natural looking.

Their living habits reflect a stylish, unkempt appearance; large bookcases, scuffed wooden floors, antique chairs.

### What level of maintenance would you care to have?

They want very little lawn and would prefer a low-maintenance approach. Although Ann will spend lots of time tending to gardens and flowers, she doesn't want to maintain trees, shrubs, and turf.

### What are your favorite plants?

Anything that is fragrant. Gardenia, Tea Olive, Jasmine . . . things like that. Also plants that attract birds and butterflies.

Things that are unique; more specifically, things that aren't commonly found in most landscapes.

### What are your least favorite plants?

Anything that is thorny.

### Ask if there's a yard they've seen that they really like.

No. But Ann would like to replicate some of the garden styles she's seen at local botanical gardens.

### Ask about other parts of a design they may be interested in looking at.

They're not really interested in developing any other amenities in great detail.

# Grant Residence Inventory and Analysis

Let's take an example of a residence to analyze the inventory (Fig. A–1). The Grant residence will be illustrated with pictures taken on site (Fig. A–2). From the initial interview, the following information was gathered:

***Figure A–1*** **Grant Residence Camera Angles**
These are camera angles that correspond to the following figures.

***Figure A–2*  Grant Residence**
Front of house from road.

***Figure A–3*  Grant Residence**
The gardening area on side of
house. Keep access available to
front and backyard.

**How many family members are there?**

Two. Ann and her husband, Jeff.

**Are there kids and what ages are they?**

None in the house. All grown up and moved away.

**Are there any allergies to be aware of?**

None.

**Are there any pets to consider?**

Yes. A small toy poodle. He spends limited time outdoors and is too small to cause any problems in the yard.

**Are there any hobbies?**

Yes. Gardening. Ann would like to develop an area with a compost bin and bench for gardening (Fig. A–3).

*Analysis:* Develop area for gardening that has privacy and is accessible.

**Do the clients entertain guests?**

Very few. Most of their time is spent amongst themselves.

*Analysis:* Limit the entertainment area to a few people and include more privacy.

# House

### Color of the house and materials

Tan siding with light blue shutters.

### Locate doors and windows

Doors and windows were located. The kitchen window is left of the front door and about 5 feet off the ground. The office, which is a converted garage, has large bay windows that are only a few feet off the ground.

*Analysis:* Avoid tall plantings in front of the office windows.

# Circulation

## Parking

### How many cars does the client want to accommodate?

Two. Currently there is not enough room for both cars. They have difficulty getting cars out because they are parked single file (Fig. A–4). They have also expressed concern about having to back out onto the road that is often busy with traffic, and their view is partially obstructed. They would like to look at ideas of parking side-by-side and also being able to turn the car around before pulling out onto the road.

*Analysis:* Widen the driveway and develop a turnabout so that the cars are not blocked in and can get to the road without backing out.

### Where are the major paths of foot traffic?

Major foot traffic is from the driveway to the house (Fig. A–5). Currently there is no path or sidewalk established. The only sidewalk leads from the front door straight out to the road, which Ann and Jeff say is never used.

*Analysis:* Develop a hardscape path from the driveway to the front of the house to accommodate traffic from the house and road.

### How would guests approach the house?

Up the driveway.

*Figure A–4* **Grant Residence**
The driveway is not large enough to accommodate two cars. The residents would also like to develop a turnabout.

(a)

(b)

***Figure A–5*** **Grant Residence**
(a) The entrance lacks a warm, accommodating approach. The entry walk will be rerouted. (b) The most common path of primary circulation to the front door.

***Figure A–6*** **Grant Residence**
The right side of the front yard needs better definition from the neighbor. Keep secondary circulation open to the side yard.

### Is the traffic around both sides of the house or just one?

In order to get to the backyard, people walk up the driveway and around the house. Ann also walks from the front door around the right side of the house when she is gardening (Fig. A–6).

*Analysis:* Keep the access available to the right side of the house from the front.

### What about movement from the side and back doors?

There are no side doors. There is a back door that opens into the living room and out onto the back patio.

### Is there adequate space for each one?

No. The back patio is too small to sit comfortably and funnels up a narrow set of stairs (Fig. A–7).

*Analysis:* Improve the circulation over the back patio and create a more usable space.

*Figure A–7* **Grant Residence**
Entertainment area is small, lacks interest
and enclosure, and is crowded.

## Pavement

### Are the materials suitable for each path?

There are no materials for paths. The driveway contains gravel that lacks edging and
scatters out into the yard.

*Analysis:* Develop a warm path to the front door. Also improve the gravel drive contain-
ment and consider a warmer material.

### Is the material in good condition?

The loose gravel is appropriate for the informal style of Ann and Jeff's yard. There could
be a better material that is warmer.

### Does it look visually appealing?

No. Primarily due to the lack of edging.

### Is it functional?

No. It is too small for the cars and does not facilitate foot traffic.

## Secondary Paths

### Is the turf suitable?

Yes. There's not enough traffic to require hard pavement.

### What about inexpensive paths of mulch and gravel?

Leaving an opening around the right side of the front, possibly mulch, would be suitable.

# Utilities

### Is there a septic tank?

No.

### Are there overhead lines?

Yes. Along the road over the right-of-way and from the front corner of the yard to the
front right corner of the house.

*Analysis:* Avoid tall plantings that would interfere with the overhead lines.

**Are there air-conditioning units and washer/dryer exhaust?**

The air-conditioning unit is on the right side of the house.

*Analysis:* The air-conditioning unit does not appear to be a visual nuisance.

**Are there other visual utilities that still need access such as gas meters?**

Yes. Ann doesn't like the telephone pole that is in the front right corner of the yard.

*Analysis:* Screen the telephone pole from the house.

# Additions

**Are there any additions that don't appear on the site plan?**

Yes. There is a storage shed in the backyard.

*Analysis:* Keep the access available to the shed. Consider moving the shed to allow adequate space for the addition.

**Are there any future additions that will be accounted for?**

Yes. They will build an enclosed sunroom onto the back of the house.

# Views

## Bad Views

Yes. They don't care for the view of the neighbor's privacy fence along side of the yard and would like to screen it. Also, they would like to screen the telephone pole in the front yard.

*Analysis:* Plant to break up the long empty space of the neighbor's privacy fence.

## Good Views

There's an outstanding view to the marsh in the backyard that should not be obstructed (Fig. A–8).

*Analysis:* Avoid tall plantings in the backyard that would obstruct the view. Also, consider framing the view.

(a)

(b)

***Figure A–8*  Grant Residence**
(a) Outstanding view to marshy area from the house across large backyard. Keep the view unobstructed.
(b) View to right part of the backyard can use some visual interest and definition.

(a)

(b)

***Figure A–9*** **Grant Residence**
(a) View from office needs to remain unobstructed to marshy area. (b) View from office to front yard needs to remain open, but screen the view from the road into the office.

## Important Views

*Entertainment Area*

This will be the view to the marsh.

*Inside Views*

The bay window in the office looks out through the backyard to the marsh (Fig. A–9). The bay window looks into the front yard and is open to passing traffic. They both have expressed a desire to screen the view from the road.

*Analysis:* Screen the view of the traffic from the office window without obstructing the view of the front yard (Fig. A–9b).

*Kitchen Window*

They would like to create a view from the kitchen window since they spend a moderate amount of time in front of it.

*Analysis:* Create a view from the kitchen window into the front yard.

# Exposure

## Sun

*Full Sun*

The backyard is mostly full sun (Fig. A–10).

*Analysis:* The backyard plants need to be full-sun tolerant.

*Full Shade*

The front yard is mostly shade to partial shade due to the northern exposure and over-head trees.

*Analysis:* The front yard needs to be tolerant of partial shade.

**Figure A–10** **Grant Residence**
Backyard of residence.

*Time of Exposure*

Back of the house will be in the shade in the mid to late afternoon, while the front of the house will get dappled sun at that time.

# Wind

**Is the prevailing wind a problem?**

No.

# Temperature

**Is the Southwest exposure a problem?**

No.

# Salt

Brackish water in marsh.

Analysis: Use salt-tolerant plants.

# Existing Plants

**Do the owners want to get rid of any particular plants? Keep any?**

All plants are expendable except for the Live Oak and Pecan in the front yard.

*Analysis:* Avoid disturbing the existing Live Oak and Pecan.

# Soil

## Texture

Sandy soil. Beds should be amended with organic matter for moisture retention.

*Analysis:* Recommend amending planting beds with organic matter where possible.

## Soil Test

pH is good at 6.9. No other deficiencies.

# Drainage

### Foundation

House is built on a slab.

### Surface

No problems except for a low spot in the middle of the backyard. However, sandy soil drains rapidly.

### Downspouts and Gutters

There are no gutters. Runoff from roof does not appear to be a problem; the house is built on a slab.

# Traffic

Previously mentioned problem with view into office.

### Are there any concerns with obstructed views of traffic when pulling out of the driveway?

Difficult pulling out of driveway due to large Live Oak.

*Analysis:* Minimize plantings at the entrance. Allow for cars to pull out forward.

### Are there concerns with traffic and children?

No.

# Other Observations

The ditch. Ann and Jeff expressed a dislike for the drainage ditch running along the road in the front because it was difficult to maintain.

*Analysis:* Consider groundcover in the drainage ditch to reduce mowing, or installing drain pipe.

Wildlife. They love to attract birds, butterflies, and other wildlife and expressed an interest in developing a small habitat outside the office window in the backyard.

*Analysis:* Develop a wildlife habitat outside of office window in the backyard.

No turf. Ann didn't care for turf and asked for solutions that would reduce the amount of lawn in the front yard.

*Analysis:* Expand the beds in front yard to reduce lawn.

# Presenting the Master Plan

*The following is an abbreviated approach to presenting the master plan to the clients. Take note of how it explains how and why the design is laid out and plants are selected. Also note that pictures or examples of materials are shown to the client during the presentation, either printed on paper or from a laptop. All pictures can be burned to a CD and given to the client at the end of the presentation. Keep in mind that this design is located in hardiness zone 8b/9a.*

Before we get started, let me explain a few things about the design so you will get the most out of the presentation. This is a plan drawing that is like a bird's-eye view of your property, looking straight down on it from above. Here is your front door (pointing) and this is the back door (pointing). It is drawn to a 1/8″ scale, which means that every 1/8 of an inch is equivalent to 1 foot. You will also notice there is a plant list on the plan. Each one of the symbols is labeled with a key that can be found in the plant list that will identify it by the botanical and common name.

All right, if you have any questions about the design while I am presenting it, do not hesitate to ask. Let us start in the front yard and we will work our way toward the back.

Based on the interview, I have put together a plan that allows for plenty of planting space and working areas for gardening. It includes low-maintenance plants that provide a lot of variety and interest. These include plants of fragrance and attraction to birds and butterflies. You will find that this design not only provides you with a rich variety of sights, smells, and sounds but also creates a useful plan that addresses the activities of your home and property.

You had concerns about backing out of the driveway onto the busy road. As a result, the driveway has been expanded to allow room for a turnabout to pull out onto the road forward. The same crushed aggregate will remain in the drive, but the borders will be defined with edging materials to contain the aggregate and maintain a sharp edge. Off the end of the driveway, the neighbor's fence, which you didn't care to see, will be covered with Crossvine, which has vivid orange, tubular flowers in the spring and, in addition, attracts hummingbirds.

The entry walk that went directly out to the street and was seldom used has been removed from the middle of the yard and routed from the turnabout of the driveway. Guests from the road or parking will approach the house up the driveway. The walkway will be constructed with a beige flagstone (example of material shown to client), which is an irregular stone that is a few inches thick and will pick up the color of the siding. This stone will continue onto the step and porch.

The rest of the front yard has been designed to reduce the amount of turf and increase the bed space. The turf in the front yard, as well as the back, will be St. Augustine, which handles the shade and full sun.

I have kept fragrance in mind by placing a Tea olive near the entrance that will flower in the late winter and early spring with a potent essence that should drift into the house during warm weather. You will see the Tea olive, as well as other plants and materials, repeated throughout the property in order to provide some continuity.

There are a variety of colors that will develop throughout the growing season. In the early spring the Loropetulam will flower bright pink with a dark burgandy foliage throughout the rest of the year; Crape myrtle will flower white in late spring with an interesting mottled trunk during the winter; Clethra will flower white in profuse numbers in midsummer; in late summer–early fall, Sweetgrass, planted in mass along the driveway, will bloom a soft, pink color while the Inkberry will set an interesting black fruit.

Also, at the entrance you will find the Fatsia, an interesting large, coarse foliage that will contrast nicely with the Inkberry along with a uniquely black, low-growing Mondograss, which will pick up the black fruit of the Inkberry. In addition there will be a cutleaf Japanese maple, which grows slow and low with a graceful form and soft texture.

At the ditch near the road where you wanted to reduce the maintenance, we discussed the possibility of filling in the ditch with a drainpipe but came to the conclusion it was too expensive. Instead, the ditch can be planted with a groundcover,

Liriope, which is a dark green, grassy plant that will spread effectively. It is a real tough plant that will cover the ground and require very little maintenance. This plant, as well as the Sweetgrass on the other side of the driveway, are low growing and will not hinder the view to the road when pulling out.

Here, where you were concerned with the view from the road into the office window, a Loropetulum will create a screen and the Sago palm will be a nice focal point to enhance the view from the office.

Over here is the telephone pole that you would like to screen from the house. This Arizona cypress, which is a bluish evergreen conifer, grows quickly and handles dry, hot conditions well.

Around the right side of the house there is an informal path that is paved in the planting bed with the same flagstone used on the front walk. It goes to the work area that is on the south side of the house where you will find plenty of space on a workbench to store pots and materials for gardening, in addition to the compost bin. The large oak trees in the neighbor's yard protect the southern exposure, so this will be a comfortable place to work. The area is framed by Crape myrtles for overhead enclosure during the summer; you will also have Tea olives to provide fragrance in late winter and early spring. From the work area there is direct access to the storage shed that is relocated to allow room for the sunroom addition.

In the backyard there are two large areas reserved for herbs, annuals, or perennials. The right side of the yard is defined with a bed that extends to the back property line and partially screens the view from the neighbor's yard. The bed includes Elaeagnus, which is a tough shrub with unique evergreen foliage that will grow 8 to 10 feet or taller; Abelia has attractive, shiny reddish foliage that flowers white in the spring; the Sweetgrass that is planted along the driveway is also planted in mass along the back; Pampasgrass grows 8- to 10-feet tall with outstanding plumes in the summer. The Lantana, which are low-growing perennials, flower yellow all summer long and attract butterflies.

The view to the marsh is preserved with an open area on the left and low plantings along the right. Right outside the office window there are several plantings that attract birds, hummingbirds, and butterflies. They are low growing and will not obstruct the view to the marsh. There is also a Gardenia planted near the office window that has extremely fragrant flowers in the summer and will fill the corner and office with a wonderful smell.

This large tree outside the office is called a Goldenrain tree. It is covered with yellow flowers in the spring and sets fruit in a cluster of dry capsules in the late summer, which rustles in the wind like rain is falling.

Further down the fence is a group of shrubs called Butterfly bushes that, as the name implies, are very attractive to butterflies. In front of the shrubs is Lantana, which also attacts butterflies.

Since the back deck was very cramped and provided little more than a walkway from the back door, I have expanded it to include bench seating for a couple of people and planters for annuals to provide color that can also be seen from inside the house. The Natchez crape myrtle is planted next to the deck in order to provide some overhead enclosure and color from the bark and flowers. The same flagstone used in the front yard and work area will create a wide landing area at the bottom of the steps and continue through the planting bed to the left side of the house.

That concludes the presentation of the landscape design, are there any questions that I can answer for you?

# ANALYSIS

**Graphical Analysis**
The analysis of the inventory done graphically on the site plan.

CONCEPT A

**Concept Plans**

Three concept plans organize the ground plane in a different arrangement, each one addresses the analysis.

*(continues)*

**Concept Plans—continued**

Three concept plans organize the ground plane in a different arrangement, each one addresses the analysis.

*(continues)*

CONCEPT C

## Concept Plans—continued

Three concept plans organize the ground plane in a different arrangement, each one addresses the analysis.

PRELIMINARY SKETCH A

## Preliminary Sketches

Using a concept plan, or combinations of concept plans, a preliminary design takes shape. Sketches are useful in defining the ground plane and getting a rough idea of plant size and placement.

*(continues)*

PRELIMINARY SKETCH B

## Preliminary Sketches—continued

Using a concept plan, or combinations of concept plans, a preliminary design takes shape. Sketches are useful in defining the ground plane and getting a rough idea of plant size and placement.

PRELIMINARY PLAN A

GRANT RESIDENCE
724 WEST MARKET ST
ANYTOWN, USA

PELICAN DESIGNS

## Preliminary Design

Two preliminary designs are developed with generic plant symbols and ground plane textures. They convey the arrangement, flow, and balance of the design concept without the details of specific plants and materials. They will be used to get feedback from the client.

*(continues)*

PRELIMINARY PLAN B

NORTH

GRANT RESIDENCE
724 WEST MARKET ST
ANYTOWN, USA

PELICAN DESIGNS

## Preliminary Design—continued

Two preliminary designs are developed with generic plant symbols and ground plane textures. They convey the arrangement, flow, and balance of the design concept without the details of specific plants and materials. They will be used to get feedback from the client.

## Master Sketch

A sketch of the master plan helps specify the ideas of the master plan.

The master plan includes a plant key/legend table:

| KEY | BOTANICAL NAME | COMMON NAME | QTY | SIZE | NOTES |
|---|---|---|---|---|---|
| AEG | Abelia x 'Edward Goucher' | Edward Goucher Abelia | 21 | 3 gal | |
| AP | Acer palmatum 'Dissectum' | Cutleaf Japanese Maple | 1 | 10 gal | |
| BC | Bignonia capreolata | Crossvine | 7 | 1 gal | |
| BT | Berberis thunbergii var. Atropurpurea 'Crimson Pygmy' | Japanese Barberry | 1 | 3 gal | |
| CA | Clethra alnifolia 'Compacta' | Summersweet | 7 | 3 gal | |
| CB | Callistemon citrinus 'Compacta' | Dwarf Bottlebrush | 3 | 3 gal | |
| CR | Cycas revoluta | Sago Palm | 2 | 30 gal | |
| CS | Cortaderia selloana | Pampas Grass | 1 | 3 gal | |
| CAR | Cupressus arizonica | Arizona Cypress | 1 | 30 gal | |
| EP | Elaeagnus pungens | Elaeagnus | 5 | 5 gal | |
| FJ | Fatsia japonica | Fatsia | 3 | 3 gal | |
| FS | Feijoa sellowiana | Pineapple Guava | 5 | 3 gal | |
| GA | Gardenia augusta | Gardenia | 5 | 3 gal | |
| IG | Ilex glabra 'Densa' | Inkberry | 15 | 1 gal | |
| KP | Koelreuteria paniculata | Goldenraintree | 1 | 1.5" cal | |
| LC | Lantana camara | Lantana | 17 | 1 gal | |
| LCH | Loropetalum chinense | Fringetree | 9 | 5 gal | |
| LN | Lagerstroemia x 'Natchez' | Natchez Crape Myrtle | 3 | 30 gal | |
| LS | Liriope spicata | Liriope | 300 | 4" | 12" O.C. |
| MB | Mahonia bealei | Mahonia | 3 | 3 gal | |
| MC | Muhlenbergia capillaris | Sweetgrass | 54 | 1 gal | |
| OF | Osmanthus fragrans | Tea Olive | 3 | 5 gal | |
| OP | Ophiopogon planiscapus 'Nigrescens' | Black Mondograss | 50 | 4" | 6" O.C. |
| QV | Quercus virginiana | Live Oak | 1 | 1.5" cal | |
| WF | Weigela florida | Weigela | 1 | 3 gal | |

MASTER PLAN

GRANT RESIDENCE
724 WEST MARKET ST
ANYTOWN, USA

PELICAN DESIGNS

## Master Plan

The master plan is the final plan in the design process; it specifies all plants and other materials.

# B  Software and Books

Most of the following books and software are sold by the American Nurseryman Publishing Company (http://www.amerinursery.com), or at other book retailers.

## Software

*Betrock's Guide to Landscape Palms CD*, Alan W. Meerow, Ph.D.
*The Color Encyclopedia of Ornamental Grasses on CD-ROM*, Rick Darke
*Field Notes CD-ROM*, American Nurseryman Publishing Company
Horticopia Titles
  *Horticopia A–Z*
  *Horticopia: Herbaceous SE Library*
  *Horticopia: Woody SE Library*
  *Horticopia Professional XE Package*
*The Interactive Guide for Herbaceous Perennial Plants*, Allan M. Armitage
*The Interactive Manual of Woody Landscape Plants on CD-ROM*, Michael A. Dirr
*Landscaping Plants and Trees*, Delmar Publishers
*Michael A. Dirr's Photo-Library of Woody Landscape Plants on CD-ROM*, Michael A. Dirr
*Ornamental Plants Plus 3.5*, Michigan Landscape and Nursery Association and Michigan State University Extension
*This is Gardening*, Allan Armitage (annuals and perennials)
*Water Gardening CD-ROM*

## Internet Links

### Google

*http://www.google.com*

> When in doubt, go to Google and click the "Images" tab, then search for the plant.
> Your search will yield all the photos of that plant on the Internet found by Google.

### Salisbury University Arboretum

*http://www.salisbury.edu/arboretum/*

> Salisbury University in Maryland; Great photos!

### Landscape Plants of the Upper Midwest

*http://www.midwestlandscapeplants.org*

> University of Wisconsin; Great photos and plant selector, also an audio file to pronounce names

## Oregon State University, Landscape Plants, Volume 1

*http://oregonstate.edu/dept/ldplants/*

Oregon State University; Excellent photos from large database

## Connecticut College Arboretum

*http://arboretum.conncoll.edu/*

Connecticut College; Adequate photos arranged by family

## Ornamental Plants plus Version 3.0

*http://www.msue.msu.edu/msue/imp/modzz/masterzz.html*

Michigan State University; No photos on Web site, can purchase photos on CD

## Missouri Botanical Gardens

*http://www.mobot.org/MOBOT/otherwww.html*

Missouri Botanical Garden; Comprehensive list of links

## Horticulture on the Internet

*http://www.ces.ncsu.edu/depts/hort/consumer/hortinternet/*

NC State University; Great comprehensive list of photos, links, and horticulture information

## Gymnosperm Database: Links

*http://www.botanik.uni-bonn.de/conifers/links.htm#1*

Gymnosperm Database; Numerous links to other plant databases

## The University of Delaware Botanical Gardens

*http://ag.udel.edu/udbg/botanic_garden/Visit%20the%20garden.html*

University of Delaware Botanical Gardens; Good collection of plant descriptions and photos

## University of Connecticut Plant Database

*http://www.hort.uconn.edu/plants/index.html*

University of Connecticut; Excellent database of photos and plant selector, also an audio file to pronounce names

## US National Arboretum Plant Photo Gallery

*http://www.usna.usda.gov/PhotoGallery/index.html*

United States National Arboretum; Photos of daylilies, crape myrtles, and azaleas

## PLANTS National Database

*http://plants.usda.gov/*

United States Dept of Agriculture; Source of plant photos and information

### Floridata

*http://www.floridata.com/*

Floridata Marketplace; Good source of photos, descriptions, and other horticulture related items, organized into plant categories including flowers, herbs, trees, palms, etc.

### Palm and Cycad Societies of Florida

*http://www.plantapalm.com/*

Source of palm photos and information

### Evergreen Nursery

*http://www.qualitygroundcovers.com/*

Evergreen Nursery, Inc; Great source of groundcover photos

### San Felasco Nurseries, Inc.

*http://www.sanfelasco.com/g_products.asp*

San Felasco Nurseries; Great source for photos and links

### Monrovia Nursery

*http://www.monrovia.com*

Monrovia Nurseries; Great source of photos and criteria filter

### HortiPlex Plant Database

*http://hortiplex.gardenweb.com/plants/*

Very extensive database of plant information and pictures

### Plants Database

*http://plantsdatabase.com/*

Locate plant information and pictures by name

### Plantfacts

*http://plantfacts.osu.edu/*

Lots of plant photos! Easy to navigate through the site.

### Greathouse Butterfly Farm, Inc.

*http://www.greathousebutterflies.com/*

Good information of butterflies and gardening

# Books

### Trees and Shrubs

*The American Horticultural Society A–Z Encyclopedia of Garden Plants,* C. Brickell and J. Zuk
*The American Horticultural Society Encyclopedia of Garden*
*The American Horticultural Society Gardening Manual,* Gillian Roberts

*Botanica's Trees and Shrubs*
*The Botanical Garden*, R. Phillips and M. Rix
*Broad-Leaved Evergreens*, Stephen G. Haw
*Choosing Plant Conbinations*, Cathy Wilkinson Barash
*The Complete Plant Selection Guide for Landscape Design*, Marc C. Stoecklein
*Conifers*, D. M. Van Gelderen and J. R. P. Van Hoey Smith
*Dirr's Hardy Trees and Shrubs*, Michael A. Dirr
*Dirr's Trees and Shrubs for Warm Climates*, Michael A. Dirr
*The Encyclopedia of North American Trees*, Sam Benvie
*The Encyclopedia of Planting Combinations*, Tony Lord
*Garden Plants*, C. Brickell and J. Zuk
*Gardening with Conifers*, Adrian Bloom
*Great Plant Guide*, The American Horticultural Society
*The Illustrated Book of Trees*, W. C. Grimm
*Landscape Plants*, Ferrell M. Bridwell
*Manual of Woody Landscape Plants*, Michael A. Dirr
*Native Trees, Shrubs, and Vines*, William Cullina
*Native Trees, Shrubs, and Vines for Urban and Rural America*, Gary L. Hightshoe
*Pictorial Library of Landscape Plants, Vol. 1*, Dr. Jane Coleman Helmer; *Vol. 2*,
    Dr. Ruth Fortune Woods
*Plants*, Christopher Brickell and John Elsley
*Plants for American Landscape*, N. G. Odenwald, ASLA, C. F. Fryling, Jr., ASLA, and
    T. E. Pope
*The Random House Book of Shrubs*, Roger Phillips and Martyn Rix
*The Random House Book of Trees of North America and Europe*, Roger Phillips
*Right Plant, Right Place*, Nicola Ferguson
*Trees and Shrubs for Flowers*, Glyn Church
*Trees and Shrubs for Foliage*, Glyn Church
*Trees and Shrubs for Fragrance*, Glyn Church
*Trees for Urban and Suburban Landscapes*, Edward F. Gilman
*Xeriscape Plant Guide*, David Winger

## Herbaceous Plants (Flowers, Groundcovers, Herbs, etc.)

*Annuals and Biennials*, R. Phillips and M. Rix
*Annuals with Style*, M. A. Ruggiero and T. Christopher
*Armitage's Garden Perennials*, Allan M. Armitage
*Armitage's Manual of Annuals, Biennials, and Half-Hardy Perennials*, Allan
    M. Armitage
*Bamboo for Gardens*, Ted Jordan Meredith
*Botanica's Annuals and Perennials*,
*Continuous Bloom*, Pam Duthie
*Designing with Perennials*, Pamela J. Harper
*An Encyclopedia of Shade Perennials*, W. George Schmid
*Hardy Herbaceous Perennials*, Leo Jelitto and Wilhelm Schacht
*Herbaceous Perennial Plants*, Allan M. Armitage
*Landscaping with Herbs*, James Adams
*Manual of Herbaceous Ornamental Plants*, Steven M. Still
*Perennial Combinations*, C. Colston Burrell

*Perennial Ground Covers*, David S. MacKenzie
*Perennials*, R. Phillips and M. Rix
*Taylor's Guide to Ground Covers*, N. Sinton and D. C. Michener
*The Well-Tended Perennial Garden*, Tracy DiSabato-Aust

## Ornamental Grasses

*Color Encyclopedia of Ornamental Grasses*, Rick Darke
*The Encyclopedia of Ornamental Grasses*, John Greenlee
*Gardening with Grasses*, M. King and P. Oudolf
*Taylor's Guide to Ornamental Grasses*, Edited by R. Holmes and F. Tenenbaum

## Palms

*Betrock's Guide to Landscape Palms*, Alan W. Meerow
*Cultivated Palms of the World*, D. Ellison and A. Ellison
*Ornamental Palm Horticulture*, Tim Broschat and Alan Meerow
*Tropical Ornamentals*, W. Arthur Whistler

## Estimation

*Estimating for Landscape and Irrigation Contractors*, James Huston
*Grounds Maintenance Estimating Guidelines*, Professional Grounds Management Society
*Landscape Designer and Estimator's Guide*, National Landscape Association
*Lanscape Estimating and Contract Administration*, S. Angley, E. Horsey and D. Roberts
*Landscape Estimating Methods*, Sylvia Hollman Chattin
*Means Site Work and Landscape Cost Data*
*Time-Saver Standards for Landscape Architecture*, C. Harris and N. Dines

## Water Gardening

*The American Horticultural Socitey Complete Guide to Water Gardening*, Peter Robinson
*Gardening*, Peter Robinson
*The Master Book of the Water Garden*, Philip Swindells
*Rock and Water Gardening*, Peter Robinson
*The Ultimate Water Garden Book*, Jean-Claude Arnoux
*The Water Garden Design Book*, Y. Rees and P. May

## Hardscaping

*Brick in the Landscape*, Rob W. Sovinski
*Complete Construction*, Christine Beall
*A Guide to Dry Stone Walling*, Andy Radford
*Landscape Specification Guidelines*, Landscape Contractor Association
*Stonework*, Charles McRaven

# C | Estimating the Materials

Some designers continue on beyond the design and prepare a materials list and bid for installation. A freelance designer may prepare a formal bid and give it to several companies for installation. There are some basic calculations that can be made to get an accurate estimate of the materials in the design.

## Square Footage

Materials like sod and hardscaping will require the amount of square footage to estimate amounts (Fig. C–1). There are four basic geometric shapes that can be used to estimate square footage:

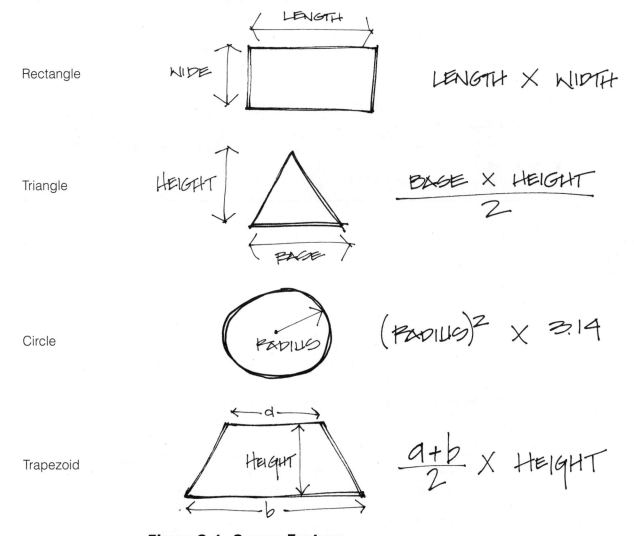

Rectangle

Triangle

Circle

Trapezoid

**Figure C–1   Square Footage**
Square footage of basic geometric areas include rectangle, triangle, circle, and trapezoid.

### *Figure C–2*  **Estimating Area on the Plan**
With a piece of tracing paper over the master plan, square footage can be estimated with a scale by dividing large areas into smaller geometric areas to calculate total amount of material requirements.

These simple formulas can be easily applied to shapes that conform to a rectangle, triangle, circle or trapezoid . Unfortunately most often the areas are irregular and don't fit to a single shape. Irregular areas are estimated by breaking them up into smaller components of rectangles, circles, triangles, and trapezoids until all of the space is accounted for, then the smaller parts can be summed up to equal the total square footage.

These estimates can be calculated by placing tracing paper over the master plan and using a scale to sketch out square footage (Fig. C–2).

---

### *Tip Box*

Many items are estimated by the number of **palettes** to complete the job, such as sod or stone. Palettes can be estimated by dividing the total square footage of area by the square footage a palette will cover.

---

# Volume

Materials like mulch, sand, and gravel will require estimates of volume (Fig. C–3). Mulch, for instance, can be supplied in bulk in cubic yards or bags in cubic feet. To calculate volume,

1. Calculate the square footage of the area
   To estimate mulching requirements of a bed, estimate the square footage of the bed. For example, 200 square feet.

2. Determine how deep the material required needs to be.
   For example, 4 inches deep

3. Convert depth into feet.
   If the depth is in inches, divide by 12 to convert to depth in feet. (For example, four inches divided by 12 = 0.33 feet deep.) This is to keep all the measurements in the same units, square feet and depth in feet, in order to correctly calculate cubic feet. They cannot be calculated if measurements are feet and inches.

***Figure C–3a*** **Volume**
Volume can be calculated with the use of square footage and depth.

4. Calculate cubic feet
   Multiply square footage and depth. For example, 200 square feet X 0.33 feet deep = 66 cubic feet.

5. Calculate cubic yards
   Divide cubic feet by 27. For example, 66 cubic feet divided by 27 = 2.4 cubic yards.

CUBIC FEET ——→ CUBIC YARDS

$$\text{CUBIC FEET} \div 27 = \text{CUBIC YARDS}$$

CUBIC YARD

3'

3'

3'

ONE CUBIC YARD $= 3' \times 3' \times 3'$

$= 27 \text{ CUBIC FEET}$

***Figure C–3b*** **Volume**
Volume can be calculated with the use of square footage and depth.

# Materials

The following are common materials in the design that will have to be estimated by square footage, palettes, cubic feet, or yards.

# Sod

Sod will require square footage for an estimate and most often palettes of sod will be required. Sod is sold in rolls or square pieces but is often delivered in bulk on palettes for large jobs (Fig. C–4). In many cases, depending on the type of turf, one palette of sod will cover approximately 500 square feet (check with supplier).

To estimate the number of palettes required, divide the total square footage by 500 square feet (Fig. C–5).

**Figure C–4   Palette of Sod**
Sod is usually ordered and delivered on palettes that normally cover about 500 square feet (check with the supplier).

**Figure C–5   Estimating Palettes**
Divide total square by the number of square feet a palette will cover.

# Concrete

Concrete will require square footage for an estimate. In most cases, a 4-inch deep slab is suitable and will be subcontracted by a concrete company. They will use the square footage to give an estimate.

# Pavers

Pavers require square footage for an estimate. In order to estimate the number of pavers required, it will take some additional math.

1. Get square inches of the paver.

   For instance, a brick paver may measure 8 inches by 4 inches (Fig. C–6). Calculate square inches of the paver by multiplying length times width.

   $$8 \times 4 = 32 \text{ square inches}$$

2. Convert square inches to square footage.

   Every paver occupies 32 square inches of space. The area of the brick will be divided into the total square footage of the paving. But first it must be converted into square feet, the same units of the total area. One square foot = 144 square inches. To convert square inches into square feet, divide by 144 (Fig. C–7).

   $$32 \text{ square inches} \div 144 \text{ square inches} = 0.22 \text{ square feet}$$

3. Divide the total area by the square footage of the paver

   This will get the total number of pavers.

   $$\text{Total area} \div 0.22 = \text{Number of pavers}$$

(a)

(b)

***Figure C–6*  Estimating Pavers**
To estimate paver requirements, measure the (a) length and (b) width of the paver.

8" 4"
PAVER
= 32 SQUARE INCHES

32 SQUARE INCHES ÷ 144 = 0.22 SQUARE FEET

TOTAL SQUARE FEET ÷ SQUARE FEET OF PAVER = NUMBER OF PAVERS

1' 1'
1 SQUARE FOOT

12" 12"
144 SQUARE INCHES

SQUARE INCHES ÷ 144 = SQUARE FEET

*Figure C–7* **Converting Square Inches into Square Feet**
To convert square inches into square feet, divide by 144.

Handwritten on figure:

4" ÷ 12" = 0.3

4" → 0.33'

40 SQUARE FEET × 0.33' DEEP = 13.3 CUBIC FEET

13.3 CUBIC FEET ÷ 27 = 0.5 CUBIC YARD

1 CUBIC YARD SAND ≈ 1.5 TON

0.5 CUBIC YARD × 1.5 = 0.75 TON SAND

**Figure C–8  Estimating Foundation Material**
Estimate the volume of materials, such as sand, to lay the foundation of a paved area. Aggregate material such as sand is often sold in tons.

# Base Material

Depending on how the pavers or stone are to be constructed, the base materials can also be estimated. For dry-laid, there is typically a 4-inch layer of crushed limestone or other suitable material (Fig. C–8). Over this is a 1-inch layer of setting sand.

Estimate the volume in cubic feet or yards. Sand and other aggregate material is often ordered in tons. For instance, 1 cubic yard of sand is approximately equal to 1.5 tons. Be sure to check with supplier before ordering

1 cubic yard of sand = Approximately 1.5 tons

# Flagstone

Estimating flagstone requires the total square footage of the flagstone area. Since flagstone comes in various sizes, the number of stones is difficult to estimate. Instead, the number of palettes required can be estimated (Fig. C–9). The number of square feet that a palette will cover depends on the type of stone used. Typically a palette will cover 120 to 200 square feet, but check with a supplier on the type of stone to be estimated.

***Figure C–9*** **Stone Palettes**
Stone is sold on palettes. The area of one palette varies depending on the type of stone, but is often 120 to 200 square feet. Check with the supplier. To estimate number of palettes, calculate the same as sod: the total square feet divided by the square footage of a palette.

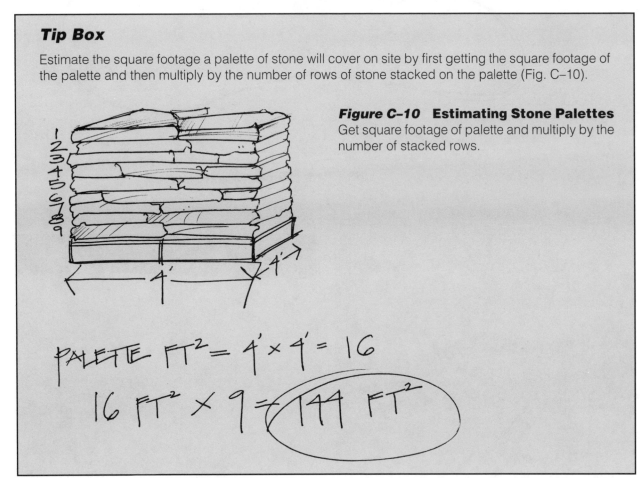

**Tip Box**

Estimate the square footage a palette of stone will cover on site by first getting the square footage of the palette and then multiply by the number of rows of stone stacked on the palette (Fig. C–10).

***Figure C–10*** **Estimating Stone Palettes**
Get square footage of palette and multiply by the number of stacked rows.

$$\text{PALETTE FT}^2 = 4' \times 4' = 16$$

$$16 \text{ FT}^2 \times 9 = 144 \text{ FT}^2$$

Estimate the number of palettes by dividing the total square footage of the area by the square footage of the palette.

Total square footage / 120 square feet = Number of palettes

# Edging

The amount of edging is estimated by linear feet. Edging will be installed primarily between turf and planting beds. To get an estimate of the linear requirements of edging, use a flex curve to follow the bed lines and anywhere else edging will be installed. Know the length of the flex curve to scale and calculate the edging by using it as a flexible scale or digital scale (Fig. C–11).

(a)

(b)

(c)

***Figure C–11*** **Estimating Edging**
(a) Edging is estimated in linear feet. To estimate the total length of edging required, use a (b) flex curve or (c) digital wheel that tabulates much like a measuring wheel, the scale can be changed according to plan.

Once the total number of linear feet is known, calculate the number of edging units required to complete the work (Fig. C–12). Divide the total linear feet by the unit feet of the a length of edging. For instance, a piece of steel edging is 8 feet long.

Total number of linear feet ÷ 8 feet = Number of edging pieces

# Mulch

Estimate the mulch requirements in cubic feet or cubic yards (Fig. C–13). Most bulk mulch is sold in cubic yards, while bagged mulch is sold in cubic feet. First calculate the number of cubic feet that the mulched areas will require at a given depth.

***Figure C–12* Units of Edging**
Edging is sold in lengths. Steel edging, for instance, is sold in 8-foot lengths. Divide the total length of edging by the length of one edging unit.

(a)

(b)

***Figure C–13* Mulch**
Mulch can be acquired in (a) bags, measured in cubic feet, or (b) bulk, measured in cubic yards.

For instance, the mulch will be applied 3 inches deep (Fig. C–14). Converting depth of inches to depth of feet and multiply by the square footage to get the cubic feet. If estimating for bulk mulch supply, then the cubic feet can be converted to cubic yards by dividing by 27.

If estimating for the number of bags required, then divide the total number of cubic feet by the number of cubic feet in a bag. If a bag contains 3 cubic feet,

Total cubic feet ÷ 3 cubic feet = Number of bags

$$3'' \div 12'' = 0.25'$$

2500 SQUARE FEET × 0.25' DEEP = 625 CUBIC FEET (FT³)

BAG = 3 CUBIC FEET

625 CUBIC FEET ÷ 3 CUBIC FEET (ONE BAG) = 208 BAGS

CUBIC YARD = 27 CUBIC FEET

625 CUBIC FEET ÷ 27 CUBIC YARDS = 23 CUBIC YARD (YD³)

**Figure C–14  Estimating Mulch Requirements**
Estimate the volume of mulch requirements. Then an estimate of bags, based on cubic feet, or bulk, based on cubic yards, can be calculated.

The number of palettes of bagged mulched can be estimating by dividing the total number of bags by the number of bags on a palette.

Total bags ÷ Bags on a palette = Number of palettes required

# Weed Barrier

The amount of weed barrier can be estimated by the square footage of the beds that will be covered (Fig. C–15). To estimate the number of rolls required to do the job, determine the square footage of the weed barrier roll. For instance, if a roll that is 3 feet × 100 feet would cover 300 square feet of ground. Once the square footage of a roll is determined, calculate the number of rolls by dividing the total square footage of beds by the square footage of the roll (Fig. C–16).

Total square footage ÷ 300 square feet (roll) = Number of rolls

# Groundcover

To estimate the quantity of plants to fill an area of groundcover, first the spacing between the plants must be determined (Fig. C–17). For instance, plants may be planted on 4, 6, 8, 10, or 12 inch centers (or larger). This is usually specified as "on center."

Second, determine how many square inches each plant would occupy.

***Figure C–15* Weed Barrier**
Weed barrier is sold in rolls of various widths and lengths.

= 300 SQUARE FEET

100' ROLL

TOTAL SQUARE FEET ÷ SQUARE FEET PER ROLL = NUMBER OF ROLLS

**Figure C–16  Estimate Weed Barrier**
Estimate the weed barrier requirements by dividing total area of beds by the square foot one roll will cover.

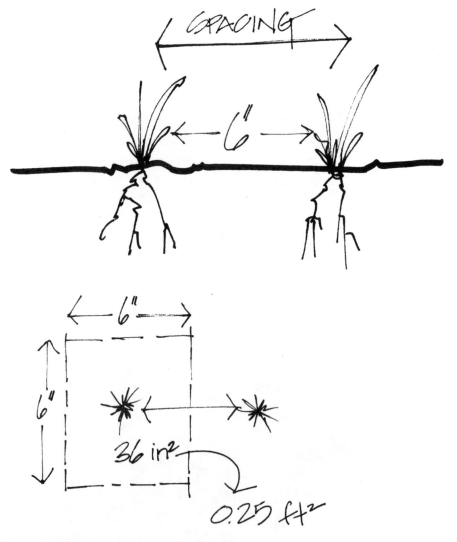

SPACING

6"

6"

6"

36 in²

0.25 ft²

**Figure C–17  Groundcover Estimate**
Once the spacing is determined, calculate the square footage a plant will occupy then divide into the entire groundcover area.

### Example

*If a groundcover is to be planted 6 inches on center, then each individual plant will occupy a square space that is 6 inches by 6 inches. This would equal 36 square inches.*

Third, calculate how many square feet each plant will occupy by dividing the square inches by 144.

### Example

*If the groundcover occupies 36 square inches, then the square footage is 0.25.*

Fourth, determine the total square footage of the area to be planted.

### Example

*The total area is 10 feet by 20 feet, equal to 200 square feet.*

Fifth, estimate the total number of plants required to fill the determined area. Take the total area divided by the square footage of each plant.

### Example

*In this case, 200 square feet is divided by 0.25 square feet to equal 800 ground-cover plants.*

# Cost Estimate

The bid for the installation will cover the companies cost and profit and is based on several factors: materials, driving distance, estimated man-hours, soil conditions, and so forth. The bids will vary from company to company. To get an approximate estimate of what range of bids to expect, some designers look at the cost of the materials and figure the installation will be between two to three times the cost of materials.

Cost of materials x 2 or 3 = Approximate cost of installation

### Estimate Example

*The following is a materials estimate of the master plan. The area calculations are located at Figure C–18.*

# Turfgrass

Amount of sod required for lawn

*Square footage*

Front yard = 787.5 square feet

Side yard = 208 square feet

Back yard = 5875 square feet

**Total square footage = 6870.5 square feet**

*An estimate of the amount of sod required*

Palette of sod = 500 square feet

6870.5 total square footage / 500 square feet of palette = **13.7 or 14 palettes**

**Figure C-18 Estimate**
Example of estimating material for master plan.

# Mulch

Amount of mulch required for planting beds

*Square footage of planting beds*

Front = 1983.5 square feet

Back and side yard = 4862 square feet

**Total square footage of beds = 6845.5 square feet**

*Volume of mulch required if three inches deep*

Cubic feet = 6845.5 square feet × 0.25′ (three inches deep) = **1711 cubic feet**

Cubic yards = 1711 cubic feet / 27 cubic feet = **63.4 cubic yards**

# Weed Barrier

The amount of weed barrier required to cover all planting beds

**Total square footage of beds = 6845.5 square feet**

Roll of weed barrier = 6′ wide and 500′ long = **3000 square foot of coverage per roll**

*Number of rolls required to cover all planting beds*

Total square footage of beds = 6845.5 / 3000 square feet = **2.3 or 3 rolls**

# Edging

The amount of edge required to separate planting beds from turf

**Total linear feet = 486 linear feet**

*Number of steel edge pieces required*

One piece of steel edging = 8′

486 total linear feet / 8′ per piece = **60.75, or 61 pieces of steel edging**

# Driveway

A stone aggregate will be used for the driveway

**Driveway = 676 square feet**

*Tons of stone aggregate required to fill driveway four inches deep*

Cubic feet = 676 square feet of driveway × 0.33′ (four inches deep) = **225.3 cubic feet**

Cubic yards = 225.3 cubic feet / 27 cubic feet = **8.3 cubic yards**

Tons = 8.3 cubic yards × 1.5 tons = **12.5 tons**

# Stone

The amount of stone required for front and back walk

**Total square footage of flagstone = 261 square feet**

Number of palettes required for flagstone construction

261 square feet / 120 square feet of palette = 2.2 palettes

Amount of crushed granite required for base material 4″ deep

Cubic feet = 261 square feet of stone × 0.33′ (four inches deep) = **86.1 cubic feet**

Cubic yards = 86.1 cubic feet / 27 cubic feet = **3.2 cubic yards**

Tons = 3.2 cubic yards × 1.5 tons = **4.8 tons**

# D Computer Graphics

Computer-aided-drafting systems are referred to as CAD. AutoCAD is a software program that allows the user to draw lines, arcs, and circles in addition to many other functions. For the landscape designer, however, it lacked a symbol library early in its development. LANDCADD, released in 1984, evolved from AutoCAD to include numerous symbols and applications that relates to landscape design, irrigation, estimating, and construction details, among others. Larger companies, such as landscape architecture, engineering, or commercial landscaping, commonly use AutoCAD or LANDCADD. But for many landscape designers, it is very expensive, difficult to learn, and more software than needed.

The advantages to software design are numerous. Site surveys can be readily scanned to file and designing can begin without having to draw the site. Symbols can be sized and instantly duplicated throughout the plan. Revisions are easily done without redrawing, symbols can be moved, deleted, or added as needed. All materials can be tagged with specifications and exported to develop a complete materials list and estimation. Files can easily be printed at various sizes or e-mailed.

## Software Products

Since the mid-1980s, design software other than AUTOCAD and LANDCADD have developed to include imaging, plan drawing, and estimators. Many of these products are easier to learn, relatively inexpensive, and more applicable for many landscape designers.

If considering design software other than AUTOCAD and LANDCADD, be sure to purchase high-quality design software. They are much different than the programs that are on the shelf at a local store and selling for less than $50. Although inexpensive, they are limited in their applications, quality, and database of images. As a landscape designer, the professional grade software offers a wide range of applications, high-quality prints, in addition to program and database upgrades.

This appendix is not intended to promote any of the products that are listed at the end of the section. They all have some outstanding qualities. But regardless of which product is learned by the user, there are several common techniques used by each program. This appendix is not intended to teach you how to use each program since the actual execution of the commands will vary between products. Its intention is, however, to give you an idea of what design software can do and what kind of finished products they create. If you decide to pursue design software, most products have very good tutorials that will walk you through the design process step by step.

Also, this appendix is not complete in the extent of what each program can do. In fact, most the programs that I have experienced can do much more than the basic commands. However, what is described in the following is the basic approach to using design software.

In considering purchasing a product, shop around at the various retailers listed at the end of this appendix. Some can send you the fully operational product that will run for a 30-day trial before requiring the user to purchase a password to unlock it for further use.

# Plan Drawing and Estimator Software

Once a site survey is scanned to file, the operating scale is set. One of the most basic functions of the plan drawing software is the ability to draw lines (Fig. D–1). These lines can be straight, curves, arcs, or any number of options, depending on the software. Beds, patios, walks, driveways, and other areas can be drawn on the ground plane. Many programs have the capability to estimate the square footage of the area as well as calculate volume, which can then be used to estimate materials such as mulch or pavers (Fig. D–2). With the drawing in scale, a dimension tool can be used to automatically specify distances for layout (Fig. D–3).

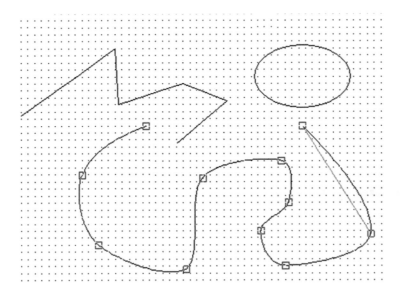

***Figure D–1   Line Tool***
The most basic function of design software is to draw lines, arcs, and shapes.

***Figure D–2   Estimating Tool***
Area and volume is automatically calculated to estimate materials.

*Figure D–3* **Dimension Tool**
Lines and areas can have dimensions added for layout.

*Figure D–4* **Symbol Database**
Symbols can be added to the design from a database.

The image database contains a collection of plant symbols that can be dropped onto the design (Fig. D–4). These symbols can then be sized and transformed to the correct scale. Properties can also be assigned to the symbol. These can include, but are not limited to, the plant name, planting size, price, and inventory number. The symbols can be duplicated quickly with a copy command that places the same exact symbol with every click. When all the symbols are placed, the design can be quickly labeled (Fig. D–5). Most programs have an automatic labeling command that will place the name of the symbol on the label without having to type it again. All it takes is selecting a symbol and then placing the label. Since the properties of the symbol contain the name, the command can automatically assign the name to the label. This makes labeling a snap that is completed in seconds.

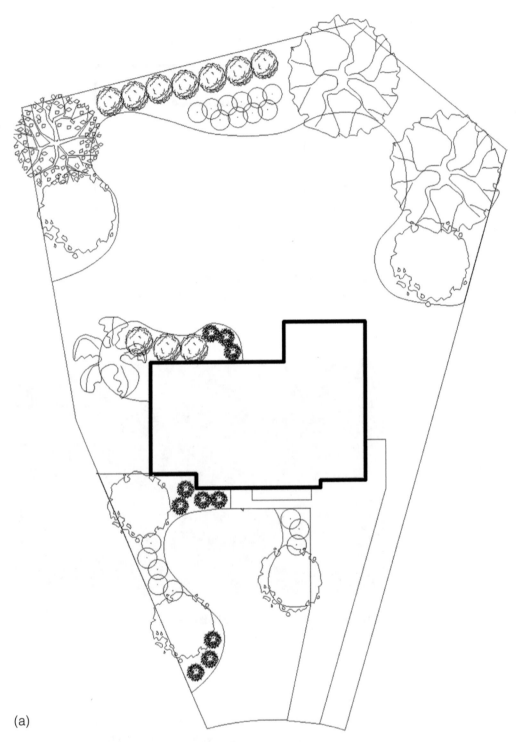

(a)

**Figure D–5   Symbols and Labeling**
(a) Once symbols are sized and placed,

*(continues)*

(b)

**Figure D–5  Symbols and Labeling—continued**
(b) labels can be quickly added.

Some programs have the capability to color the plans for presentation. The plan can then be printed on high-quality paper for presentation or e-mail to the client.

When the plan drawing is complete, all the plants and other materials can be exported to an estimator program. The estimator can organize all the material and assigned properties, as well as square footage and volume of ground plane areas, into a proposal format that can add up the cost of materials for an estimate (Fig. D–6). This software can be customized for your company as a proposal template that can be printed and presented to the client.

**Pepperdam Nursery and Landscaping**

| | | | | | |
|---|---|---|---|---|---|
| John Doe | | Tel: (843) 555-1143 | | | Date 8/15/2001 |
| 111 Carolina Lane | | Fax: (843) 555-1433 | | | Estimate # 00000153 |
| Charleston, SC 29111 | | | | | |

| Name | Qty. | Size | Price | Tax | Total |
|---|---|---|---|---|---|
| CLEYERA | 3 | 5 gallon | 20.00 | 3.75 | 63.75 |
| DOGWOOD | 1 | 5 gallon | 25.00 | 1.56 | 26.56 |
| JUNIPER | 6 | 3 gallon | 12.00 | 4.50 | 76.50 |
| RIVER BIRCH | 1 | 15 gallon | 55.00 | 3.44 | 58.44 |
| SPIREA | 8 | 3 gallon | 12.00 | 6.00 | 102.00 |
| | | | | | |
| Tax Total | | | | 19.25 | |
| Grand Total | | | | | 327.25 |
| | | | | | |

Signature                    Date

*Figure D–6*  **Estimator Program**
All materials can be exported and formatted for a proposal.

# Imaging Software

Landscape design imaging has been used to simulate landscape designs on an actual photo of the site. Older versions often times had the result of a photo with pictures of plants, like refrigerator magnets, stuck on top of it. Although this was helpful, it wasn't believable. Imaging software has advanced to point that realistic photos of proposed designs, where objects and textures could be blended into a photo of the site, can be easily created. As a result, a much more tangible product is created where clients see a picture of what they are purchasing instead of an artist's drawing. Rather than relying on descriptions and vague imagery to "paint" a picture of the design, a client sees what actual plants and hardscape material look like.

First, a picture of the site is acquired, either digitally or from scanning a photo. The picture is opened in the software program to design. The picture can be cropped and sharpened to improve the quality. Existing objects can often be erased from the picture, if needed, using a cloning tool (Fig. D–7). A database of images, similar to the symbols database, is opened that contains trees, shrubs, grass, sidewalks, driveways, and more (Fig. D–8). The objects, such as trees, can be loaded onto the picture, just as symbols were loaded onto the plan drawing, and adjusted for size and color, then duplicated as needed (Fig. D–9). As more objects are loaded onto the picture, they "stack" like objects on a table and can be moved forward and backward. Shadows can also be added to the objects for additional depth (Fig. D–10).

Once the image is finalized, it can be printed on high-quality paper and presented along with the plan to the clients (Fig. D–11). It can also be e-mailed.

(a)

(b)

**Figure D–7   Cloning Tool**
(a) Erasing an existing object on the photo,
(b) a cloning tool borrows texture from the
photo, such as turf in the case, to paint over
the object (c) making it appear as if it were
never there.

(c)

**Figure D–8   Object Database**
Objects such as trees, shrubs, pavers, and turf are added to the photo.

***Figure D–9*** **Duplicating**
Objects from the database can be added
to the photo, transformed, and duplicated
with a few clicks of the mouse.

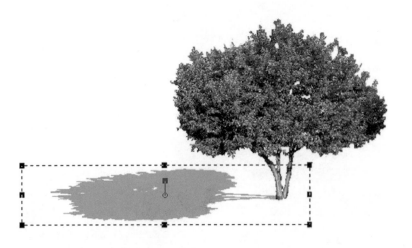

***Figure D–10*** **Shadows**
To create more realism and perspective, shadows can be added to objects.

(a)

(b)

(c)

(d)

**Figure D–11  Imaging Examples**
Before and after pictures. *(Photos courtesy of Visual Impact Imaging)*

# Software Products

## DesignWare and Planscape

*http://designimaginggroup.com*

*Design Imaging Group, Inc.*
320 Long Island Avenue
Holtsville, NY 11742
Phone (816) 842-4955

## PRO Landscape

*http://www.drafix.com/*

*Draftix Software, Inc.*
105 East 5th Street, Suite 201
Kansas City MO 64106
Phone (816) 842-4955

### Earthscapes

*http://www.visualimpactimaging.com/*

*Visual Impact Imaging*
3533 W. Bath Road
Akron, OH 44333
Phone: (330) 665-9080

### Picture Perfect and Visual Landscaping

*http://www.eaglepoint.com/*

*Eagle Point Software*
4131 Westmark Drive
Dubuque, IA 52002-2627
Phone: (319) 556-8392
Toll Free: (800) 678-6565

### Dynascape and Gardenworks

*http://www.gardengraphics.com*

*Garden Graphics*
3425 Harvester Road, Suite 217
Burlington, ON L7N-3N1
1.800.710.1900
fax: 905.639.9108

### RainCAD and Photoscape

*http://www.raincad.com*

*Software Republic, L.L.P.*
Houston, Texas
*Phone:* **(281) 463-8804**

### Night Vision

*http://www.vistapro.com*

*Vista Professional Outdoor Lighting*
1625 N. Surveyor Ave
Simi Valley, CA 93063
*Phone:* **(800) 766-8478**

# E Butterfly Gardening

Plants offer constantly changing colors throughout the year with flowers, foliage, fruit, and stems, but they can also attract interesting colors in the form of butterflies. Butterflies are naturally seen in any landscape, but there are several design approaches to increase butterfly diversity and presence by developing a butterfly garden.

## Puddling

Groups of butterflies can often be found sitting on a wet, muddy area. This is referred to as **puddling.** Butterflies will feed on minerals and salts from the wet ground to get nutrients. Preparing a low area that remains wet naturally or connected to a low-flow water source can be a way to attract butterflies. This can be enhanced by burying a shallow container, like a bird bath, to hold moisture for a longer period of time.

## Basking

Butterflies require warm weather to fly, ideally when temperatures are between 85 and 100 degrees Fahrenheit. They will warm their bodies by spreading their wings to absorb the sun's heat, often on a rock or concrete. Flagstones and rocks may provide space for butterflies to **bask.**

## Protection

Plan a butterfly garden in an area protected from the wind. Butterflies are more likely to spend time in a garden that does not require fighting the wind. Planting a dense shrub protection around the area will create a more calm, quiet microclimate.

## Hibernation

Most species of butterflies overwinter in the same region. The monarch is the only butterfly that migrates to another area to overwinter, and in that case all the way to Mexico. They will hibernate, depending on the species, as larva, pupa, or adults in protected areas such as loose bark, debris, buildings, or logs.

### Hibernation Boxes

**Hibernation boxes** are decorative houses with narrow slots on one side. It is intended to attract butterflies to shelter over the winter. However, most butterflies do not overwinter as adults. Many experts believe that the value of hibernation boxes is mainly as a garden decoration. While they might attract insects and spiders, rarely do butterflies utilize them.

# Reduce Pesticides

Pesticide usage will kill caterpillars and butterflies just as it does the pests. Many insecticides are **contacts,** meaning that the butterfly or insect only has to come in contact with a treated surface to kill it.

# Food Source

Butterflies have two growth stages: caterpillar (larval) and butterfly (adult). Attract both stages by planting the appropriate food source.

# Host Plants

Host plants provide food for caterpillars. Butterflies will search out a particular plant to lay eggs, so that upon hatching the caterpillar will immediately have an appropriate food source. Host plants will be consumed like an insect pest, sometimes completely defoliated, so these plants are often considered expendable because the caterpillar will pupate into a butterfly. Host plants are often located in low-visibility areas.

# Nectar Plants

Nectar is produced by flowers and consumed by butterflies. Butterflies uncoil a long tubular mouthpart, called a proboscis, to siphon nectar from flowers. They are often attracted to bright, warm colors such as pink, red, yellow, and orange. Butterflies will seek out nectar all season long when temperatures are above 60 degrees Fahrenheit through frost.

### Abbreviated List of Host Plants for Butterflies

**Butterfly—Host Plant**
Poplar Admiral—Poplar, aspen
Red Admiral—Nettle
Apollo—Stonecrops, houseleeks
Silvery Blue—Lupine
Yellow Brimstone—Senna
Buckeye—Platain, gerardia
Comma—Nettle, hops, elm
Meadow Fritillary—Violets
Pearl-Bordered Fritillary—Violets
Shepherd's Fritillary—Violets
Silver-washed Fritillary—Violets
Purple Emperor—Willow, poplars, aspen
Colorado Hairstreak—Oak
Purple Hairstreak—Oak
Monarch—Milkweed
Mourning Cloak—Willow, birch, elm
Mylitta Crescentspot—Thistles
Orange Tip—Cuckoo-flower

Sara Orange Tip—Wild mustard
Two-tailed Pasha—Strawberry tree
Painted Lady—Thistles, nettles, yarrow
The Peacock—Nettles
Swallowtail—Fennel, milk parsley, queen Anne's lace
Black Swallowtail—Carrot, celery, parsley, fennel
Giant Swallowtail—Hop Tree, Citrus
Tiger Swallowtail—Black cherry
Cloudless Sulphur—Senna
Orange-barred Sulphur—Peas
Small Tortoiseshell—Nettle
The Queen—Milkweed

## Nectar plants

### Botanical Common Name

*Arabis alpina* Alpine rockcress
*Aster species* Aster
*Rudbeckia hirta* Black-Eyed Susan
*Ajuga species* Bugleweed
*Buddleja davidii* Butterfly Bush
*Silene Campion* Catchfly
*Caragana aurantiaca* Pea tree
*Nepeta* x *faassenii* Catnip
*Allium schoenoprasum* Chives
*Origanum vulgare* Common marjoram
*Bellis perennis* Daisy
*Hemerocallis species* Daylily
*Eryngium species* Field eryngo
*Tagetes patula* French marigold
*Solidago canadensis* Golden rod
*Heliopsis helianthoides* Heliopsis
*Eupatorium purpureum* Hemp agrimony
*Lonicera species* Honeysuckle
*Hyssopus officinalis* Hyssop
*Vernonia species* Ironweed
*Centaurea species* Knapweed
*Lavandula angustifolia* Lavendar
*Syringa species* Lilacs
*Doronicum species* Leopards-bane
*Daphne species* Daphne
*Cerastium species* Mouse-ear
*Phlox species* Phlox
*Dianthus species* Pink
*Scabiosa species* Pincushion flower
*Primula species* Primrose
*Echinaea purpurea* Purple coneflower
*Lythrum salicaria* Purple loosestrife

*Lathyrus species* Sweet pea
*Salvia species* Sage
*Scilla sibiria* Siberian squill
*Liatris spicata* Snakeroot
*Veronica species* Speedwell
*Stokesia laevis* Stoke's Aster
*Sedum species* Stonecrops
*Asclepias incarnata* Swamp milkweed
*Armeria species* Thrift rose
*Cirsium species* Thistle
*Coreopsis species* Tickseed
*Verbena species* Vervain
*Vicia species* Vetch
*Anthemis tinctoria* Yellow chamomile
*Viburnum species* Viburnum
*Zinnia elegans* Zinnia

# F  Deer

Much like insects cause problems by consuming plants for food, deer, also in much the same way, are pests. It is often a problem at the edge of woods where deer will graze in the evening and then return to the safety of the wooded area to sleep during the day. They will rip the foliage from trees and shrubs, trim all the flowers from an annual bed, and even feed on turf in the summer. Deer problems are more pronounced during droughty summers when nutritious, green food is scarce; deer are more likely to wander further from the woods in search of food. The winter following a hard drought is especially tough on deer that have less fat stored, which perhaps sets the stage for more severe deer problems. In search of green food, they will eat plants in the winter that they will ordinarily leave untouched in the summer.

In the fall, other problems can occur when deer are mating. They will damage the trunks of trees by rubbing their antlers on them to remove the fuzz from the new antlers. Tree trunks may need protection from gouging.

## Deer-Resistant Plants

The most effective way to reduce damage from deer is using deer-resistant plants. For one reason or another, deer will not feed on certain plants unless near starvation, and for some plants not even then. Some plants develop physiological defenses to ward off deer, such as thorns, spines, or prickles. Others defend themselves by tasting foul or even poisonous (to deer, not necessarily humans). Deer typically do not care for bitter tasting plants.

In regions where deer are a serious problem, deer-resistant plants are the best means of deterrence. Research or check with local plant nurseries for plants that are deer resistant. If plants are not deer resistant, there are a few other approaches to protecting plants from being eaten.

## Deer Deterrents

Deer will stay away from plants and areas that taste or smell offensive to deer, not necessarily us. Taste repellence will sustain some feeding damage before deer stop. If plants that are not deer resistant are used, an area or plant that is regularly sprayed or planted with an offensive taste or smell can steer deer away. If the plants are edible to humans, the repellent needs to be able to wash off easily, thus effective for longer periods of time. Be aware the repellent is only protective on what is sprayed. New growth will not be protected so reapplication is required. Rotate repellents to prevent deer from becoming used to one product. Some products claim to remain active for two to three months, check the product for application.

### Odor Repellents

Odor repellents work better in warm weather because the colder weather reduces the effectiveness of scent. One of the more popular odor deterrents is **egg solids.** They are very safe and last one to three months. **Garlic** and **soaps** are recommended for edible plants because they wash off easily and become ineffective after rain. **Meal meat** is placed in sachets and hung around the plants for protection, and it requires no spraying. It's effective for several months and rain makes it even more effective. **Predator urine** signals to the deer that danger is in the area making them leave to feed in safer pastures. It is not applied to the plants but placed in dispensers near plants or applied around them.

## Taste Repellents

Taste repellents are preferred in colder weather. When applied, the foliage and flowers need to remain dry for approximately 10 hours. **Hot pepper,** much like garlic, is good for edible plants. **Denatonium Benzoate** is a bittering agent that is absorbed by the plant and creates a bitter taste that is said to last for years. Some products like **Thiram,** the fungicide, and **blood-type ingredients** are effective as a taste and odor repellent.

# Deer Barriers

**Deer fence** or **netting** is typically a six-and-a-half-feet-tall barrier to keep deer away from an area. It is effective for large areas, but unsightly and often unacceptable in residential and many commercial areas. **Baited electric fences** attract deer to touch the wires and deliver a harmless shock that chases them from the area. **Wireless baited electric fencing** has also been developed (www.wirelessdeerfence.com).

## Abbreviated List of Deer-Resistant Plants

### Perennials

*Achillea filipendulina* Yarrow

*Aconitum napellus* Monkshood

*Agastache species* Hyssop

*Ajuga reptans* Bugleweed

*Anemone nemorosa* Windflower

*Aquilegia species* Columbine

*Artemisia schmidtiana* Wormwood

*Asarum canadense* Wild ginger

*Asarum europaeum* European wild ginger

*Asclepias species* Butterfly weed

*Aster species* Aster

*Astilbe arendsii* False spiraea

*Belamcanda chinensis* Blackberry lily

*Boltonia asteroides* Boltonia

*Carex species* Sedge

*Caryopteris clandonensis* Bluebeard

*Chrysanthemum superbum* Shasta daisy

*Convallaria majalis* Lily-of-the-valley

*Coreopsis lanceolata* Coreopsis

*Coronilla species* Crown vetch

*Delphinium species* Larkspur

*Dicentra eximia* Fringed bleeding heart

*Dicentra spectabilis* Bleeding heart

*Digitalis species* Foxglove

*Echinacea purpurea* Purple coneflower

*Eschscholzia californica* California poppy

*Euphorbia species* Spurge

*Gaillardia grandiflora* Blanket flower

*Galium odoratum* Sweet woodruff

*Gaura lindheimeri* Whirling butterflies

*Helleborus species* Hellebore

*Heuchera specie* Coralbells

*Hibiscus moscheutos* Rose mallow

*Kniphofia uvaria* Red-hot-poker

*Lamiastrum galeobdolon* Yellow archangel

*Lamium maculatum* Dead nettle

*Lavandula angustifolia* English lavender

*Liatris spicata* Gayfeather

*Ligularia dentata* Bigleaf ligularia

*Matteuccia struthiopteris* Ostrich fern

*Monarda didyma* Beebalm

*Myosotis scorpioides* True forget-me-not

*Nepeta species* Catmint

*Opuntia compressa* Prickly pear cactus

*Osmunda cinnamomea* Cinnamon fern

*Paeonia species* Peony

*Papaver orientale* Oriental poppy

*Perovskia atriplicifolia* Russian sage

*Polygonatum species* Solomon's seal

*Polystichum acrostichoides* Christmas fern

*Pulmonaria saccharata* Bethlehem sage

*Salvia nemorosa* Perennial sage

*Santolina chamaecyparissus* Lavender-cotton

*Sedum species* Stonecrop

*Sempervirens tectorum* Hens and chicks

*Solidago species* Goldenrod

*Stachys byzantina* Lamb's ears

*Thymus species* Thyme

*Yucca filamentosa* Adam's needle

## Groundcover

*Ajuga reptans* Bugleweed

*Asarum canadense* Wild ginger

*Asarum europaeum* European wild ginger

*Brunnera macrophylla* Siberian bugloss

*Convallaria majalis* Lily-of-the-valley

*Coronilla species* Crown vetch

*Cyrtomium falcatum* Holly fern

*Galium odoratum* Sweet woodruff

*Juniperus procumbens* Japanese garden juniper

*Lamiastrum galeobdolon* Yellow archangel

*Lamium maculatum* Dead nettle

*Lantana camara* Lantana

*Leymus arenarius* Lyme grass

*Liriope species* Lilyturf

*Myosotis scorpioides* True forget-me-not

*Nepeta species* Catmint

*Pachysandra procumbens* Allegheny spurge

*Pachysandra species* Pachysandra

*Perovskia atriplicifolia* Russian sage

*Phalaris arundinacea* Ribbon grass

*Polygonatum species* Great Solomon's seal

*Sedum species* Stonecrop

*Stachys byzantina* Lamb's ears

## Shrubs

*Abelia* X *grandiflora* Glossy abelia

*Berberis thunbergii* Japanese barberry

*Buxus species* Boxwood

*Callicarpa species* Beautyberry

*Camellia japonica* Camellia

*Cephalotaxus harringtoniana* Japanese plum yew

*Cephalotaxus* species False yew

*Cornus alba* Red twigged dogwood

*Cornus mas* Cornelian cherry dogwood

*Cycas revoluta* Sago palm

*Cytisus species* Broom

*Daphne species* Mezereon

*Elaeagnus pungens* Elaeagnus

*Feijoa sellowiana* Pineapple guava

*Gardenia augusta* Gardenia

*Hamamelis species* Witch hazel

*Hypericum species* St. John's wort

*Ilex* species Holly

*Illicium* species Anise

*Juniperus chinensis* Hollywood juniper

*Juniperus procumbens* Japanese garden juniper

*Kalmia latifolia* Mountain laurel

*Leucothoe species* Leucothoe

*Ligustrum* species Privet

*Lonicera species* Honeysuckle

*Loropetalum chinense* Chinese fringe

*Mahonia aquifolium* Oregon grape holly

*Mahonia* species Mahonia

*Nandina domestica* Heavenly bamboo

*Nerium oleander* Oleander

*Osmanthus fragrans* Tea olive

*Picea pungens* Spruce

*Pieris floribunda* Mountain Pieris

*Pieris japonica* Lily-of-the-valley shrub

*Pieris species* Pieris

*Podocarpus species* Podocarpus

*Potentilla fruticosa* Shrubby cinquefoil

*Prunus laurocerasus* Cherry laurel

*Rosa rugosa* Rose

*Rosmarinus officinalis* Creeping rosemary

*Spiraea bumalda* Spiraea

*Viburnum rhytidophyllum* Leatherleaf viburnum

*Viburnum suspensum* Viburnum

## Trees

*Acer griseum* Paperbark maple

*Acer japonicum* Japanese maple

*Acer palmatum* Coralbark maple

*Acer palmatum* Japanese maple

*Acer saccharum* Sugar maple

*Betula nigra* River birch

*Butia capitata* Pindo palm

*Cedrus atlantica* Blue atlas cedar

*Cercidiphyllum japonicum* Katsura

*Cornus florida* Flowering dogwood

*Cornus kousa* Kousa dogwood

*Fagus sylvatica* European beech

*Magnolia virginiana* Sweetbay magnolia

*Myrica cerifera* Wax myrtle

*Picea pungens* Colorado spruce

*Prunus subhirtella* Higan cherry

*Stewartia pseudocamellia* Japanese stewartia

*Styrax japonicus* Japanese snowbell

# G Xeriscaping

**Xeriscaping** is a practice that utilizes native plants and proper planning to conserve water and maintenance costs in the landscape. "Xeros" is Greek for *dry* and "scape" means *view* or *scene,* which equates to drought-tolerant plants in the landscape. This approach to landscape design is critical in arid regions, such as the Southwest, where restrictions on water use limit irrigation. Elements of xeriscaping include proper design, limited turf areas, mulching, efficient irrigation practices, and proper landscape management.

## Proper Design

As this book has stressed, thoughtful planning and design will make the landscape useful as well as practical for the homeowner. Identifying microclimates and selecting appropriate plants will limit problems and maintenance requirements. In particular, using plants adapted to dry conditions will require less water.

## Turf Areas

In arid regions where xeriscaping is much more common, it is easy to notice limited, if any, turf areas. They are often smaller turf panels surrounded by large planting beds often mulched with rock that does not need to be replenished. This reduces irrigation since turf often requires more water than many trees and shrubs that have deeper root systems.

## Mulch

Mulch is an integral component of the landscape around trees, shrubs, and groundcover. As discussed in the Plants & Hardscapes chapter, it conserves water by reducing the amount of evaporation from the soil surface. It keeps the soil cooler by protecting it from the direct sunlight. It also reduces weeds that would otherwise grow on exposed soil and compete with landscape plants.

## Irrigation

Good irrigation design is more efficient at delivering water to the plants and reducing waste. Poor irrigation design often applies water to sidewalks, parking lots, and other areas outside of the target plants. As a result, more water is used to get the proper amount to the plants.

Whenever possible, *drip irrigation* is very efficient at delivering water to the root systems of plants in beds. There is little water loss to evaporation since it is dripped through emitters at the base of each plant. Also, no water is applied outside the root zone between plants where weeds would grow.

# Proper Management

Although landscape design may have less of an impact on maintenance, analyzing and recommending proper preparation of the soil should preclude design recommendations. Improve the soil by first having a soil test to study the pH and nutrients and then adding organic matter to improve the structure and adding other amendments as recommended by the soil test.

Other management practices, such as fertilization, pruning, and pest control, will be minimized if proper planning and design are done. Good plant selection and placement will reduce the need for pruning, allowing the plants to fill in the area. There should also be few pest problems if the plants are adapted to the region as well as the microclimate.

With fewer clippings from mowing and pruning there is less waste that will end up in the landfill. Proper design will also reduce the number of inputs used to maintain the landscape.

# Index